NEW

PENGUIN BOOKS

POLISH PHRASE BOOK

POLISH
PHRASE BOOK

THIRD EDITION

JILL NORMAN
MAGDA HALL

PENGUIN BOOKS

PENGUIN BOOKS

Published by the Penguin Group
Penguin Books Ltd, 27 Wrights Lane, London W8 5TZ, England
Penguin Books USA Inc., 375 Hudson Street, New York, New York 10014, USA
Penguin Books Australia Ltd, Ringwood, Victoria, Australia
Penguin Books Canada Ltd, 10 Alcorn Avenue, Toronto, Ontario, Canada M4V 3B2
Penguin Books (NZ) Ltd, 182-190 Wairau Road, Auckland 10, New Zealand

Penguin Books Ltd, Registered Offices: Harmondsworth, Middlesex, England

First published 1973
Second edition 1979
Third edition 1993
1 3 5 7 9 10 8 6 4 2

Illustrations by Zafer Baran

Printed in England by Clays Ltd., St Ives plc

CONTENTS

TRAVEL ■ 17

DIRECTIONS ■ 32

DRIVING ■ 35

CYCLING ■ 50

HOTELS & GUEST HOUSES ■ 53

CAMPING ■ 63

SHOPPING & SERVICES 104

POST OFFICE 133

SIGHTSEEING 138

ENTERTAINMENT 144

SPORTS & GAMES 147

INTRODUCTION

In this series of phrase books only those words and phrases that might be called essential to a traveller have been included, but the definition of 'traveller' has been made very wide, to include not only the business traveller and the holiday-maker, whether travelling alone, with a group or the family, but also the owner of a house, an apartment or a time-share. Each type of traveller has his own requirements, and for easy use the phrases are arranged in sections which deal with specific situations.

Pronunciation is given for each phrase and for all words in the extensive vocabulary. An explanation of the system used for the pronunciation guide is to be found on pages xii–xv. It is essential to read this section carefully before starting to use this book.

Some of the Polish phrases are marked with an asterisk* – these attempt to give an indication of the kind of reply you might get to your question, and of questions you may be asked in your turn.

For those who would like to know a little more about the Polish language, a brief survey of the main points of its grammar is provided at the end of the book (pages 194–205).

PRONUNCIATION

The pronunciation guide is intended for people with no knowledge of Polish. As far as possible the system is based on English pronunciation. This means that complete accuracy may be lost for the sake of simplicity. However, the reader should be able to understand Polish pronunciation and make himself understood if he reads this section carefully. In addition each word in the vocabulary is given with a pronunciation guide based on the symbols given below.

Polish spelling is largely phonetic, i.e. one letter of the alphabet corresponds to one sound. Some sounds, however, are marked by combinations of two letters: cz, dz, dż, dź, sz, rz, ch. Others are indicated by letters of the alphabet with diacritical marks: ą, ć, ę, ń, ó, ś, ż, ź.

The following sounds are pronounced as in English: b, d, f, k, l, m, n, p, s, t, z. The others are given below:

a	as **u** in cut	symbol **a**	**mapa** – map (mapa)
ą	as French *on*, nasal equivalent of **o**	symbol **o**^{n}	**mąż** – husband (mo^{n}zh)
c	as **ts** in cats	symbol **ts**	**cukier** – sugar (tsookyer)

ć, ci	very soft **ch**	symbol **ch**	**być** – to be (bich)
ci	before vowels	symbol **chy**	**ciocia** – aunt (chyochya)
ch	as **h** in half	symbol **h**	**chleb** – bread (hleb)
cz	as **ch** in church	symbol **ch**	**czysty** – clean (chisti)
dz	as **ds** in woods	symbol **dz**	**bardzo** – very (bardzo)
dź	as **dg** in budget, but much softer	symbol **dg**	**łódź** – boat (woodg)
dzi	is pronounced as **dź** before vowels	symbol **dgy**	**dziadek** – grandfather (dgyadek)
dż	as **j** in jump	symbol **j**	**dżokej** – jockey (jockey)
e	as **e** in bed	symbol **e**	**teraz** – now (teraz)
ę	as French *vin*, nasal equivalent of **e**	symbol **e^{n}**	**ręka** – hand (re^{n}ka)
g	as **g** in go	symbol **g**	**góra** – mountain (goora)
h	as **h** in half	symbol **h**	**hotel** – hotel (hotel)
i	as **i** in machine, but shorter; never as short as **i** in ship	symbol **ee**	**wino** – wine (veeno)
i	before vowels	symbol **y**	**biec** – to run (byets)
j	as **y** in yellow	symbol **y**	**jajko** – egg (yayko)
ł	as **w** in water	symbol **w**	**łosoś** – salmon (wososh)

ń	soft **n**, as **ni** in onion	symbol **n**	**koń** – horse (kon)
ni	is pronounced as **ń** before vowels	symbol **ny**	**stocznia** – shipyard (stochnya)
o	as **o** in not	symbol **o**	**okno** – window (okno)
ó	as **oo** in book	symbol **oo**	**córka** – daughter (tsoorka)
r	is clearly trilled	symbol **r**	**rana** – wound (rana)
rz	as **s** in pleasure or as **sh** in ship	symbol **zh**	**rzeka** – river (zheka)
		and **sh**	**przez** – across (pshez)
ś, si	very soft sh	symbol **sh**	**światło** – light (shvyatwo)
si	before vowels	symbol **shy**	**siano** – hay (shyano)
sz	as **sh** in ship	symbol **sh**	**szafa** – cupboard (shafa)
u	as **oo** in book	symbol **oo**	**ulica** – street (ooleetsa)
w	as **v** in voice or as **f** in fire	symbol **v** and **f**	**woda** – water (voda)
			wcześnie – early (fcheshnye)
y	as **i** in rich	symbol **i**	**syn** – son (sin)
ż	as **s** in pleasure (*see* **rz**)	symbol **zh**	**żaba** – frog (zhaba)
ź, zi	very soft **s** as in pleasure	symbol **zh**	**źródło** – source (zhroodwo)
			zima – winter (zheema)

zi	before vowels	symbol **zhy**	**ziemia** – ground (zhyemya)

STRESS

In words of more than one syllable the stress falls on the last syllable but one.

szafa – wardrobe   śnia**da**nie – breakfast

Monosyllabic words unite with the preceding or following word.

pod **sto**łem – under the table   jak **dłu**go – how long

In the vocabulary stressed syllables are printed in **bold type.**

ESSENTIALS

FIRST THINGS

Yes	**Tak**	tak
No	**Nie**	nye
Please	**Proszę**	pro-she^{n}
Thank you	**Dziękuję**	dgye^{n}-koo-ye^{n}
You're welcome	**Proszę bardzo**	pro-she^{n} bar-dzo
Sorry; excuse me	**Przepraszam**	pshe-pra-sham

LANGUAGE PROBLEMS

I'm English/American	**Jestem Anglikiem (Angielką)/ Amerykaninem (Amerykanką)**	yes-tem an-glee-kyem (an-gyel-ko^{n}) /a-me-ri-ka-nee-nem (a-me-ri-kan-ko^{n})

Do you speak English?	**Czy pan(i) mówi po angielsku?**	chi pan (pa-nee) moo-vee po an-gyel-skoo
Does anybody here speak English?	**Czy ktoś tu mówi po angielsku?**	chi ktosh too moo-vee po an-gyel-skoo
I don't speak Polish	**Nie mówię po polsku**	nye moo-vye^{n} po pol-skoo
Do you understand?	***Czy pan(i) rozumie?**	chi pan (pa-nee) ro-zoo-mye
I don't understand	**Nie rozumiem**	nye ro-zoo-myem
Would you say that again, please?	**Czy może pan(i) to powtórzyć?**	chi mo-zhe pan (pa-nee) to pof-too-zhich
Please speak slowly	**Proszę mówić powoli**	pro-she^{n} moo-veech po-vo-lee
What does that mean?	**Co to znaczy?**	tso to zna-chi
Can you translate this for me?	**Czy może mi pan(i) to przetłumaczyć?**	chi mo-zhe mee pan (pa-nee) to pshe-twoo-ma-chich
Please write it down	**Proszę to napisać**	pro-she^{n} to na-pee-sach
What is it called in Polish?	**Jak to się nazywa po polsku?**	yak to shye^{n} na-zi-va po pol-skoo
I understand	**Rozumiem**	ro-zoo-myem
I speak a little Polish	**Mówię trochę po polsku**	moo-vye^{n} tro-he^{n} po pol-skoo
Please show me the word in the book	**Proszę mi pokazać to słowo w książce**	pro-she^{n} mee po-ka-zach to swo-vo fkshyo^{n}zh-tse
I will look it up in my phrase book	**Poszukam tego w książce**	po-shoo-kam te-go fkshyo^{n}zh-tse

QUESTIONS

Who?	**Kto?**	kto
Where is/are …?	**Gdzie jest/są …?**	gdgye yest/so^n
When?	**Kiedy?**	kye-di
How?	**Jak?**	yak
How much is/are …?	**Ile kosztuje/ kosztują …?**	ee-le kosh-too-ye/kosh-too-yo^n
How far?	**Jak daleko?**	yak da-le-ko
How much/many?	**Ile?**	ee-le
How long?	**Jak długo?**	yak dwoo-go
What's this?	**Co to jest?**	tso to yest
What do you want?	**Czego pan(i) sobie życzy?**	che-go pan (pa-nee) so-bye zhi-chi
What must I do?	**Co mam zrobić?**	tso mam zro-beech
Why?	**Dlaczego?**	dla-che-go
Have you …/ do you sell …?	**Czy jest/są …?**	chi yest/so^n
Is there …?	**Czy jest …?**	chi yest
Where can I find …?	**Gdzie znajdę …?**	gdgye znay-de^n
Have you seen …?	**Czy pan(i) widział (-a) …?**	chi pan (pa-nee) vee-dgyaw (dgya-wa)
May I have …?	**Czy mogę prosić o …?**	chi mo-ge^n pro-shich o
I want/should like …	**Chcę/chciałbym (-abym) …**	htse^n /hchyaw-bim (hchya-wa-bim)
I don't want …	**Nie chcę …**	nye htse^n

What is the matter?	**O co chodzi?**	o tso **ho**-dgee
Can you help me?	**Czy może pan(i) mi pomóc?**	chi **mo**-zhe pan (**pa**-nee) mee **po**-moots
Can I help you?	**Czy mogę panu(i) pomóc?**	chi **mo**-ge^{n} **pa**-noo (**pa**-nee) **po**-moots
Can you tell/give/ show me ...?	**Czy może pan(i) mi powiedzieć/dać/ pokazać ...?**	chi **mo**-zhe pan (**pa**-nee) mee po-**vye**-dgyech/ dach/po-**ka**-zach

USEFUL STATEMENTS

It is ...	**To jest ...**	to yest
It isn't ...	**To nie jest ...**	to nye yest
Here it is	**Tutaj jest**	**too**-tay yest
There they are	**Tam są**	tam so^{n}
There is/are ...	**Jest/są ...**	yest/so^{n}
Here is/are ...	**Tutaj jest/są ...**	**too**-tay yest/so^{n}
There isn't any/there aren't any	**Nie ma**	nye ma
OK/that's fine	**W porządku**	fpo-**zho^{n}d**-koo
I have ...	**Mam ...**	mam
I don't have ...	**Nie mam ...**	nye mam
I want ...	**Chcę ...**	htse^{n}
I would like ...	**Chciałbym (-abym) ...**	**hchyaw**-bim (hchya-**wa**-bim)
I need ...	**Potrzebuję ...**	po-tshe-**boo**-ye^{n}
I (don't) like it	**(Nie) podoba mi się to**	(nye) po-**do**-ba mee shye^{n} to
I (don't) know	**(Nie) wiem**	(nye) vyem

I didn't know	**Nie wiedziałem (-am)**	nye vye-**dgya**-wem (-wam)
I think so	**Chyba tak**	**hi**-ba tak
I'm hungry/tired	**Jestem głodny (-a)/ zmęczony (-a)**	yes-tem **gwod**-ni (-na)/ zme^{n}-**cho**-ni (-na)
I'm thirsty	**Chce mi się pić**	htse mee shye^{n} peech
I'm ready	**Jestem gotowy (-a)**	yes-tem go-**to**-vi (-va)
I'm in a hurry	**Spieszę się**	**shpye**-she^{n} shye^{n}
I'm lost	**Zgubiłem (-łam) się**	zgoo-**bee**-wem (-wam) shye^{n}
We're looking for …	**Szukamy …**	shoo-**ka**-mi
It's important	**To jest ważne**	to yest **vazh**-ne
It's urgent	**To jest pilne**	to yest **peel**-ne
You're right	**Ma pan(i) rację**	ma pan (**pa**-nee) **ra**-tsye^{n}
You're wrong	**Pan(i) się myli**	pan (**pa**-nee) shye^{n} **mi**-lee
You're mistaken	**Pan(i) się myli**	pan (**pa**-nee) shye^{n} **mi**-lee
It's cheap	**To jest tanio**	to yest **ta**-nyo
It's too expensive	**To jest za drogo**	to yest za **dro**-go
That's all	**To wszystko**	to **fshist**-ko
Leave me alone	**Proszę mnie zostawić w spokoju**	**pro**-she^{n} mnye zos-**ta**-veech fspo-**ko**-yoo
Just a minute	***Chwileczkę**	hvee-**lech**-ke^{n}
This way, please	***Tędy, proszę**	**te**^{n}-di **pro**-she^{n}
Take a seat	***Proszę siadać**	**pro**-she^{n} **shya**-dach
Come in!	***Proszę!**	**pro**-she^{n}

GREETINGS

Good morning/good day	**Dzień dobry**	dgyen do-bri
Good afternoon	**Dzień dobry**	dgyen do-bri
Good evening	**Dobry wieczór**	do-bri vye-choor
Good night	**Dobranoc**	do-bra-nots
How are you?	**Jak się pan(i) czuje?**	yak shye^n pan (pa-nee) choo-ye
Very well, thank you	**Bardzo dobrze, dziękuję**	bar-dzo dob-zhe dgye^n-koo-ye^n
Good-bye	**Do widzenia**	do vee-dze-nya
See you soon	**Do zobaczenia**	do zo-ba-che-nya
See you tomorrow	**Do zobaczenia jutro**	do zo-ba-che-nya yoo-tro
Thanks for a pleasant time	**Dziękuję za wszystko**	dgye^n-koo-ye^n za fshist-ko
Thanks for the invitation	**Dziękuję za zaproszenie**	dgye^n-koo-ye^n za za-pro-she-nye
Have a good journey	**Szczęśliwej podróży**	shche^n-shlee-vey po-droo-zhi
Have a nice time	**Życzę przyjemnego spędzenia czasu**	zhi-che^n pshi-yem-ne-go spe^n-dze-nya cha-soo
Good luck/all the best	**Powodzenia/wszystkiego najlepszego**	po-vo-dze-nya/fshist-kye-gonay-lep-she-go

POLITE PHRASES

Sorry/excuse me	**Przepraszam**	pshe-**pra**-sham
Excuse me (*to pass*)	**Przepraszam**	pshe-**pra**-sham
With pleasure	**Proszę bardzo/z przyjemnością**	**pro**-she^n **bar**-dzo/spshi-yem-**nosh**-chyo^n
That's all right	**Nic nie szkodzi**	neets nye **shko**-dgee
Not at all	**Nie szkodzi**	nye **shko**-dgee
Don't mention it (*after thanks*)	**Proszę bardzo**	**pro**-she^n **bar**-dzo
Everything all right?	**Wszystko w porządku?**	**fshist**-ko fpo-**zho^{n}d**-koo
Can't complain	**Nie mogę narzekać**	nye **mo**-ge^n na-**zhe**-kach
Don't worry	**Proszę się nie przejmować**	**pro**-she^n shye^n nye pshey-**mo**-vach
It doesn't matter	**Nie szkodzi**	nye **shko**-dgee
I beg your pardon?	**Słucham?**	**swoo**-ham
Am I disturbing you?	**Czy nie przeszkadzam?**	chi nye pshesh-**ka**-dzam
I'm sorry to have troubled you	**Przepraszam, że przeszkodziłem (-am)**	pshe-**pra**-sham zhe pshesh-ko-**dgee**-wem (-wam)
Good/that's fine	**Dobrze/doskonale**	**do**-bzhe/dos-ko-**na**-le
Thank you for your help	**Dziękuję za pomoc**	dgye^n-**koo**-ye^n za **po**-mots
That's very kind of you	**Bardzo uprzejmie z pańskiej strony**	**bar**-dzo oop-**shey**-mye **span**-skyey **stro**-ni
It's nice/beautiful	**Przyjemnie/ślicznie**	pshi-**yem**-nye/**shleech**-nye

OPPOSITES

before/after	**przed/po**	pshed/po
early/late	**wcześnie/późno**	fchesh-nye/poozh-no
first/last	**pierwszy/ostatni**	pyerv-shi/os-tat-nee
now/later, then	**teraz/później, wtedy**	te-raz/poozh-nyey, fte-di
far/near	**daleko/blisko**	de-le-ko/blees-ko
here/there	**tutaj/tam**	too-tay/tam
in/out	**w/poza**	v/po-za
inside/outside	**wewnątrz/na zewnątrz**	vev-no^{n}tsh/na zev-no^{n}tsh
under/over	**pod/nad**	pod/nad
big, large/small	**duży, wielki/mały**	doo-zhi, vyel-kee/ma-wi
deep/shallow	**głęboki/płytki**	gwe^{n}-bo-kee/pwit-kee
empty/full	**pusty/pełny**	poos-ti/pew-ni
fat/lean	**tłusty/chudy**	twoos-ti/hoo-di
heavy/light	**ciężki/lekki**	chye^{n}zh-kee/lek-kee
high/low	**wysoki/niski**	vi-so-kee/nees-kee
long/short	**długi/krótki**	dwoo-gee/kroot-kee
narrow/wide	**wąski/szeroki**	vo^{n}s-kee/she-ro-kee
tall/short	**wysoki/niski**	vi-so-kee/nees-kee
thick/thin	**gruby/cienki**	groo-bi/chyen-kee
least/most	**najmniej/najwięcej**	nay-mnyey/nay-vye^{n}-tsey
many/few	**wiele/mało**	vye-le/ma-wo
more/less	**więcej/mniej**	vye^{n}-tsey/mnyey

much/little	dużo/mało	doo-zho/ma-wo
beautiful/ugly	piękny/brzydki	pye^{n}k-ni/bzhid-kee
better/worse	lepszy/gorszy	lep-shi/gor-shi
cheap/dear	tani/drogi	ta-nee/dro-gee
clean/dirty	czysty/brudny	chis-ti/brood-ni
cold/hot, warm	zimny/gorący, ciepły	zheem-ni/go-ro^{n}-tsi, chyep-wi
easy/difficult	łatwy/trudny	wat-vi/trood-ni
fresh/stale	świeży/nieświeży	shvye-zhi/nye-shvye-zhi
good/bad	dobry/zły	dob-ri/zwi
new, young/old	nowy, młody/stary	no-vi, mwo-di/sta-ri
nice/nasty	przyjemny/ nieprzyjemny	pshi-yem-ni/ nye-pshi-yem-ni
right/wrong	właściwy/ niewłaściwy	vwash-chee-vi/ nye-vwash-chee-vi
free/taken	wolny/zajęty	vol-ni/za-ye^{n}-ti
open/closed, shut	otwarty/zamknięty	ot-var-ti/zam-knye^{n}-ti
quick/slow	szybki/powolny	shib-kee/po-vol-ni
quiet/noisy	cichy/hałaśliwy	chee-hi/ha-wash-lee-vi
sharp/blunt	ostry/tępy	os-tri/te^{n}-pi

SIGNS & PUBLIC NOTICES[1]

Bank	Bank
Bilety wysprzedane	House full (cinema etc.)
Ciągnąć	Pull
Damski/dla kobiet/dla pań	Ladies
Do wynajęcia	To let
Informacja	Information
Kasa	Cash desk/cashier
Męski/dla mężczyzn/dla panów	Gentlemen
Policja	Police station
Na sprzedaż	For sale
Nie …	Do not …
Niebezpieczeństwo	Danger
Nie do picia	Not for drinking
Nie palić/palenie wzbronione	No smoking

1. See also SIGNS TO LOOK FOR AT AIRPORTS AND STATIONS (p. 20) and ROAD SIGNS (p. 37).

bcym wstęp wzbroniony	Trespassers will be prosecuted
twarte od ... do ...	Open from ... to ...
hać	Push
esi	Pedestrians
ciągnąć	Pull
czta	Post Office
kój do wynajęcia	Room to let
oszę dzwonić	Ring
oszę nie dotykać	Please do not touch
oszę pukać	Knock
zewodnik	Guide
umacz	Interpreter
ylko miejsca stojące	Standing room only
prasza się nie ...	You are requested not to ...
waga	Caution
C/△ men/O women	Lavatory
ejście	Entrance
inda	Lift/elevator
oda do picia	Drinking water
olny	Vacant/free/unoccupied
stęp bezpłatny/wolny	Admission free
stęp wzbroniony	No entrance/no admission
yjście	Exit
yjście/drzwi zapasowe	Emergency exit
ysprzedaż	Sale
jęty	Engaged/occupied

Zamknięte/nieczynne	Closed
Zarezerwowane	Reserved

ABBREVIATIONS

Al.	avenue
b.m.	this month
b.r.	this year
CEPELIA	folk art and souvenir shops
CPN	petrol station
DESA	souvenirs and antiques
dr.	doctor
dyr.	director
EWG	EC
godz.	hour
inż.	civil engineer
IT	tourist information
m. *(followed by a number)*	flat, apartment
mgr.	MA, MSc.
min.	minute
ORNO	shops for silver jewellery
pan	Mr (*in written address:* W. Pan)
pani	Mrs (*in written address:* W. Pani)
PKP	Polish Railways
PKS	coach service

PTTK	Polish Tourist Association
spółka	company (limited)
Ul.	street, road
w/w	above mentioned

MONEY

Is there an exchange bureau near here?	**Czy jest w pobliżu biuro wymiany walut?**	chi yest fpo-**blee**-zhoo **byoo**-ro vi-**mya**-ni **va**-loot
Do you change travellers' cheques?	**Czy można tu wymienić czeki podróżnicze?**	chi **mozh**-na too vi-**mye**-neech **che**-kee po-droozh-**nee**-che
Where can I change travellers' cheques?	**Gdzie mogę wymienić czeki podróżnicze?**	gdgye **mo**-ge^{n} vi-**mye**-neech **che**-kee po-droozh-**nee**-che
Please cash this Eurocheque	**Proszę mi spieniężyć ten czek**	**pro**-she^{n} mee spye-**nye**^{n}-zhich ten chek
May I see your passport?	**Poproszę o paszport**	po-**pro**-she^{n} o **pash**-port
I want to change some pounds/dollars	**Chcę wymienić kilka funtów/dolarów**	htse^{n} vi-mye-neech **keel**-k foon-toov/do-**la**-roov
How much do I get for a pound/dollar?	**Ile dostanę za funta/za dolara?**	**ee**-le dos-**ta**-ne^{n} za **foon**-ta/za do-**la**-ra

What is the current rate of exchange?	**Jaki jest obecny kurs wymiany?**	ya-kee yest o-**bets**-ni koors vi-**mya**-ni
Can you give me some small change?	**Czy mogę prosić o drobne?**	chi **mo**-ge^{n} **pro**-sheech o **drob**-ne
Where do I sign?	**Gdzie mam podpisać?**	gdgye mam pod-**pee**-sach
Sign here, please	***Proszę tutaj podpisać**	**pro**-she^{n} **too**-tay pod-**pee**-sach
Go to the cashier	***Proszę iść do kasy**	**pro**-she^{n} eeshch do **ka**-si
I arranged for money to be transferred from England, has it arrived yet?	**Załatwiłem (-łam) przelew pieniędzy z Anglii, czy już te pieniądze przyszły?**	za-wat-**vee**-wem (-wam) pshe-lev pye-**nye**^{n}-dzi **zan**-glee, chi yoozh te pye-**nyo**^{n}-dze **pshish**-wi
I want to open a bank account	**Chcę otworzyć konto bankowe**	htse^{n} o-**tvo**-zhich **kon**-to ban-**ko**-ve
Please credit this to my account	**Proszę to wpłacić na moje konto**	**pro**-she^{n} to **vpwa**-cheech na **mo**-ye **kon**-to
I'd like to get some cash with my credit card	**Chciałbym (-abym) podjąć gotówkę na kartę kredytową**	**hchyaw**-bim (hchya-**wa**-bim) **pod**-yo^{n}ch go-**toov**-ke^{n} na **kar**-te^{n} kre-di-**to**-vo^{n}
Will you take a credit card?	**Czy państwo przyjmują karty kredytowe?**	chi **pan**-stvo pshiy-**moo**-yo^{n} **kar**-ti kre-di-**to**-ve
Current account	**Konto bieżące**	**kon**-to bye-**zho**^{n}-tse
Deposit account	**Konto oszczędnościowe/ zablokowane**	**kon**-to osh-che^{n}d-nosh-**chyo**-ve/ za-blo-ko-**va**-ne
Statement	**Wyciąg**	**vi**-chyo^{n}g

Balance	**Stan konta**	stan kon-ta
Cheque book	**Książeczka czekowa**	kshyo^{n}-zhech-ka che-ko-v
Cheque card	**Karta czekowa**	kar-ta che-ko-va

CURRENCY

100 groszy = 1 złoty

'RAVEL

ARRIVAL

ASSPORTS

ssport control	***Kontrola paszportowa**	kon-tro-la pash-por-to-va
our passport, please	***Paszport proszę**	pash-port proshe^{n}
ay I see your reen card please?	***Proszę pokazać zaświadczenia międzynarodowego ubezpieczenia?**	pro-she^{n} po-ka-zach zash-vyad-che-nye mye^{n}-dzi-na-ro-do-ve-go oo-bez-pye-che-nya
e you together?	***Czy państwo są razem?**	chi pan-stvo so^{n} ra-zem
n travelling alone	**Podróżuję sam(a)**	po-droo-zhoo-ye^{n} sam (sa-ma)
n travelling with my vife/a friend	**Jestem z żoną ze znajomym (-mą)**	yes-tem z zho-no^{n}/ze zna-yo-mim (-mo^{n})

I'm here on business/ on holiday	**Jestem tutaj służbowo/na wakacjach**	yes-tem too-tay swoozh-bo-vo/na va-kats-yah
What is your address in Warsaw?	***Jaki jest pana(i) adres w Warszawie?**	ya-kee yest pa-na (-ne a-dres v var-sha-vye
How long are you staying here?	***Jak długo się pan(i) tutaj zatrzyma?**	yak dwoo-go shye^{n} pan (pa-nee) too-tay za-tshi-

CUSTOMS

Customs	***Kontrola celna**	kon-tro-la tsel-na
Which is your luggage?	***Gdzie jest pana(i) bagaż?**	gdgye yest pa-na (-nee ba-gazh
Do you have any more luggage?	***Czy ma pan(i) jakieś inne bagaże?**	chi ma pan (pa-nee) ya-kesh een-ne ba-ga-
This is (all) my luggage	**To jest mój (cały) bagaż**	to yest mooy (tsa-wi) ba-gazh
You must fill in a customs form	***Musi pan(i) wypełnić deklarację celną**	moo-shee pan (pa-ne vi-pew-nich de-kla- tsye^{n} tsel-no^{n}
Have you anything to declare?	***Czy ma pan(i) coś do oclenia?**	chi ma pan (pa-nee) tsosh do o-tsle-nya
I have only my personal things in it	**Tu są tylko moje rzeczy osobiste**	too so^{n} til-ko mo-ye zhe-chi o-so-bees-t
I have a carton of cigarettes and a bottle of gin/wine	**Mam karton papierosów i butelkę ginu/wina**	mam kar-ton pa-pye- soov ee boo-tel-ke^{n} jee-noo/vee-na
You will have to pay duty on this	***Musi pan(i) zapłacić za to cło**	moo-shee pan (pa-ne za-pwa-cheech za to t
Open this bag, please	***Proszę otworzyć walizkę**	pro-she^{n} o-tvo-zhich va-leez-ke^{n}

Can I shut my case now?	**Czy mogę już zamknąć walizkę?**	chi mo-ge^{n} yoozh zam-kno^{n}ch va-leez-ke^{n}
How much money have you got?	***Ile ma pan(i) pieniędzy?**	ee-le ma pan (pa-nee) pye-nye^{n}-dzi
I have ... pounds/dollars	**Mam ... funtów/dolarów**	mam ... foon-toov/do-la-roov
May I go?	**Czy mogę odejść?**	chi mo-ge^{n} o-deyshch

LUGGAGE

My luggage has not arrived	**Nie ma mojego bagażu**	nye ma mo-ye-go ba-ga-zhoo
My luggage is damaged	**Mój bagaż jest uszkodzony**	mooy ba-gazh yest oo-shko-dzo-ni
One suitcase is missing	**Brakuje jednej walizki**	bra-koo-ye yed-ney va-leez-kee
Are there any luggage trolleys?	**Czy są wózki bagażowe?**	chi so^{n} vooz-kee ba-ga-zho-ve
Where is the left luggage office?	**Gdzie jest przechowalnia bagażu?**	gdgye yest pshe-ho-val-nya ba-ga-zhoo
Luggage lockers	**Schowek na bagaż**	s-ho-vek-na ba-gazh

MOVING ON

Porter!	**Bagażowy!**	ba-ga-zho-vi
Would you take these bags to a taxi/the bus?	**Czy może pan zanieść te walizki do taksówki/autobusu?**	chi mo-zhe pan za-nyeshch te va-leez-kee do tak-soov-kee/a-oo-to-boo-soo

What's the price for each piece of luggage?	**Jaka jest cena od sztuki?**	ya-ka yest tse-na od shtoo-kee
I shall take this myself	**Sam (-a) to poniosę**	sam (sa-ma) to po-nyo-se
That's not mine	**To nie moje**	to nye mo-ye
Would you call a taxi?	**Proszę mi sprowadzić taksówkę?**	pro-she^{n} mee spro-va-dgeech tak-soov-ke^{n}
How much do I owe you?	**Ile jestem panu winien/(winna)?**	ee-le yes-tem pa-noo vee-nyen (veen-na)
Is there a bus/train into the town?	**Czy jest autobus/pociąg do miasta?**	chi yest a-oo-to-boos/po-chyo^{n}g do myas-ta
How can I get to ...?	**Jak dostanę się do ...?**	yak dos-ta-ne^{n} shye^{n} do

SIGNS TO LOOK FOR AT AIRPORTS AND STATIONS

Arrivals	**Przyjazd/przylot**	pshi-yazd/pshi-lot
Booking office	**Kasa biletowa**	ka-sa bee-le-to-va
Buses	**Autobusy**	a-oo-to-boo-si
Car rental	**Rent-a-car**	rent-e-kar
Departures	**Odjazd/odlot**	od-yazd/od-lot
Exchange	**Wymiana walut**	vi-mya-na va-loot
Gentlemen	**Męski/dla mężczyzn/dla panów**	me^{n}s-kee/dla me^{n}zh-chizn dla pa-noov
Hotel reservations	**Rezerwacje hotelowe**	re-zer-vats-ye ho-te-lo-v
Information	**Informacja**	een-for-ma-tsya
Ladies' room	**Damski/dla kobiet/dla pań**	dam-skee/dla ko-byet/dla pan

Left luggage	**Przechowalnia bagażu**	pshe-ho-val-nya ba-ga-zhoo
Lost property	**Biuro rzeczy znalezionych**	byoo-ro zhe-chi zna-le-zhyo-nih
News-stand	**Kiosk z gazetami**	kyosk zga-ze-ta-mee
Non-smoker	**Dla niepalących**	dla nye pa-lo^{n}-tsih
Refreshments	**Bufet**	boo-fet
Reservations	**Rezerwacje**	re-zer-va-tsye
Smoker	**Dla palących**	dla pa-lo^{n}-tsih
Suburban lines	**Linie podmiejskie**	lee-nye pod-myey-skye
Taxis	**Taksówki**	tak-soov-kee
Tickets	**Bilety**	bee-le-ti
Tourist office	**Biuro obsługi turystycznej**	byoo-ro ob-swoo-gee too-ris-tich-ney
Transit desk	**Tranzyt**	tran-zit
Waiting room	**Poczekalnia**	po-che-kal-nya

BUYING A TICKET

Where's the nearest travel agency/tourist office?	**Gdzie jest najbliższe biuro podróży/biuro obsługi turystycznej?**	gdgye yest nay-bleezh-she byoo-ro po-droo-zhi/ byoo-ro ob-swoo-gee too-ris-tich-ney
Have you a timetable, please?	**Czy ma pan(i) rozkład jazdy?**	chi ma pan (pa-nee) roz-kwad yaz-di
What's the tourist return fare to ...?	**Ile kosztuje bilet powrotny do ...?**	ee-le kosh-too-ye bee-let po-vrot-ni do
How much is it first class to ...?	**Ile kosztuje pierwsza klasa do ...?**	ee-le kosh-too-ye pyerv-sha kla-sa do

A second class single to …	**Druga klasa w jedną stronę do …**	droo-ga **kla**-sa vyed-no^{n} **stro**-ne^{n} do
Three singles to …	**Trzy w jedną stronę do …**	tshi **vyed**-no^{n} **stro**-ne^{n} do
Is there a special rate for children?	**Czy jest zniżka dla dzieci?**	chi yest **zneezh**-ka dla **dgye**-chee
How old is he/she?	***Ile on/ona ma lat?**	ee-le on/o-na ma lat
How long is this ticket valid?	**Jak długo jest ważny ten bilet?**	yak **dwoo**-go yest **vazh**-ni ten **bee**-let
A book of tickets, please	**Poproszę bloczek biletowy**	po-**pro**-she^{n} **blo**-chek bee-le-**to**-vi
Is there a supplementary charge?	**Czy jest dodatkowa opłata?**	chi yest do-dat-**ko**-va o-**pwa**-ta
Is there a cheaper fare?	**Czy są jakieś tańsze bilety?**	chi so^{n} **ya**-kyesh **tan**-she bee-**le**-ti
A day return to …	**Powrotny do …**	po-**vrot**-ni do
When are you coming back?	***Kiedy będzie pan(i) wracać?**	**kye**-di **be**^{n}-dgye pan (**pa**-nee) **vra**-tsach

BY TRAIN[1]

RESERVATIONS AND INQUIRIES

Where's the railway station?	**Gdzie jest dworzec kolejowy?**	gdgye yest **dvo**-zhets ko-le-**yo**-vi
Where is the ticket office?	**Gdzie jest kasa biletowa?**	gdgye yest **ka**-sa bee-le-**to**-va

1. For help in understanding the answers to these and similar questions see TIME (p. 179), NUMBERS (p. 185), DIRECTIONS (p. 32).

Two seats on the … tomorrow to …	**Dwa bilety na jutro na pociąg … do …**	dva bee-le-ti na yoo-tro na po-chyo^{n}g …do
I want a window seat/ a corner seat/ a seat in a non-smoking compartment	**Poproszę o miejsce przy oknie/w rogu/ w przedziale dla niepalących**	po-pro-she^n o myey-stse pshi o-knye/vro-goo/ fpshe-dgya-le dla nye-pa-lo^n-tsih
I want to reserve a sleeper	**Chcę zarezerwować miejsce w wagonie sypialnym**	htse^n za-re-zer-vo-vach myey-stse v va-go-nye si-pyal-nim
How much does a couchette cost?	**Ile kosztuje kuszetka?**	ee-le kosh-too-ye koo-shet-ka
I want to register this luggage through to …	**Chcę nadać ten bagaż do …**	htse^n na-dach ten ba-gazh do
When is the next train to …?	**Kiedy jest następny pociąg do …?**	kye-di yest nas-te^{n}p-ni po-chyo^{n}g do
Is it an express or a local train?	**Czy to jest pociąg ekspresowy czy podmiejski?**	chi to yest po-chyo^{n}g eks-pre-so-vi chi pod-myey-skee
Is there a later/earlier train?	**Czy jest późniejszy/ wcześniejszy pociąg?**	chi yest poozh-nyey-shi/ fchesh-nyey-shi po-chyo^{n}g
Is there a restaurant car on the train?	**Czy jest w tym pociągu wagon restauracyjny?**	chi yest ftim po-chyo^n-goo va-gon res-ta-oo-ra-tsiy-ni

CHANGING

Is there a through train to …?	**Czy jest bezpośredni pociąg do …?**	chi yest bez-po-shred-nee po-chyo^{n}g do
Is there a through carriage to …?	**Czy jest bezpośredni wagon do …?**	chi yest bez-po-shred-nee va-gon do
Do I have to change?	**Czy muszę się przesiadać?**	chi moo-she^n shye^n pshe-shya-dach

Where do I change?	**Gdzie się mam przesiadać?**	gdgye shye^n mam pshe-**shya**-dach
What time is there a connection to …?	**Kiedy jest połączenie do …?**	kye-di yest po-wo^n-**che**-nye do
Change at … and take the local train	***Proszę się przesiąść w … i wziąć podmiejski pociąg**	**pro**-she^n shye^n **pshe**-shyo^{n}shch v … ee vzhyo^{n}ch pod-**myey**-skee **po**-chyo^{n}g

DEPARTURE

When does the train leave?	**Kiedy ten pociąg odjeżdża?**	kye-di ten **po**-chyo^{n}g od-**yezh**-ja
Which platform does the train to … leave from?	**Z którego peronu odjeżdża pociąg do ...?**	sktoo-**re**-go pe-**ro**-noo od-**yezh**-ja **po**-chyo^{n}g do
Is this the train for …?	**Czy to jest pociąg do ...?**	chi to yest **po**-chyo^{n}g do
There will be a delay of …	***Będzie opóźnienie ...**	**be**^{n}-dgye o-poozh-**nye**-nye

ARRIVAL

When does it get to …?	**O której przyjeżdżamy do …?**	o **ktoo**-rey pshi-yezh-**ja**-mi do
Does the train stop at …?	**Czy ten pociąg zatrzymuje się w …?**	chi ten **po**-chyo^{n}g za-tshi-**moo**-ye shye^n v
How long do we stop here?	**Jak długo się tu zatrzymujemy?**	yak **dwoo**-go shye^n too za-tshi-moo-**ye**-mi
Is the train late?	**Czy pociąg jest opóźniony?**	chi **po**-chyo^{n}g yest o-poozh-**nyo**-ni
When does the train from … get in?	**Kiedy przyjeżdża pociąg z …?**	kye-di pshi-**yezh**-ja **po**-chyo^{n}g z
At which platform?	**Z którego peronu?**	sktoo-**re**-go pe-**ro**-noo

ON THE TRAIN

We have reserved seats	**Mamy miejsca zarezerwowane**	ma-mi myey-stsa za-re-zer-vo-va-ne
Is this seat free?	**Czy to miejsce jest wolne?**	chi to myey-stse yest vol-ne
This seat is taken	**To miejsce jest zajęte**	to myey-stse yest za-ye^{n}-te
Conductor	**Konduktor**	kon-doo-ktor
Is this a smoking/ non-smoking compartment?	**Czy to jest przedział dla palących/ niepalących?**	chi to yest pshe-dgyaw dla pa-lo^{n}-tsih/ nye-pa-lo^{n}-tsih
Dining car	**Wagon restauracyjny**	va-gon res-taoo-ra-tsiy-ni
When is the buffet car open?	**Kiedy jest otwarty bufet?**	kye-di yest ot-var-ti boo-fet
Where is the sleeping car?	**Gdzie jest wagon sypialny?**	gdgye yest va-gon si-pyal-ni
Which is my sleeper?	**Gdzie jest moje miejsce sypialne?**	gdgye yest mo-ye myeys-tse si-pyal-ne
The heating is too high/too low	**Ogrzewanie jest nastawione za wysoko/za nisko**	ogzhe-va-nye yest na-sta-vyo-ne za vi-so-ko/za nees-ko
I can't open/close the window	**Nie mogę otworzyć/ zamknąć okna**	nye mo-ge^{n} ot-vo-zhich/ zam-kno^{n}ch o-kna
What station is this?	**Jaka to jest stacja?**	ya-ka to yest sta-tsya
How long do we stop here?	**Jak długo się tu zatrzymamy?**	yak dwoo-go shye^{n} too za-tshi-ma-mi

BY AIR

Where's the LOT office?	**Gdzie jest biuro LOT-u?**	gdgye yest **byoo**-roo **lo**-too
I'd like to book two seats on Monday's plane to …	**Chcę zamówić dwa miejsca na poniedziałek, na samolot do …**	htse^{n} za-**moo**-veech dva **myey**-stsa na po-nye-**dgya**-wek na sa-**mo**-lot do
Is there a flight to …?	**Czy jest lot do …?**	chi yest lot do
What is the flight number?	**Jaki jest numer lotu?**	ya-kee yest **noo**-mer **lo**-too
When does it leave/arrive?	**Kiedy odlatuje/ przylatuje?**	**kye**-di od-la-**too**-ye/ pshi-la-**too**-ye
When does the next plane leave?	**Kiedy odlatuje następny samolot?**	**kye**-di od-la-**too**-ye na-**ste**^{n}p-ni sa-**mo**-lot
Is there a coach to the town/the airport?	**Czy jest autobus do miasta/na lotnisko?**	chi yest a-oo-to-**boos** do **myas**-ta/na lot-**nees**-ko
When must I check in?	**Kiedy mam się zgłosić na lotnisku?**	**kye**-di mam shye^{n} **zgwo**-sheech na lot-**nees**-koo
Please cancel my reservation to …	**Proszę unieważnić moją rezerwację do …**	**pro**-she^{n} oo-nye-**vazh**-neech **mo**-yo^{n} re-zer-**va**-tsye^{n} do
I'd like to change my reservation to …	**Chcę zmienić rezerwację na …**	htse^{n} **zmye**-neech re-zer-**va**-tsye^{n} na
I have an open ticket	**Mam otwarty bilet**	mam ot-**far**-ti **bee**-let
Can I change my ticket?	**Czy mogę zmienić bilet?**	chi **mo**-ge^{n} **zmye**-neech **bee**-let
Will it cost more?	**Czy to będzie drożej kosztować?**	chi to **be**^{n}-dgye **dro**-zhey kosh-**to**-vach

BY BOAT

Is there a ferry/boat from here to …?	**Czy jest stąd prom/ statek do …?**	chi yest sto^{n}d prom/ sta-tek do
How long does it take to get to …?	**Jak długo trwa podróż do …?**	yak **dwoo**-go trva po-droozh do
How often do the boats leave?	**Jak często odpływają statki?**	yak **che**^{n}-sto od-pwi-va-yo^{n} stat-kee
Where does the boat put in?	**Gdzie statek przybija do brzegu?**	gdgye **sta**-tek pshi-**bee**-ya do **bzhe**-goo
Does it call at …?	**Czy statek zatrzymuje się w …?**	chi **sta**-tak za-tshi-**moo**-ye shye^{n} v
When does the next boat leave?	**Kiedy odpływa następny statek?**	**kye**-di od-**pwi**-va na-**ste**^{n}p-ni **sta**-tek
Can I book a single-berth cabin?	**Czy mogę zarezerwować kabinę jednoosobową?**	chi **mo**-ge^{n} za-re-zer-**vo**-vach ka-**bee**-ne^{n} yed-no-o-so-**bo**-vo^{n}
How many berths are there in this cabin?	**Ile łóżek jest w tej kabinie?**	**ee**-le **woo**-zhek yest ftey ka-**bee**-nye
How do we get on to the deck?	**Jak dostaniemy się na pokład?**	yak dos-ta-**nye**-mi shye^{n} na **po**-kwad
When must we go on board?	**Kiedy mamy się zgłosić na statku?**	**kye**-di **ma**-mi shye^{n} **zgwo**-sheech na **stat**-koo
When do we dock?	**Kiedy przypływamy do portu?**	**kye**-di pshi-pwi-**va**-mi do **por**-too
How long do we stay in port?	**Jak długo zatrzymamy się w porcie?**	yak **dwoo**-go za-tshi-**ma**-mi shye^{n} **fpor**-tchye

Hovercraft	**Poduszkowiec**	po-doosh-**ko**-vyets
Hydrofoil	**Wodolot**	vo-**do**-lot
Lifebelt	**Pas ratunkowy**	pas ra-toon-**ko**-vi
Lifeboat	**Łódź ratunkowa**	woodg ra-toon-**ko**-va

BY BUS OR COACH

Where's the bus station?	**Gdzie jest stacja autobusowa?**	gdgye yest **sta**-tsya a-oo-to-boo-**so**-va
Where is the bus stop?	**Gdzie jest przystanek autobusowy?**	gdgye yest pshi-**sta**-nek a-oo-to-boo-**so**-vi
Where's the coach station?	**Gdzie jest stacja autokarowa?**	gdgye yest **sta**-tsya a-oo-to-ka-**ro**-va
Bus stop	***Przystanek autobusowy**	pshi-**sta**-nek a-oo-to-boo-**so**-vi
Request stop	***Przystanek na żądanie**	pshi-**sta**-nek na zho^{n}-**da**-nye
When does the coach leave?	**Kiedy odjeżdża autokar?**	kye-di od-**yezh**-ja a-oo-**to**-kar
What time do we get to …?	**O której godzinie przyjeżdżamy do …?**	o **ktoo**-rey go-**dgee**-nye pshi-yezh-**ja**-mi do
What stops does it make?	**Gdzie się zatrzymujemy po drodze?**	gdgye shye^{n} za-tshi-moo-**ye**-mi po-**dro**-dze
Is it a long journey?	**Czy to jest długa podróż?**	chi to yest **dwoo**-ga **po**-droozh
We want to take a sightseeing tour round the city	**Chcielibyśmy się wybrać na zwiedzanie miasta**	hchye-lee-**bish**-mi shye^{n} vi-**brach** na zvye-**dza**-nye **myas**-ta

Is there a sightseeing tour?	**Czy jest wycieczka po mieście?**	chi yest vi-**chyech**-ka po **myesh**-tsye
What is the fare?	**Jaka jest opłata?**	**ya**-ka yest o-**pwa**-ta
Does the bus/coach stop at our hotel?	**Czy autobus/autokar zatrzymuje się przed naszym hotelem?**	chi a-oo-**to**-boos/a-oo-**to**-kar za-tshi-**moo**-ye shye^{n} pshed na-shim ho-**te**-lem
Is there an excursion to ...tomorrow?	**Czy jest jutro wycieczka do ...?**	chi yest **yoo**-tro vi-**chyech**-ka do
What time is the next bus?	**O której godzinie jest następny autobus?**	o **ktoo**-rey go-**dgee**-nye yest na-**ste^{n}p**-ni a-oo-**to**-boos
How often does the 25 run?	**Jak często chodzi dwadzieścia pięć?**	yak **che^{n}s**-to **ho**-dgee dwa-**dgyesh**-cha pye^{n}ch
Has the last bus gone?	**Czy odjechał ostatni autobus?**	chi **odye**-haw o-**stat**-ni a-oo-**to**-boos
Does this bus go to the centre?	**Czy ten autobus jedzie do centrum?**	chi ten a-oo-**to**-boos **ye**-dgye do **tsen**-troom
Does this bus go to the beach/to the station?	**Czy ten autobus jedzie na plażę/na dworzec?**	chi ten a-oo-**to**-boos **ye**-dgye na **pla**-zhe^{n}/na **dvo**-zhets
Does it go near ...?	**Czy on jedzie w pobliże ...?**	chi on **ye**-dgye fpo-**blee**-zhe
Where can I get a bus to ...?	**Gdzie jest autobus do ...?**	gdgye yest a-oo-**to**-boos do
Is this the right stop for ...?	**Czy to jest przystanek na ...?**	chi to yest pshi-**sta**-nek na
I want to get off at ...	**Chcę wysiąść przy ...**	htse^{n} vi-**shyo^{n}shch** pshi
I want to go to ...	**Chcę jechać do ...**	htse^{n} **ye**-hach do
Where do I get off?	**Gdzie mam wysiąść?**	gdgye mam **vi-shyo^{n}shch**
The bus to ... stops over there	***Autobus do ... zatrzymuje się tam**	a-oo-**to**-boos do ... za-tshi-**moo**-ye shye^{n} tam

A number 30 goes to ...	***Numer trzydzieści jedzie do ...**	noo-mer tshi-dgyesh-chee ye-dgye do
You must take a number 24	***Musi pan(i) wsiąść w numer dwadzieścia cztery**	moo-shee pan (pa-nee) fshyo^{n}shch v noo-mer dva-dgyesh-chya chte-ri
You get off at the next stop	***Będzie pan(i) wysiadać na następnym przystanku**	be^n-dgye pan (pa-nee) vi-shya-dach na nas-te^{n}p-nim pshi-stan-koo
The buses run every ten minutes/every hour	***Autobusy jeżdżą co dziesięć minut/co godzinę**	a-oo-to-boo-si yezh-jo^n tso dgye-shye^{n}ch mee-noot/tso go-dgee-ne^n

BY TAXI

Please get me a taxi	**Proszę mi zawołać taksówkę**	pro-she^n mee za-vo-wach ta-ksoov-ke^n
Where can I find a taxi?	**Gdzie znajdę taksówkę?**	gdgye znay-de^n tak-soov-ke^n
Are you free?	**Czy pan jest wolny?**	chi pan yest vol-ni
Please take me to Hotel Central/the station/this address	**Proszę mnie zawieźć do Hotelu Central/ na stację/ na dworzec/ pod ten adres**	pro-she^n mnye za-vyezhch do ho-te-loo tsen-tral/ na stats-ye^n/ na dvo-zhets/ pod ten a-dres
Can you hurry, I'm late?	**Czy może się pan pośpieszyć? Jestem spóźniony (-a)**	chi mo-zhe shye^n pan posh-pye-shich? yes-tem spoozh-nyo-ni (-na)
I want to go through the centre	**Chciałbym (-abym) pojechać przez centrum**	hchyaw-bim (hchya-wa-bim) po-ye-hach pshez tsen-troom

Please wait a minute	**Proszę chwilę zaczekać**	pro-she^n hvee-le^n za-che-kach
Please stop here	**Proszę się tutaj zatrzymać**	pro-she^n shye^n too-tay za-tshi-mach
Is it far?	**Czy to jest daleko?**	chi to yest da-le-ko
How far is it to …?	**Jak daleko jest do …?**	yak da-le-ko yest do
Turn right/left at the next corner	**Proszę skręcić w prawo/w lewo za następnym rogiem**	pro-she^n skre^n-chich fpra-vo/vle-vo za nas-te^{n}p-nim ro-gyem
Straight on	**Prosto**	pros-to
How much do you charge by the hour/for the day?	**Ile pan liczy za godzinę/za dzień?**	ee-le pan lee-chi za go-dgee-ne^n/za dgyen
I'd like to go to … How much would you charge?	**Chciałbym (-abym) pojechać do … Ile to będzie kosztować?**	hchyaw-bim (hchya-wa-bim) po-ye-hach do …ee-le to be^n-dgye kosh-to-vach
How much is it?	**Ile to kosztuje?**	ee-le to kosh-too-ye
That's too much	**To za drogo**	to za dro-go
I am not prepared to spend that much	**Nie jestem przygotowany (-a) na taki wydatek**	nye yes-tem pshi-go-to-va-ni (-na) na ta-kee vi-da-tek
It's a lot, but all right	**To bardzo drogo, ale zgadzam się**	to bar-dzo dro-go a-le zga-dzam shye^n

DIRECTIONS

Excuse me – could you tell me ...	**Przepraszam – czy może mi pan(i) powiedzieć ...**	pshe-pra-sham – chi mo-zhe mee pan (pa-nee) po-vye-dgyech
Where is ...?	**Gdzie jest ...?**	gdgye yest
Is this the way to ...?	**Czy tędy do ...?**	chi te^n -di do
Which is the road for ...?	**Która droga prowadzi do ...?**	ktoo-ra dro-ga pro-va-dgee do
Is this the right road for ...?	**Czy to jest droga do ...?**	chi to yest dro-ga do
How far is it to ...?	**Jak daleko jest do ...?**	yak da-le-ko yest do
How many kilometres?	**Ile kilometrów?**	ee-le kee-lo-me-troov
How far is the next village/petrol station?	**Jak daleko do następnej wsi/stacji benzynowej?**	yak da-le-ko do na-ste^{n}p-ney fshee/ sta-tsyee ben-zi-no-vey
We want to get on to the motorway to ...	**Chcemy się dostać na autostradę do ...**	htse-mi shye^n do-stach na a-oo-to-stra-de^n do
Which is the best road to ...?	**Jaka jest najlepsza droga do ...?**	ya-ka yest nay-lep-sha dro-ga do

Is there a scenic route to ...?	**Czy jest ładna droga do ...?**	chi yest **wad**-na **dro**-ga do
You are going the wrong way	***Pan(i) jedzie w złą stronę**	pan (**pa**-nee) **ye**-dgye vzwo^n **stro**-ne^n
Follow signs for ...	***Proszę jechać według znaków na ...**	**pro**-she^n **ye**-hach **ve**-dwoog **zna**-koov na
Where does this road lead to?	**Dokąd ta droga prowadzi?**	**do**-ko^{n}d ta **dro**-ga pro-**va**-dgee
Is it a good road?	**Czy to jest dobra droga?**	chi to yest **do**-bra **dro**-ga
Is it a motorway?	**Czy to jest autostrada?**	chi to yest a-oo-to-**stra**-da
Is the tunnel/pass open?	**Czy tunel/przejazd jest otwarty?**	chi **too**-nel/**pshe**-yazd yest ot-**var**-ti
Is the road to ... clear?	**Czy droga do ... jest otwarta?**	chi **dro**-ga do ... yest ot-**var**-ta
Will we get to ... by evening?	**Czy dojedziemy na wieczór do ...?**	chi do-ye-**dgye**-mi na **vye**-choor do
How long will it take by car/ by bicycle/ on foot?	**Jak długo to zajmie samochodem/ na rowerze/ na piechotę?**	yak **dwoo**-go to **zay**-mye sa-mo-**ho**-dem/ na ro-**ve**-zhe/ na pye-**ho**-te^n
Where are we now?	**Gdzie jesteśmy teraz?**	gdgye yes-**tesh**-mi **te**-raz
What is the name of this place?	**Jak się to miejsce nazywa?**	yak shye^n to **myey**-stse na-**zi**-va
Please show me on the map	**Proszę mi pokazać na mapie**	**pro**-she^n mee po-**ka**-zach na **ma**-pye
It's that way	***To w tę stronę**	to fte^n **stro**-ne^n
It isn't far	***To jest niedaleko**	to yest nye-da-**le**-ko

Follow this road for 5 kilometres	***Pojedzie pan(i) tą drogą przez pięć kilometrów**	po-**ye**-dgye pan (**pa**-nee) to^{n} **dro**-go^{n} pshez **pye^{n}ch** kee-lo-**met**-roov
Keep straight on	***Cały czas prosto**	tsa-wi chas **pro**-sto
Turn right at the crossroads	***Proszę skręcić w prawo na skrzyżowaniu**	**pro**-she^{n} **skre^{n}**-cheech **fpra**-vo na skshi-zho-**va**-nyoo
Take the second road on the left	***Proszę skręcić w drugą przecznicę po lewej stronie**	**pro**-she^{n} **skre^{n}**-cheech **vdroo**-go^{n} pshe-**chnee**-tse^{n} po **le**-vey **stro**-nye
Turn right at the traffic-lights	***Proszę skręcić w prawo przy światłach drogowych**	**pro**-she^{n} **skre^{n}**-cheech **fpra**-vo pshi **shvyat**-wah dro-**go**-vih
Turn left after the bridge	***Proszę skręcić w lewo za mostem**	**pro**-she^{n} **skre^{n}**-cheech **vle**-vo za **mos**-tem
The best road is the …	***Najlepsza droga jest …**	nay-**lep**-sha **dro**-ga yest
Take this road as far as … and ask again	***Proszę jechać tą drogą aż do … i potem znowu kogoś zapytać**	**pro**-she^{n} **ye**-hach to^{n} **dro**-go^{n} azh do … ee **po**-tem **zno**-voo **ko**-gosh za-**pi**-tach
One-way system	**System jedno-kierunkowy**	**sis**-tem **yed**-no kye-**roon**-ko-vi
North	**Północ**	**poow**-nots
South	**Południe**	po-**wood**-nye
East	**Wschód**	**fs**-hood
West	**Zachód**	**za**-hood

DRIVING

Have you a road map, please?	**Czy mogę prosić o mapę drogową/ samochodową?**	chi **mo**-ge^{n} pro-sheech o **ma**-pe^{n} dro-**go**-vo^{n}/ sa-mo-ho-**do**-vo^{n}
Where is a car park?	**Gdzie jest parking?**	gdgye yest **par**-keeng
Can I park here?	**Czy mogę tutaj zaparkować?**	chi **mo**-ge^{n} **too**-tay za-par-**ko**-vach
How long can I park here?	**Jak długo mogę tutaj zaparkować?**	yak **dwoo**-go **mo**-ge^{n} **too**-tay za-par-**ko**-vach
No parking	***Zakaz parkowania**	**za**-kaz par-ko-**va**-nya
Is this your car?	***Czy to jest pana (pani) samochód?**	chi to yest **pa**-na (nee) sa-**mo**-hood
May I see your licence, please?	***Proszę pokazać prawo jazdy**	**pro**-she^{n} po-**ka**-zach **pra**-vo **yaz**-di
Logbook	**Dowód rejestracyjny**	**do**-vood re-yes-tra-**tsiy**-ni
Where is the nearest petrol station?	**Gdzie jest najbliższa stacja benzynowa?**	gdgye yest nay-**bleezh**-sha **sta**-tsya ben-zi-**no**-va

How far is the next petrol station?	**Jak daleko jest do następnej stacji benzynowej?**	yak da-le-ko yest do nas-te^{n}p-ney sta-tsye ben-zi-no-vey
Have you any change for the meter, please?	**Czy ma pan(i) drobne na parkometr?**	chi ma pan (pa-nee) drob-ne na par-ko-me
Speed limit	**Ograniczenie szybkości**	o-gra-nee-che-nye shib-kosh-chee
Pedestrian precinct	**Strefa piesza**	stre-fa pye-sha

CAR HIRE

Where can I hire a car?	**Gdzie można wynająć samochód?**	gdgye mo-zhna vi-na-yo^{n} sa-mo-hood
I want to hire a car and a driver/a self drive car	**Chciałbym (-abym) wynająć samochód z kierowcą/bez kierowcy**	hchyaw-bim (hchya-wa-bim vi-na-yo^{n}ch sa-mo-hoo skye-rov-tso^{n}/bez kye-rov-tsi
I want to hire an automatic	**Chcę wynająć samochód z automatyczną skrzynką biegów**	htse^{n} vi-na-yo^{n}ch sa-mo-hood z a-oo-to-ma-tich-no^{n} skshin-ko^{n} bye-goov
Is there a weekend rate/a midweek rate?	**Czy jest specjalna taryfa w soboty i niedziele/w środku tygodnia?**	chi yest spets-yal-na ta-ri-fa v so-bo-ti ee nye-dgye-le/ v shrod-koo ti-god-ny
How much is it by the hour/ day/ week?	**Ile to kosztuje za godzinę/ dziennie/ tygodniowo?**	ee-le to kosh-too-ye za go-dgee-ne^{n}/ dgyen-nye/ ti-god-nyo-vo

I need it for two days/ a week	**Potrzebny mi na dwa dni/tydzień**	po-**tsheb**-ni mee na dva dnee/**ti**-dgyen
Does that include mileage?	**Czy jest włączona opłata za ilość przejechanych kilometrów?**	chi yest vwo^{n}-**cho**-na o-**pwa**-ta za **ee**-loshch pshe-ye-**ha**-nih kee-lo-**me**-troov
The charge per kilometre is …	***Opłata za kilometr jest …**	o-**pwa**-ta za kee-**lo**-metr yest
Do you want full insurance?	***Czy chce pan(i) pełne ubezpieczenie?**	chi htse pan (**pa**-nee) **pew**-ne oo-bez-pye-**che**-nye
May I see your driving licence?	***Poproszę o prawo jazdy?**	po-**pro**-she^{n} o **pra**-vo **yaz**-di
Do you want a deposit?	**Czy mam zostawić kaucję?**	chi mam zos-**ta**-vich **kaoo**-tsye^{n}
I will pay by credit card	**Zapłacę kartą kredytową**	za-**pwa**-tse^{n} **kar**-to^{n} kre-di-**to**-vo^{n}
Can I return it to your office in …?	**Czy mogę go zwrócić do pańskiego biura w …?**	chi **mo**-ge^{n} go **zvroo**-cheech do pan-**skye**-go **byoo**-ra v
Could you show me the controls/ lights?	**Czy może mi pan pokazać wszystkie przyrządy/światła?**	chi **mo**-zhe mee pan po-**ka**-zach **fshist**-kye pshi-**zho**^{n}-di/**shvya**-twa

ROAD SIGNS

Dopuszcza się ruch lokalny	Local traffic only
Droga zamknięta	Road closed
Jeden kierunek ruchu	One-way street

Koniec	End of ...(cancellation of sign to which the word is attached)
Niebezpieczeństwo	Danger
Objazd	Diversion
Parking	Parking allowed/car park
Parking tylko dla samochodów osobowych	Parking for private cars
Parkowanie wzbronione	No parking
Ruch przelotowy	Through traffic
Ślepa uliczka	Dead end
Uwaga	Caution/attention
Wjazd zamknięty	No entry
Zakaz wyprzedzania	Overtaking prohibited

AT THE GARAGE OR PETROL STATION

Fill it up	**Proszę nalać do pełna**	pro-she^{n} na-lach do pew-na
... litres of standard/ premium petrol, please	**Proszę ... litrów niskooktanowej/ wysokooktanowej**	pro-she^{n} ... leet-roov nees-ko-o-kta-no-vey/ vi-so-ko-o-kta-no-vey
... litres of diesel	**... litrów oleju napędowego**	leet-roov o-le-yoo na-pe^{n}-do-ve-go
... zlotys' worth of petrol, please	**Proszę o benzynę za ... złotych**	pro-she^{n} o ben-zi-ne^{n} za ... zwo-tih
How much is petrol a litre?	**Ile kosztuje litr benzyny?**	ee-le kosh-too-ye leetr ben-zi-ni

Please check the oil and water/ the battery/ the brakes/ the oil/ the transmission fluid/ the tyre pressure, including the spare tyre	**Proszę sprawdzić olej i wodę/ akumulator/ hamulce/ olej/ płyn przekładni automatycznej/ ciśnienie w oponach łącznie z zapasową oponą**	pro-she^n sprav-dgeech o-ley ee vo-de^n/ a-koo-moo-la-tor/ ha-mool-tse o-ley pwin pshe-kwad-ni a-oo-to-ma-tich-ney/ cheesh-nye-nye vo-po-nah wo^{n}ch-nye z za-pa-so-vo^n o-po-no^n
Could you check the brake/ transmission fluid	**Proszę sprawdzić płyn hamulcowy/ przekładni automatycznej**	pro-she^n sprav-dgeech pwin ha-mool-tso-vi/ pshe-kwad-nee a-oo-to-ma-tich-ney
The oil needs changing	**Trzeba zmienić olej**	tshe-ba zmye-neech o-ley
Check the tyre pressure, please	**Proszę sprawdzić ciśnienie w oponach**	pro-she^n sprav-dgeech cheesh-nye-nye vo-po-nah
Would you clean the windscreen, please?	**Proszę wyczyścić przednią szybę?**	pro-she^n vi-cheesh-cheech pshed-nyo^n shi-be^n
Please wash the car	**Proszę umyć samochód**	pro-she^n oo-mich sa-mo-hood
Can I garage the car here?	**Czy mogę tu zostawić samochód?**	chi mo-ge^n too zos-ta-veech sa-mo-hood
What time does the garage close?	**O której godzinie zamyka się garaż?**	o ktoo-rey go-dgee-nye za-mi-ka shye^n ga-razh
Where are the toilets?	**Gdzie są toalety?**	gdgye so^n to-a-le-ti

REPAIRS

Can you give me a lift to a telephone?	**Czy może mnie pan(i) podwieźć do telefonu?**	chi mo-zhe mnye pan (pa-nee) **pod**-vyezhch do te-le-**fo**-noo
Please tell the next garage to send help	**Proszę zawiadomić najbliższy garaż żeby przysłali pomoc**	**pro**-she^n za-vya-**do**-meech nay-**bleezh**-shi **ga**-razh **zhe**-bi pshi-**swa**-lee **po**-mots
My car's broken down	**Mój samochód się zepsuł**	mooy sa-**mo**-hood shye^n **ze**-psoow
Can I use your phone?	**Czy mogę skorzystać z telefonu?**	chi **mo**-ge^n sko-**zhis**-tach z te-le-**fo**-noo
Where is there a Ford agency?	**Gdzie jest filia firmy Ford?**	gdgye yest **feel**-ya **feer**-mi ford
Have you a breakdown service?	**Czy mają państwo pogotowie awaryjne?**	chi **ma**-yo^n **pan**-stvo po-go-**to**-vye a-va-**riy**-ne
Is there a mechanic?	**Czy jest tu mechanik?**	chi yest too me-**ha**-neek
Can you send someone to look at it/ tow it away?	**Czy może pan(i) przysłać kogoś żeby obejrzał samochód/ odholował go?**	chi **mo**-zhe pan (**pa**-nee) **pshi**-swach **ko**-gosh **zhe**-bi o-**bey**-zhaw sa-**mo**-hood/ od-ho-**lo**-vaw go
It is an automatic and cannot be towed	**To jest samochód z automatyczną skrzynią biegów i nie może być holowany**	to yest sa-**mo**-hood z a-oo-to-ma-**tich**-no^n **skshin**-ko^n **bye**-goov ee nye **mo**-zhe bich ho-lo-**va**-ni
Where are you?	***Gdzie pan(i) jest?**	gdgye pan (**pa**-nee) yest

Where is your car?	*Gdzie jest pański samochód?	gdgye yest **pan**-skee sa-**mo**-hood
I am on the road from … to … near kilometre post …	Jestem na drodze z … do … niedaleko znaku kilometrowego …	**yes**-tem na **dro**-dze z … do … nye-da-**le**-ko **zna**-koo kee-lo-me-tro-**ve**-go
How long will you be?	Jak długo zajmie panu dojazd?	yak **dwoo**-go **zay**-mye **pa**-noo **do**-yazd
I want the car serviced	Proszę skontrolować mój samochód i zrobić konieczne naprawy	**pro**-she^n skon-tro-**lo**-vach mooy sa-**mo**-hood ee **zro**-bich ko-**nyech**-ne na-**pra**-vi
The battery is flat, it needs charging	Akumulator się wyładował, proszę go naładować	a-koo-moo-**la**-tor shye^n vi-wa-**do**-vaw, **pro**-she^n go na-wa-**do**-vach
The tyre is flat/ punctured	Ta opona jest przebita/ przedziurawiona	ta o-**po**-na yest pshe-**bee**-ta/ pshe-dgyoo-ra-**vyo**-na
The exhaust is broken	Wydech jest zepsuty	**vi**-deh yest ze-**psoo**-ti
The windscreen wipers do not work	Wycieraczki nie działają	vi-chye-**rach**-kee nye dgya-**wa**-yo^n
The valve is leaking	Wentyl jest nieszczelny	**ven**-til yest nye-**shchel**-ni
The radiator is leaking	Chłodnica przecieka	hwod-**nee**-tsa pshe-**chye**-ka
I've lost my car key	Zgubiłem (-am) klucz do mojego samochodu	zgoo-**bee**-wem (-wam) klooch do mo-**ye**-go sa-mo-**ho**-doo
The lock is broken/ jammed	Zamek się zepsuł/ zaciął	**za**-mek shye^n **ze**-psoow/ **za**-cho^{n}w
My car won't start	Silnik nie pali	**sheel**-neek nye **pa**-lee

It's not running properly	Nie działa prawidłowo	nye dgya-wa pra-veed-wo-vo
The engine is overheating	Silnik się przegrzewa	sheel-neek shye^{n} pshe-gzhe-va
The engine is firing badly	Silnik nie pali prawidłowo	sheel-neek nye pa-lee pra-veed-wo-vo
The engine knocks	Silnik stuka	sheel-neek stoo-ka
Can you change this plug?	Czy może pan zmienić tę świecę?	chi mo-zhe pan zmye-nich te^{n} shvye-tse^{n}
There's a petrol/ oil leak	Benzyna/ olej przecieka	ben-zi-na/ o-ley pshe-chye-ka
There's a smell of petrol/rubber	Ulatnia się zapach benzyny/gumy	oo-lat-nya shye^{n} za-pah ben-zi-ni/goo-mi
The radiator is blocked/leaking	Chłodnica jest zatkana/przecieka	hwod-nee-tsa yest zat-ka-na/pshe-chye-ka
Something is wrong with my car/	Coś jest niewporządku z moim samochodem/	tsosh yest nye fpo-zho^{n}d-koo z mo-eem sa-mo-ho-dem/
the engine/	z silnikiem/	z sheel-nee-kyem/
the lights/	ze światłami/	ze shvyat-wa-mee/
the clutch/	ze sprzęgłem/	ze spshe^{n}g-wem/
the gearbox/	ze skrzynką biegów/	ze skshin-ko^{n} bye-goov/
the brake/	z hamulcami/	z ha-mool-tsa-mee/
the steering	z kierownicą	z kye-rov-nee-tso^{n}
There's a squeak/ whine/ rumble/ rattle	Coś skrzypi/ świszczy/ turkocze/ klekocze	tsosh skshi-pee/ shveesh-chi/ toor-ko-che/ kle-ko-che
It's a high/low noise	To jest głośny/ stłumiony dźwięk	to yest gwosh-ni/ stwoo-myo-ni dgvye^{n}k

It's intermittent/ continuous	**To jest przerywany/ ciągły**	to yest pshe-ri-va-ni/ chyo^{n}g-wi
The carburettor needs adjusting	**Trzeba wyregulować karburator/gaźnik**	tshe-ba vi-re-goo-lo-vach kar-boo-ra-tor/gazh-neek
Can you repair it?	**Czy może pan to naprawić?**	chi mo-zhe pan to na-pra-vich
How long will it take to repair?	**Ile czasu zajmie naprawa?**	ee-le cha-soo zay-mye na-pra-va
What will it cost?	**Ile to będzie kosztować?**	ee-le to be^{n}-dgye kosh-to-vach
When can I pick the car up?	**Kiedy mogę odebrać samochód?**	kye-di mo-ge^{n} o-deb-rach sa-mo-hood
I need it as soon as possible	**Potrzebuję go jak najszybciej**	po-tshe-boo-ye^{n} go yak nay-shib-chyey
I need it in three hours/ tomorrow morning	**Potrzebuję go za trzy godziny/jutro rano**	po-tshe-boo-ye^{n} go za tshi go-dgee-ni/yoo-tro ra-no
It will take two days	***To zajmie dwa dni**	to zay-mye dva dnee
We can repair it temporarily	***Możemy to naprawić prowizorycznie**	mo-zhe-mi to na-pra-vich pro-vi-zo-rich-nye
We haven't got the right spares	***Nie mamy odpowiednich części zapasowych**	nye ma-mi od-po-vyed-nih che^{n}sh-chee za-pa-so-vih
We have to send for the spares	***Musimy zamówić części zapasowe**	moo-shee-mi za-moo-vich che^{n}sh-chee za-pa-so-ve
You will need a new …	***Potrzebny jest nowy …**	po-tsheb-ni yest no-vi
Could I have an itemized bill, please?	**Czy mogę prosić o rachunek z wyszczególnieniem kosztów?**	chi mo-ge^{n} pro-sheech o ra-hoo-nek z vish-che-gool-nye-nyem kosh-toov

PARTS OF A CAR AND OTHER USEFUL WORDS

accelerate (to)	**przyśpieszać**	pshish-pye-shach
accelerator	**przyśpiesznik**	pshish-pyesh-neek
air pump	**sprężarka**	spre^{n}-zhar-ka
alignment	**regulacja**	re-goo-la-tsya
alternator	**prądnica**	pro^{n}d-nee-tsa
anti-freeze	**anti-freeze/glikol**	an-tee freez/glee-kol
automatic transmission	**automatyczna skrzynka biegów**	a-oo-to-ma-tich-na skshin-ka bye-goov
axle	**oś**	osh
axleshaft	**wał osiowy**	vaw o-sho-vi
battery	**akumulator**	a-koo-moo-la-tor
beam	**snop światła**	snop shvyat-wa
full beam	**pełne światła**	pew-ne shvyat-wa
bonnet/hood	**maska**	mas-ka
boot/trunk	**bagażnik**	ba-gazh-neek
brake	**hamulec**	ha-moo-lets
disc brakes	**hamulce tarczowe**	ha-mool-tse tar-cho-ve
drum brakes	**hamulce szczękowe**	ha-mool-tse shche^{n}-ko-ve
footbrake	**hamulec nożny**	ha-moo-lets nozh-ni
brake fluid	**płyn hamulcowy**	pwin ha-mool-tso-vi
brake lights	**światła stopu**	shvyat-wa sto-poo

brake lining	okładzina szczęk hamulca	o-kwa-dgee-na shche^{n}k ha-mool-tsa
breakdown	awaria	a-var-ya
bulb	żarówka	zha-roov-ka
bumper	zderzak	zde-zhak
carburettor	gaźnik, karburator	gazh-neek, kar-boo-ra-tor
car wash	mycie samochodów	mi-chye sa-mo-ho-doov
choke	ssanie	ssa-nye
clutch	sprzęgło	spshe^{n}-gwo
clutch plate	tarcza sprzęgłowa	tar-cha spshe^{n}-gwo-va
coil	cewka	tsev-ka
condenser	kondensator	kon-den-sa-tor
cooling system	system chłodzenia	sis-tem hwo-dze-nya
crankshaft	korba	kor-ba
cylinder	cylinder	tsi-leen-der
differential gear	dyferencjał	di-fe-ren-tsyaw
dip stick	prętowy wskaźnik poziomy	pre^{n}-to-vi fskazh-neek po-zho-mi
distilled water	woda destylowana	vo-da des-ti-lo-va-na
distributor	rozdzielacz, rozrząd	roz-dgye-lach, roz-zho^{n}d
door	drzwi	dzhvee
doorhandle	klamka	klam-ka
drive (to)	prowadzić samochód	pro-va-dgeech sa-mo-hood
driver	kierowca	kye-rov-tsa
dynamo	dynamo	di-na-mo

electrical trouble	**kłopot z częściami elektrycznymi**	kwo-pot sche^{n}sh-chya-me e-lek-trich-ni-mee
engine	**silnik**	sheel-neek
exhaust	**wydech**	vi-deh
fan	**dmuchawa**	dmoo-ha-va
fanbelt	**pasek dmuchawy**	pa-sek dmoo-ha-vi
(oil) filter	**filtr (oleju)**	feeltr (o-le-yoo)
foglamp	**światła przeciwmgielne**	shvyat-wa pshe-cheev-mgyel-ne
fusebox	**bezpiecznik**	bez-pyech-neek
gasket	**uszczelka**	oosh-chel-ka
gear	**bieg**	byeg
gear box	**skrzynka biegów**	skshin-ka bye-goov
gear lever	**dźwignia biegów**	dgveeg-nya bye-goov
grease (to)	**smarować**	sma-ro-vach
hand brake	**hamulec ręczny**	ha-moo-lets re^{n}ch-ni
headlights	**reflektor główny**	re-flek-tor gwoov-ni
heater	**grzejnik**	gzhey-neek
horn	**klakson**	klak-son
hose	**rura gumowa**	roo-ra goo-mo-va
ignition	**zapłon**	za-pwon
ignition coil	**cewka zapłonu**	tsev-ka za-pwo-noo
ignition key	**klucz do stacyjki**	klooch do sta-tsiy-kee
indicator	**wskaźnik**	fskazh-neek
inner tube	**dętka**	de^{n}t-ka
jack	**lewarek**	le-va-rek

lights	**światła**	shvyat-wa
lock/catch	**zamek**	za-mek
mechanical trouble	**awaria mechaniczna**	a-var-ya me-ha-neech-na
mirror	**lusterko**	loos-ter-ko
number plate	**tablica rejestracyjna**	ta-blee-tsa re-yes-tra-tsiy-na
nut	**nakrętka**	na-kre^{n}t-ka
oil	**olej**	o-ley
oil pressure	**ciśnienie oleju**	cheesh-nye-nye o-le-yoo
oil pump	**pompa olejowa**	pom-pa o-le-yo-va
overdrive	**nadbieg**	nad-byeg
parking lights	**światła postojowe**	shvyat-wa pos-to-yo-ve
petrol	**benzyna**	ben-zi-na
petrol can	**kanister na benzynę**	ka-nees-ter na ben-zi-ne^{n}
petrol pump	**pompa benzynowa**	pom-pa ben-zi-no-va
petrol tank	**zbiornik na benzynę**	zbyor-neek na ben-zi-ne^{n}
piston	**tłok**	twok
piston ring	**obręcz do tłoku**	ob-re^{n}ch do two-koo
points	**platynki**	pla-tin-kee
propeller shaft	**wał napędowy**	vaw na-pe^{n}-do-vi
(fuel) pump	**pompa (paliwa)**	pom-pa (pa-lee-va)
puncture	**przebicie opony**	pshe-bee-chye o-po-ni
radiator	**chłodnica**	hwod-nee-tsa
rear axle	**tylna oś**	til-na osh
rear lights	**tylne światła**	til-ne shvyat-wa
reverse (to)	**dać wsteczny bieg**	dach fstech-ni byeg

reverse	wsteczny	fstech-ni
reversing lights	światła cofania	shvyat-wa tso-fa-nya
(sliding) roof	dach (otwierany)	dah (ot-vye-ra-ni)
roof-rack	bagażnik na dachu	ba-gazh-neek na da-hoo
screwdriver	śrubociąg	shroo-bo-chyo^{n}g
seat	siedzenie	shye-dze-nye
shock absorber	amortyzator	a-mor-ti-za-tor
sidelights	światła boczne/ kierunkowe	shvyat-wa boch-ne/ kye-roon-ko-ve
silencer	tłumik	twoo-meek
(plug) spanner	klucz (do świec)	klooch (do shvyets)
spares	części zapasowe	che^{n}sh-chee za-pa-so-ve
spare wheel	koło zapasowe	ko-wo za-pa-so-ve
(sparking) plug	świeca	shvye-tsa
speed	szybkość	shib-koshch
speedometer	szybkościomierz	shib-kosh-chyo-myezh
spring	sprężyna	spre^{n}-zhi-na
stall (to)	zablokować silnik	za-blo-ko-vach sheel-neek
starter	starter	star-ter
starter motor	rozrusznik	roz-roosh-neek
steering	kierowanie	kye-ro-va-nye
steering wheel	kierownica	kye-rov-nee-tsa
sunroof	dach otwierany	dah o-tvye-ra-ni
suspension	amortyzator	a-mor-ti-za-tor
switch	przełącznik	pshe-wo^{n}ch-neek

tank	**zbiornik**	zbyor-neek
tappets	**popychacz**	po-pi-hach
transmission	**przekładnia, transmisja**	pshe-kwad-nya, trans-mees-ya
tyre	**opona**	o-po-na
tyre pressure	**ciśnienie w oponie**	cheesh-nye-nye v o-po-nye
valve	**wentyl**	ven-til
(distilled) water	**woda (dystylowana)**	vo-da (dis-ti-lo-va-na)
water pump	**pompa wodna**	pom-pa vod-na
wheel	**koło**	ko-wo
wheel (back, front, spare)	**koło (tylnie, przednie, zapasowe)**	ko-wo (til-nye, pshed-nye, za-pa-so-ve)
window	**okno**	ok-no
windscreen	**szyba przednia**	shi-ba pshed-nya
windscreen washers	**natryskiwacz szyby przedniej**	na-trys-kee-vach shi-bi pshed-nyey
windscreen wipers	**wycieraczki**	vi-chye-rach-kee
wing	**błotnik**	bwot-neek

CYCLING

Where can I hire a bicycle?	**Gdzie mogę wynająć rower?**	gdgye mo-ge^{n} vi-na-yo^{n}ch ro-ver
Do you have a bicycle with gears?	**Czy są rowery z przerzutką?**	chi so^{n} rove-ri sphe-zhoot-ko^{n}
The saddle is too high/ too low	**Siodełko jest za wysoko/ za nisko**	shyo-dew-ko yest za vi-so-ko/ za nees-ko
Where is the cycle shop?	**Gdzie jest sklep z rowerami?**	gdgye yest sklep zro-ve-ra-mee
Do you repair bicycles?	**Czy państwo naprawiają rowery?**	chi pan-stvo na-pra-vya-yo^{n} ro-ve-ri
The brake isn't working	**Hamulec nie działa**	ha-moo-lets nye dgya-wa
Could you tighten/ loosen the brake cable?	**Czy może pan(i) napiąć/ poluzować linkę hamulcową?**	chi mo-zhe pan (pa-nee) na-pyo^{n}ch/ po-loo-zo-vach leen-ke^{n} ha-mool-tso-vo^{n}
A spoke is broken	**Szprycha jest złamana**	shpri-ha yest zwa-ma-na

The tyre is punctured	**Opona jest przedziurawiona**	o-**po**-na yest pshe-dgyoo-ra-**vyo**-na
The gears need adjusting	**Trzeba wyregulować przerzutkę**	**tshe**-ba vi-re-goo-**lo**-vach pshe-**zhoot**-ke^{n}
Could you straighten the wheel?	**Czy może pan(i) wycentrować/ wyprostować koło?**	chi **mo**-zhe pan (**pa**-nee) vi-tsen-**tro**-vach/ vi-pros-**to**-vach **ko**-wo
The handlebars are loose	**Kierownica jest luźna**	kye-rov-**nee**-tsa yest **loozh**-na
Could you please lend me a spanner?	**Czy mogę pożyczyć klucz?**	chi **mo**-ge^{n} po-**zhi**-chich klooch

PARTS OF A BICYCLE

axle	**oś**	osh
bell	**dzwonek**	**dzvo**-nek
brake (front, rear)	**hamulec (przedni, tylny)**	ha-**moo**-lets (**pshed**-nee, **til**-ni)
brake cable	**linka hamulcowa**	**leen**-ka ha-mool-**tso**-va
brake lever	**dźwignia hamulcowa**	**dgveeg**-nya ha-mool-**tso**-va
bulb	**żarówka**	zha-**roov**-ka
chain	**łańcuch**	**wan**-tsooh
dynamo	**dynamo**	di-**na**-mo
frame	**rama**	**ra**-ma
gear lever	**dźwignia przerzutki**	**dgveeg**-nya pshe-**zhoot**-kee
gears	**przerzutka**	pshe-**zhoot**-ka
handlebars	**kierownica**	kye-rov-**nee**-tsa

inner tube	**dętka**	de^{n}t-ka
light (front, rear)	**światło (przednie, tylne)**	shvyat-wo (pshed-nye, til-ne)
mudguard	**błotnik**	bwot-neek
panniers	**bagażnik**	ba-gazh-neek
pedal	**pedał**	pe-daw
pump	**pompka**	pomp-ka
reflector	**reflektor**	re-flek-tor
rim	**obręcz**	o-bre^{n}ch
saddle	**siodełko**	shyo-dew-ko
saddlebag	**torba przy siodełku**	tor-ba pshi shyo-dew-koo
spoke	**szprycha**	shpri-ha
tyre	**opona**	o-po-na
valve	**wentyl**	ven-til
wheel	**koło**	ko-wo

HOTELS & GUEST HOUSES

BOOKING A ROOM

Receptionist	**Recepcja**	re-tsep-tsya
Rooms to let/vacancies	***Pokoje do wynajęcia**	po-ko-ye do vi-na-ye^n-chya
Have you a room for the night?	**Czy mają państwo pokój na jedną noc?**	chi ma-yo^n pan-stvo po-kooy na yed-no^n nots
I've reserved a room; my name is ...	**Zarezerwowałem (-am) pokój; moje nazwisko ...**	za-re-zer-vo-va-wem (-wam) po-kooy; mo-ye naz-vees-ko
Can you suggest another hotel?	**Czy mogą mi państwo polecić inny hotel?**	chi mo-go^n mee pan-stvo po-le-cheech een-ni ho-tel
I want a single room with a shower	**Proszę o pokój jednoosobowy z prysznicem**	pro-she^n o po-kooy yed-no-o-so-bo-vi z prish-nee-tsem

We want a room with a a double bed and a bathroom	**Prosimy o pokój z dwuosobowym łóżkiem i łazienką**	pro-shee-mi o po-kooy z dvoo-o-so-bo-vim woozh-kyem ee wa-zhyen-ko^{n}
Have you a room with twin beds?	**Czy mają państwo wolny pokój z dwoma łóżkami?**	chi ma-yo^{n} pan-stvo vol-ni po-kooy z dvo-ma woozh-ka-mee
extra bed	**dodatkowe łóżko**	do-dat-ko-ve woozh-ko
a private toilet	**prywatna łazienka**	pri-vat-na wa-zhyen-ka
How long will you be staying?	***Na jak długo pan(i) przyjechał (-a)?**	na yak dwoo-go pan (pa-nee) pshi-ye-haw (ha-wa)
Is it for one night only?	***Czy tylko na jedną noc?**	chi til-ko na yed-no^{n} nots
I want a room for two or three days/ a week/ until Friday	**Potrzebuję pokoju na dwa lub trzy dni/ na tydzień/ do piątku**	po-tshe-boo-ye^{n} po-ko-yoo na dva loob tshi dnee/ na ti-dgyen/ do pyo^{n}t-koo
What floor is the room on?	**Na którym piętrze jest ten pokój?**	na ktoo-rim pye^{n}t-she yest ten po-kooy
Is there a lift/elevator?	**Czy jest winda?**	chi yest vin-da
Are there facilities for the disabled?	**Czy jest dostęp dla niepełno sprawnych?**	chi yest do-ste^{n}p dla nye-pew-no sprav-nih
Have you a room on the first floor?	**Czy mają państwo wolny pokój na pierwszym piętrze?**	chi ma-yo^{n} pan-stvo vol-ni po-kooy na pyerv-shim pye^{n}-tshe
May I see the room?	**Czy można obejrzeć ten pokój?**	chi mozh-na o-bey-zhech ten po-kooy
I like this room, I'll take it	**Ten pokój mi się podoba, wezmę go**	ten po-kooy mee shye^{n} po-do-ba, vez-me^{n} go

I don't like this room	**Nie podoba mi się ten pokój**	nye po-**do**-ba mee shye^{n} ten **po**-kooy
Have you another one?	**Czy mają państwo jakiś inny wolny pokój?**	chi **ma**-yo^{n} **pan**-stvo **ya**-keesh **een**-ni **vol**-ni **po**-kooy
a bigger room	**większy pokój**	**vye^{n}k**-shi **po**-kooy
I want a quiet room	**Proszę o cichy pokój**	**pro**-she^{n} o **chee**-hi **po**-kooy
There's too much noise	**Za dużo tu hałasu**	za **doo**-zho too ha-**wa**-soo
I'd like a room with a balcony	**Proszę o pokój z balkonem**	**pro**-she^{n} o **po**-kooy z bal-**ko**-nem
Have you a room looking on to the street/ sea?	**Czy mają państwo pokój z widokiem na ulicę/ na morze?**	chi **ma**-yo^{n} **pan**-stvo **po**-kooy z vee-**do** kyem na oo-**lee**-tse^{n}/na **mo**-zhe
Is there a telephone/ radio/ television?	**Czy jest w pokoju telefon/ radio/ telewizor?**	chi yest fpo-**ko**-yoo te-**le**-fon/ **ra**-dyo/ te-le-**vee**-zor
We've only a double room	***Mamy tylko pokój dwuosobowy**	**ma**-mi **til**-ko **po**-kooy dvoo-o-so-**bo**-vi
This is the only room vacant	***To jest jedyny wolny pokój**	to yest ye-**di**-ni **vol**-ni **po**-kooy
We shall have another room tomorrow	***Jutro zwolni się drugi pokój**	**yoo**-tro **zvol**-nee shye^{n} **droo**-gee **po**-kooy
The room is only available tonight	***Ten pokój jest tylko wolny na tę noc**	ten **po**-kooy yest **til**-ko **vol**-ni na te^{n} nots
How much is the room per night?	**Ile ten pokój kosztuje za noc?**	**ee**-le ten **po**-kooy ko-**shtoo**-ye za nots
Have you nothing cheaper?	**Czy nie mają państwo nic tańszego?**	chi nye **ma**-yo^{n} **pan**-stvo neets tan-**she**-go

What do we pay for the child(ren)?	**Ile płacimy za dziecko (dzieci)?**	ee-le pwa-chee-mi za dgyets-ko (dgye-chee)
Could you put a cot in the room?	**Czy może pan(i) wstawić do pokoju łóżeczko dla dziecka?**	chi mo-zhe pan (pa-nee) fsta-veech do po-ko-yoo woo-zhech-ko dla dgyets-ka
How much is the room without meals?	**Ile kosztuje sam pokój bez posiłków?**	ee-le kosh-too-ye sam po-kooy bez po-sheew-koov
How much is full board/ half board?	**Ile kosztuje całkowite/ częściowe utrzymanie?**	ee-le kosh-too-ye tsaw-ko-vee-te/ che^{n}sh-chyo-ve oo-tshi-ma-nye
Is breakfast included in in the price?	**Czy śniadanie jest wliczone w cenę pokoju?**	chi shnya-da-nye yest vlee-cho-ne v ftse-ne^{n} po-ko-yoo
What is the weekly rate?	**Jaka jest taryfa tygodniowa?**	ya-ka yest ta-ri-fa ti-god-nyo-va
It's too expensive	**To za drogo**	to za dro-go
Would you fill in the registration form?	***Proszę wypełnić kartę zameldowania**	pro-she^{n} vi-pew-neech kar-te^{n} za-mel-do-va-nya
Could I have your passport, please?	***Poproszę o paszport**	po-pro-she^{n} o pash-port

IN YOUR ROOM

Chambermaid	**Pokojowa**	po-ko-yo-va
Room service	**Obsługa pokojowa**	ob-swoo-ga po-ko-yo-va

Could we have breakfast in our room, please?	**Czy możemy dostać śniadanie w naszym pokoju?**	chi mo-zhe-mi dos-tach shnya-da-nye vna-shim po-ko-yoo
Please wake me at 8.30	**Proszę mnie obudzić o ósmej trzydzieści**	pro-she^{n} mnye o-boo-dgeech o oos-mey tshi-dgyesh-chee
There's no ashtray in my room	**W moim pokoju nie ma popielniczki**	vmo-eem po-ko-yoo nye ma po-pyel-neech-kee
Can I have more hangers, please?	**Czy mogę prosić o dodatkowe wieszaki**	chi mo-ge^{n} pro-sheech o do-dat-ko-we vye-sha-kee
Is there a point for an electric razor?	**Czy jest kontakt do elektrycznej maszynki do golenia?**	chi yest kon-takt do e-lek-trich-ney ma-shin-kee do go-le-nya
What's the voltage?	**Jakie jest tutaj napięcie?**	ya-kye yest too-tay na-pye^{n}-chye
Where is the bathroom/ the lavatory?	**Gdzie jest łazienka/ ubikacja?**	gdgye yest wa-zhyen-ka/ oo-bee-ka-tsya
Is there a shower?	**Czy jest tutaj prysznic?**	chi yest too-tay prish-neets
There are no towels in my room	**W moim pokoju nie ma ręczników**	vmo-eem po-ko-yoo nye ma re^{n}ch-nee-koov
Our towels haven't been changed	**Nasze ręczniki nie były zmienione**	na-she re^{n}ch-nee-kee nye bi-wi zmye-nyo-ne
There's no soap	**Nie ma mydła**	nye ma mi-dwa
There's no (hot) water	**Nie ma (gorącej) wody**	nye ma (go-ro^{n}-tsey) vo-di
There's no plug in my washbasin	**Nie ma korka w umywalce**	nye ma kor-ka voo-mi-val-tse
There's no toilet paper in the lavatory	**W ubikacji nie ma papieru toaletowego**	voo-bee-ka-tsyee nye ma pa-pye-roo to-a-le-to-ve-go

The lavatory won't flush	**W ubikacji woda się nie spuszcza**	voo-bee-kats-yee vo-da shye^{n} nye spoosh-cha
The bidet leaks	**Bidet przecieka**	bee-det pshe-chye-ka
The light doesn't work	**Światło nie działa**	shvya-two nye dgya-wa
The lamp is broken	**Lampa jest zepsuta**	lam-pa yest ze-psoo-ta
The blind is stuck	**Żaluzja się zacina**	zha-looz-ya shye^{n} za-chee-na
The curtains won't close	**Zasłony się nie zasuwają**	za-swo-ni shye^{n} nye za-soo-va-yo^{n}
May I have the key to the bathroom, please?	**Czy mogę prosić o klucz do łazienki?**	chi mo-ge^{n} pro-sheech o klooch do wa-zhyen-kee
May I have another blanket/ another pillow?	**Czy mogę prosić o dodatkowy koc/ dodatkową poduszkę?**	chi mo-ge^{n} pro-sheech o do-dat-ko-vi kots/ do-dat-ko-vo^{n} po-doosh-ke^{n}
These sheets are dirty	**Ta pościel jest brudna**	ta posh-chyel yest brood-na
I can't open my window, please open it	**Nie mogę otworzyć okna, proszę mi pomóc**	nye mo-ge^{n} o-tvo-zhich ok-na, pro-she^{n} mee po-moots
It's too hot/cold	**Jest za gorąco/ za zimno**	yest za go-ro^{n}-tso/ za zheem-no
Can the heating be turned up/ turned down/ turned off?	**Czy można podkręcić/ skręcić/wyłączyć ogrzewanie?**	chi mozh-na pod-kre^{n}-chich/skre^{n}-chich/ vi-wo^{n}-chich o-gzhe-va-nye
Could we have a bottle of mineral water in our room, please?	**Czy możemy prosić o przyniesienie do pokoju butelki wody mineralnej?**	chi mo-zhe-mi pro-sheech o pshi-nye-shye-nye do po-ko-yoo boo-tel-kee vo-di mee-ne-ral-ney

ould you bring us another glass, please?	**Czy można prosić o jeszcze jedną szklankę?**	chi mozh-na pro-sheech o yesh-che yed-no^{n} shklan-ke^{n}
d like some ice cubes	**Proszę o kostki lodu**	pro-she^{n} o kost-kee lo-doo
ome in!	**Proszę!**	pro-she^{n}
ut it on the table, please	**Proszę to położyć na stole**	pro-she^{n} to po-wo-zhich na sto-le
ow long will the laundry take?	**Kiedy pranie będzie gotowe?**	kye-di pra-nye be^{n}-dgye go-to-ve
ave you a needle and thread?	**Czy ma pani igłę z nitką?**	chi ma pa-nee ee-gwe^{n} zneet-ko^{n}
ould you clean these shoes, please?	**Czy może pan(i) wyczyścić te buty?**	chi mo-zhe pan (pa-nee) vi-chish-cheech te boo-ti
ould you clean this dress, please?	**Czy może pan(i) wyczyścić tę sukienkę?**	chi mo-zhe pan (pa-nee) vi-chish-cheech te^{n} soo-kyen-ke^{n}
ould you press this suit, please?	**Czy może pan(i) odprasować ten garnitur?**	chi mo-zhe pan (pa-nee) od-pra-so-vach ten gar-nee-toor
hen will it be ready?	**Kiedy to będzie gotowe?**	kye-di to be^{n}-dgye go-to-ve
will be ready tomorrow	***Będzie gotowe jutro**	be^{n}-dgye go-to-ve yoo-tro

OTHER SERVICES

rter	**Bagażowy**	ba-ga-zho-vi
all porter	**Portier**	por-tyer
ge	**Goniec**	go-nyets

Manager	**Kierownik**	kye-**rov**-neek
Telephonist	**Telefonista (Telefonistka)**	te-le-fo-**nees**-ta (-tka)
My key, please	**Poproszę mój klucz**	po-**pro**-she^{n} mooy klooc
Can I leave this in your safe?	**Czy mogę to zostawić w depozycie?**	chi **mo**-ge^{n} to zos-**ta**-veec vde-po-**zi**-chye
Are there any letters for me?	**Czy są do mnie jakieś listy?**	chi so^{n} do mnye ya-kyesh **lees**-ti
Are there any messages for me?	**Czy zostawiono dla mnie jakąś wiadomość?**	chi zos-ta-**vyo**-no dla mnye **ya**-ko^{n}sh vya-**do**-moshch
Please post this	**Proszę to wysłać pocztą**	**pro**-she^{n} to **vi**-swach **poch**-to^{n}
Is there a telex?	**Czy jest telex?**	chi yest **te**-lex
Can I dial direct to England/America?	**Czy jest bezpośrednie połączenie z Anglią/Ameryką?**	chi yest bez-posh-**red**-ny po-wo^{n}-**che**-nye z **an**-glyo^{n}/a-me-**ri**-ko^{n}
If anyone phones, tell them I'll be back at 4.30	**Jak będzie do mnie telefon, proszę powiedzieć, że wracam o czwartej trzydzieści**	yak **be**^{n}-dgye do mnye te-le-fon **pro**-she^{n} po-**vye**-dgyech zhe **vra**-tsam o **chvar**-tey tshi-**dgyesh**-chee
No one telephoned	***Nikt nie dzwonił**	neekt nye **dzwo**-niw
There's a lady/gentleman to see you	***Jakaś pani/jakiś pan do pana (pani)**	ya-kash **pa**-nee/ya-kees pan do **pa**-na (nee)
Please ask her/ him to come up	**Proszę ją/go poprosić do mnie na górę**	**pro**-she^{n} yo^{n}/go po-**pro**-sheech do mny na **goo**-re^{n}
I'm coming down	**Schodzę na dół**	s-**ho**-dze^{n} na doow

Can I borrow/hire a typewriter?	**Czy moge pożyczyć/ wynająć maszynę do pisania?**	chi mo-ge^{n} po-zhi-cheech/ vi-na-yo^{n}ch ma-shi-ne^{n} do pee-sa-nya
Have you any writing paper/ envelopes/ stamps?	**Czy mają państwo papier listowy/ koperty/ znaczki?**	chi ma-yo^{n} pan-stvo pa-pyer lees-to-vi/ ko-per-ti/ znach-kee
Please send the chambermaid/ the waiter	**Proszę przysłać do mnie pokojową/ kelnera**	pro-she^{n} pshi-swach do mnye po-ko-yo-vo^{n}/ kel-ne-ra
I need a guide/ an interpreter	**Potrzebuję przewodnika/ tłumacza**	po-tshe-boo-ye^{n} pshe-vod-nee-ka/ twoo-ma-cha
Does the hotel have a babysitting service?	**Czy hotel załatwia opiekę do dziecka?**	chi ho-tel za-wat-vya o-pye-ke^{n} do dgyets-ka
Where are the toilets/ the cloakroom?	**Gdzie są toalety/ jest szatnią?**	gdgye so^{n} to-a-le-ti/ yest shat-nya
Where is the dining room?	**Gdzie jest jadalnia?**	gdgye yest ya-dal-nya
What time is breakfast/ lunch/dinner?	**O której godzinie jest śniadanie/ obiad/kolacja?**	o ktoo-rey go-dgee-nye yest shnya-da-nye/ o-byad/ko-lats-ya
Is there a garage?	**Czy jest tutaj garaż?**	chi yest too-tay ga-razh
Where can I park the car?	**Gdzie mogę zaparkować?**	gdgye mo-ge^{n} za-par-ko-vach
Is the hotel open all night?	**Czy hotel jest otwarty całą noc?**	chi ho-tel yest ot-var-ti tsa-wo^{n} nots
What time does it close?	**O której godzinie zamyka się hotel?**	o ktoo-rey go-dgee-nye za-mi-ka shye^{n} ho-tel
Please wake me at ...	**Proszę mnie obudzić o ...**	pro-she^{n} mnye o-boo-dgeech o

DEPARTURE

I have to leave tomorrow	**Muszę wyjechać jutro**	moo-she^{n} vi-ye-hach yoo-tro
Can we check out at ...?	**Czy możemy zwolnić pokój o ...?**	chi mo-zhe-mi z vol-neech po-kooy o
Can you have my bill ready?	**Czy może pan/pani przygotować mój rachunek?**	chi mo-zhe pan/pa-nee pshi-go-to-vach mooy ra-hoo-nek
There is a mistake on the bill	**W rachunku jest błąd**	v ra-hoon-koo yest bwo^{n}d
Do you accept credit cards?	**Czy państwo przyjmują karty kredytowe?**	chi pan-stvo pshiy-moo-yo^{n} kar-ti kre-di-to-ve
I shall be coming back on ...; can I book a room for that date?	**Wracam ...; czy mogę zarezerwować ten pokój na ten dzień?**	vra-tsam ...; chi mo-ge^{n} za-re-zer-vo-vach ten po-kooy na ten dgyen
Could you have my luggage brought down?	**Czy mogę prosić o zniesienie bagażu?**	chi mo-ge^{n} pro-sheech o znye-shye-nye ba-ga-zhoo
Please store the luggage, we will be back at ...	**Proszę przechować nasze bagaże, wrócimy o ...**	pro-she^{n} pshe-ho-vach na-she ba-ga-zhe, vroo-chee-mi o
Please call a taxi for me	**Proszę mi sprowadzić taksówkę**	pro-she^{n} mee spro-va-dgeech tak-soov-ke^{n}
Thank you for a pleasant stay	**Dziękuję za miły pobyt**	dgye^{n}-koo-ye^{n} za mee-wi po-bit

CAMPING

Is there a camp site nearby?	**Czy jest w pobliżu kamping?**	chi yest fpo-**blee**-zhoo **kam**-peeng
May we camp here for the night/ in your field/ on the beach?	**Czy można zatrzymać się na noc tutaj/ na pańskim polu/ na plaży?**	chi **mozh**-na za-**tshi**-mach shye^n na nots **too**-tay/ na **pan**-skeem **po**-loo/ na **pla**-zhi
Where should we put our tent/ caravan?	**Gdzie możemy rozstawić namiot/ zaparkować przyczepę kampingową?**	gdgye mo-**zhe**-mi roz-**sta**-vich **na**-myot/ za-par-**ko**-vach pshi-**che**-pe^n kem-peen-**go**-vo^n
Can I park the car next to the tent?	**Czy można zaparkować obok namiotu?**	chi **mozh**-na za-par-**ko**-vach **o**-bok na-**myo**-too
Can we hire a tent?	**Czy można wynająć namiot?**	chi **mozh**-na vi-**na**-yo^{n}ch **na**-myot

Is there drinking water/ electricity/ showers/ toilets?	**Czy jest woda do picia/ elektryczność/ są prysznice/ są toalety?**	chi yest vo-da do pee-cha/ e-lek-trich-noshch/ so^n prish-nee-tse/ so^n to-a-le-ti
What does it cost per night/ per week/ per person?	**Jaka jest cena za noc/ tydzień/ od osoby?**	ya-ka yest tse-na za nots/ ti-dgyen/ od o-so-bi
Is there a shop on the site/ a swimming pool/ a playground/ a restaurant/ a launderette?	**Czy jest na kampingu sklep/ basen/ plac gier i zabaw/ restauracja/ pralnia samoobsługowa?**	chi yest na kam-peen-goo sklep/ ba-sen/ plats gyer ee za-bav/ res-taoo-ra-tsya/ pral-nya sa-mo-ob-swoo-go-va
Can I buy ice?	**Czy można kupić kostki lodu?**	chi mozh-na koo-peech kost-kee lo-doo
Where can I buy paraffin/butane gas?	**Gdzie można kupić naftę/propan butan?**	gdgye mozh-na koo-peech naf-te^n/pro-pan boo-tan
Where do I put rubbish?	**Gdzie wyrzucać śmiecie?**	gdgye vi-zhoo-tsach shmye-chee
Where can I wash up/ wash clothes?	**Gdzie można zmywać naczynia/zrobić pranie?**	gdgye mozh-na zmi-vach na-chi-nya/zro-beech pra-nye
Is there somewhere to dry clothes/ equipment?	**Gdzie można wysuszyć pranie/ sprzęt?**	gdgye mozh-na vi-soo-shich pra-nye/ spshe^{n}t
My camping gas has run out	**Skończył mi się propan butan**	skon-chiw mee shye^n pro-pan boo-tan
The toilet is blocked	**Toaleta jest zablokowana**	to-a-le-ta yest za-blo-ko-va-na

e shower doesn't vork/is flooded	**Prysznic nie działa/ jest zalany**	prish-neets nye dgya-wa/ yest za-la-ni
hat is the voltage?	**Jakie jest napięcie?**	ya-kye yest na-pye^{n}-chye
ay we light a fire?	**Czy można rozpalić ognisko?**	chi mozh-na roz-pa-leech o-gnees-ko
ease prepare the bill, ve are leaving today	**Proszę przygotować rachunek, wyjeżdżamy dzisiaj**	pro-she^{n} pshi-go-to-vach ra-hoo-nek, vi-yezh-ja-mi dgee-shyay
w long do you want o stay?	***Jak długo pan/pani chce się zatrzymać?**	yak dwoo-go pan (pa-nee) htse shye^{n} za-tshi-mach
hat is your car egistration number?	***Jaki jest numer tablicy rejestracyjnej pańskiego samochodu?**	ya-kee yest noo-mer ta-blee-tsi re-yes-tra-tsiy-ney pan-skye-go sa-mo-ho-doo
afraid the camp site full	***Niestety, kamping jest pełny**	nyes-te-ti kam-peeng yest pew-ni
camping	**Zakaz kampingowania**	za-kaz kam-peen-go-va-nya

YOUTH HOSTELLIN(

How long is the walk to the youth hostel?	**Jak długo zajmie dojście do schroniska młodzieżowego?**	yak dwoo-go zay-mye doy-shchye do s-hro-nees-ka mwo-dgye-zho-ve-go
Is there a youth hostel here?	**Czy jest tu schronisko młodzieżowe?**	chi yest too s-hro-nees-k mwo-dgye-zho-ve
Have you a room/bed for the night?	**Czy jest pokój/łóżko na dzisiejszą noc?**	chi yest po-kooy/woozh- na dgee-shey-sho^n no
How many days can we stay?	**Na ile dni możemy się tu zatrzymać?**	na ee-le dnee mo-zhe-r shye^n too za-tshi-mac
Here is my membership card	**Moja legitymacja członkowska**	mo-ya le-gee-ti-ma-ts chwon-kov-ska
Do you serve meals?	**Czy podają państwo posiłki?**	chi po-da-yo^n pan-stv po-sheew-kee
Can I use the kitchen?	**Czy można skorzystać z kuchni?**	chi mozh-na sko-zhis-ta skooh-nee
Is there somewhere cheap to eat nearby?	**Czy jest w pobliżu jakaś tania restauracja?**	chi yest fpo-blee-zhoo ya-kash ta-nya res-taoo-ra-tsya

RENTING OR OWNING A PLACE

We have rented an apartment/villa	**Wynajęliśmy mieszkanie/willę**	vi-na-**ye^{n}**-leesh-mi myesh-**ka**-nye/**veel**-le^{n}
Here is our reservation	**To jest nasza rezerwacja**	to yest **na**-sha re-zer-**va**-tsya
Please show us around	**Proszę nas oprowadzić**	**pro**-she^{n} nas o-pro-**va**-dgeech
Is the cost of electricity/ the gas cylinder/ the maid included?	**Czy włączony jest koszt elektryczności/ butli gazowej/ pomocy domowej?**	chi vwo^{n}-**cho**-ni yest kosht e-lek-trich-**nosh**-chee/ **boot**-lee ga-**zo**-vey/ po-**mo**-tsi do-**mo**-vey
Where is the electricity mains switch/ water mains stopcock/ light switch/ power point/ fuse box?	**Gdzie jest główny wyłącznik elektryczności/ zawór wodny/ wyłącznik/ kontakt/gniazdko/ są bezpieczniki?**	gdgye yest **gwoov**-ni vi-**wo^{n}ch**-neek e-lek-trich-**nosh**-chee/ **za**-voor **wod**-ni/ vi-**wo^{n}ch**-neek/ **kon**-takt/**gnyazd**-ko/ so^{n} bez-pyech-**nee**-kee
How does the heating/ hot water work?	**Jak działa ogrzewanie/ gorąca woda?**	yak **dgya**-wa o-gzhe-**va**-nye/ go-**ro^{n}**-tsa **vo**-da

Is there a spare gas cylinder?	**Czy jest zapasowa butla gazowa?**	chi yest za-pa-so-va boot-la ga-zo-va
Do gas cylinders get delivered?	**Czy są dostarczane butle gazowe?**	chi so^{n} dos-tar-cha-ne boot-le ga-zo-ve
Please show me how this works	**Proszę mi pokazać jak to działa**	pro-she^{n} mee po-ka-zac yak to dgya-wa
Which days does the maid come?	**W jakie dni przychodzi pomoc domowa?**	vya-kye dnee pshi-ho-dgee po-mots do-mo-va
For how long?	**Na jak długo?**	na-yak dwoo-go
Is there a fly-screen?	**Czy jest moskitiera?**	chi yest mos-kee-tye-ra
When is the rubbish collected?	**Kiedy są wywożone śmiecie?**	kye-di so^{n} vi-vo-zho-ne shmye-chee
Where can we buy logs for the fire?	**Gdzie możemy kupić drewno do palenia w kominku?**	gdgye mo-zhe-mi koo-peech drev-no do pa-le-nya fko-meen-ko
Is there a barbecue?	**Czy jest rożen?**	chi yest ro-zhen
Please give me another set of keys	**Proszę mi dać zapasowe klucze**	pro-she^{n} mee dach za-pa-so-ve kloo-che
We have replaced the broken ...	**Odkupiliśmy nowe na miejsce złamanych**	od-koo-pee-leesh-mi no-v na myey-stse zwa-ma-ni
Here is the bill	**Tutaj jest rachunek**	too-tay yest ra-hoo-nek
Please return my deposit against breakages	**Proszę o zwrot kaucji**	pro-she^{n} o zvrot kaoo-tsyee

PROBLEMS

The drain is blocked/ pipe/sink	**Rura odpływowa jest zablokowana/ rura/zlew**	roo-ra od-pwi-vo-va yest za-blo-ko-va-na/ roo-ra/zlev
The toilet doesn't flush	**Woda się nie spuszcza w toalecie**	vo-da shye^{n} nye spoosh-cha fto-a-le-chye
There is no water	**Nie ma wody**	nye ma vo-di
We can't turn the water off/ shower on	**Nie możemy zakręcić kranu/ włączyć prysznica**	nye mo-zhe-mi za-kre^{n}-cheech kra-noo/ vwo^{n}-chich prish-nee-tsa
There is a leak/ a broken window	**Jest przeciek/ szyba wybita**	yest pshe-chyek/ shi-ba vi-bee-ta
The shutters won't close	**Żaluzje się nie zamykają**	zha-looz-ye shye^{n} nye za-mi-ka-yo^{n}
The window won't open	**Okno się nie otwiera**	ok-no shye^{n} nye ot-vye-ra
The electricity has gone off	**Nie ma elektryczności**	nye ma e-lek-trich-nosh-chee
The heating doesn't work/ cooker/ refrigerator/ water heater	**Nie działa ogrzewanie/ kuchenka/ lodówka/ podgrzewacz wody/ terma**	nye dgya-wa og-zhe-va-nye/ koo-hen-ka/ lo-doov-ka/ pod-gzhe-vach vo-di/ ter-ma
The lock is stuck	**Zamek się zaciął**	za-mek shye^{n} za-chyo^{n}w
This is broken	**To jest rozbite/ złamane**	to yest roz-bee-te/ zwa-ma-ne
This needs repairing	**To trzeba naprawić**	to tshe-ba na-pra-veech
The apartment/villa has been burgled	**Było włamanie do mieszkania/willi**	bi-wo vwa-ma-nye do myesh-ka-nya/veel-lee

PARTS OF THE HOUSE

balcony	**balkon**	bal-kon
bathroom	**łazienka**	wa-zhyen-ka
bedroom	**sypialnia**	si-pyal-nya
ceiling	**sufit**	soo-feet
chimney	**komin**	ko-meen
corridor	**korytarz**	ko-ri-tazh
door	**drzwi**	dzhvee
fence	**płot**	pwot
fireplace	**kominek**	ko-mee-nek
floor	**podłoga**	po-dwo-ga
garage	**garaż**	ga-razh
gate	**brama**	bra-ma
hall	**przedpokój**	pshed-po-kooy
kitchen	**kuchnia**	kooh-nya
living room	**salon**	sa-lon
roof	**dach**	dah
shutters	**żaluzje**	zha-looz-ye
stairs	**schody**	s-ho-di
terrace	**taras**	ta-ras
wall	**ściana**	sh-chya-na
window	**okno**	ok-no

FURNITURE AND FITTINGS

armchair	**fotel**	fo-tel
barbecue	**rożen**	ro-zhen
bath	**wanna**	van-na
bed	**łóżko**	woozh-ko
blanket	**koc**	kots
bolt (for door)	**zasuwa**	za-soo-va
broom	**miotła**	myot-wa
brush	**szczotka**	shchot-ka
bucket	**wiadro**	vya-dro
cassette player	**magnetofon kasetowy**	ma-gne-to-fon ka-se-to-vi
chair	**krzesło**	kshes-wo
charcoal	**węgiel drzewny**	ve^{n}-gyel dzhev-ni
clock	**zegar**	ze-gar
cooker	**kuchenka**	koo-hen-ka
cupboard	**kredens/szafka**	kre-dens/shaf-ka
curtains	**zasłony/firanki**	zas-wo-ni/fee-ran-kee
cushion	**poduszka**	po-doosh-ka
deckchair	**leżak**	le-zhak
door	**drzwi**	dzhvee
doorbell	**dzwonek do drzwi**	dzvo-nek do dzhvee
doorknob	**klamka**	klam-ka
dustbin	**pojemnik na śmieci**	po-yem-neek na shmye-chee

dustpan	**śmietniczka**	shmyet-neech-ka
hinge	**zawias**	za-vyas
immersion heater	**terma**	ter-ma
iron	**żelazko**	zhe-laz-ko
lamp	**lampa**	lam-pa
lampshade	**abażur**	a-ba-zhoor
light bulb	**żarowka**	zha-roov-ka
lock	**zamek**	za-mek
mattress	**materac**	ma-te-rats
mirror	**lustro**	loos-tro
mop	**szczotka do mycia podłogi**	shchot-ka do mi-chya po-dwo-gee
padlock	**kłódka**	kwood-ka
pillow	**poduszka**	po-doosh-ka
pipe	**rura**	roo-ra
plug (electric)	**wtyczka elektryczna**	ftich-ka e-lek-trich-na
(bath)	**korek do wanny**	ko-rek do van-ni
radio	**radio**	ra-dyo
refrigerator	**lodówka**	lo-doov-ka
sheet	**prześcieradło**	pshesh-chye-ra-dwo
shelf	**półka**	poow-ka
shower	**prysznic**	prish-neets
sink	**zlew**	zlev
sofa	**kanapa**	ka-na-pa
stool	**taboret/stołek**	ta-bo-ret/sto-wek
table	**stół**	stoow

tap	**kran**	kran
toilet	**toaleta/klozet**	to-a-le-ta/klo-zet
towel	**ręcznik**	re^{n}ch-neek
vacuum cleaner	**odkurzacz**	od-koo-zhach
washbasin	**umywalka**	oo-mi-val-ka
washing machine	**pralka**	pral-ka
window catch	**zasuwka**	za-soov-ka
window sill	**parapet**	pa-ra-pet

KITCHEN EQUIPMENT

bleach	**hlorek**	hlo-rek
bottle opener	**otwieracz do kapsli**	o-tvye-rach do kap-slee
bowl	**miska**	mees-ka
can opener	**otwieracz do puszek**	o-tvye-rach do poo-shek
candles	**świece**	shvye-tse
chopping board	**deska do krojenia**	des-ka do kro-ye-nya
clothes line	**sznur do bielizny**	shnoor do bye-leez-ni
clothes pegs	**klamerki/spinacze do wieszania bielizny**	kla-mer-kee/ spee-na-che do vye-sha-nya bye-leez-ni
coffee pot	**dzbanek do kawy**	dzba-nek do ka-vi
colander	**cedzak**	tse-dzak
coolbox	**torba lodówka**	tor-ba lo-doov-ka
corkscrew	**korkociąg**	kor-ko-chyo^{n}g
cup	**filiżanka**	fee-lee-zhan-ka

detergent	**środek do czyszczenia/ prania**	**shro**-dek do chish-**che**-nya/ **pra**-nya
fork	**widelec**	vee-**de**-lets
frying pan	**patelnia**	pa-**tel**-nya
glass	**szklanka**	**shklan**-ka
ice tray	**tacka do lodu**	**tats**-ka do **lo**-doo
kettle	**czajnik**	**chay**-neek
knife	**nóż**	noozh
matches	**zapałki**	za-**paw**-kee
pan	**rondel/garnek**	**ron**-del/**gar**-nek
plate	**talerz**	**ta**-lezh
scissors	**nożyczki**	no-**zhich**-kee
sieve	**sitko**	**sheet**-ko
spoon	**łyżka**	**wizh**-ka
tea towel	**ścierka**	**shchyer**-ka
torch	**latarka**	la-**tar**-ka
washing powder	**proszek do prania**	**pro**-shek do **pra**-nya
washing-up liquid	**płyn do zmywania naczyń**	**pwin** do zmi-**va**-nya **na**-chin

ODD JOBS[1]

bracket	**spornik**	**spor**-neek
hammer	**młotek**	**mwo**-tek
iron	**żelazo**	zhe-**la**-zo

1. See also SHOPS AND SERVICES, p. 105.

lacquer	**lakier**	la-kyer
metal	**metal**	me-tal
nails	**gwoździe**	gvozh-dgye
paint	**farba**	far-ba
paint brush	**pędzel do malowania**	pe^{n}-dzel do ma-lo-va-nya
plastic	**plastyk**	plas-tik
pliers	**obcążki**	ob-tso^{n}zh-kee
saw	**piła**	pee-wa
screwdriver	**śrubociąg**	shroo-bo-chyo^{n}g
screws	**śruby**	shroo-bi
spanner	**klucz**	klooch
steel	**stal**	stal
tile	**kafel**	ka-fel
wire	**drut**	droot
wood	**drewno**	drev-no

MEETING PEOPLE

How are you/things?	**Jak się pan(i) czuje/ co słychać?**	yak shye^{n} pan (pa-nee) choo-yee/tso swi-hach
Fine, thanks, and you?	**Doskonale, dziękuję, a pan(i)?**	dos-ko-na-le, dgye^{n}-koo-ye^{n}, a pan (pa-nee)
What is your name?	**Jak pan(i) się nazywa/ Jak panu(i) na imię?**	yak pan (pa-nee) shye^{n} na-zi-va/yak pa-noo (nee) na ee-mye^{n}
May I introduce …?	**Czy mogę przedstawić …?**	chi mo-ge^{n} pshed-sta-veech
May I introduce myself …?	**Czy mogę się przedstawić …?**	chi mo-ge^{n} shye^{n} pshed-sta-veech
My name is …	**Nazywam się …**	na-zi-vam shye^{n}
This is …	**To jest …**	to yest
Have you met …?	**Czy państwo się znają?**	chi pan-stvo shye^{n} zna-yo^{n}
Glad to meet you	**Miło mi pana (panią) poznać**	mee-wo mee pa-na (-nyo^{n} poz-nach

Am I disturbing you?	**Czy przeszkadzam?**	chi pshesh-ka-dzam
Go away	**Proszę odejść**	pro-she^n o-deyshch
Leave me alone	**Proszę mi dać spokój**	pro-she^n mee dach spo-kooy
Sorry to have troubled you	**Przepraszam za kłopot**	pshe-pra-sham za kwo-pot

MAKING FRIENDS

Do you live/are you staying here?	**Czy pan(i) tu mieszka?**	chi pan (pa-nee) too myesh-ka
Do you travel a lot?	**Czy pan(i) dużo podróżuje?**	chi pan (pa-nee) doo-zho po-droo-zhoo-ye
We've been here a week	**Jesteśmy tu od tygodnia**	yes-tesh-mi too od ti-god-nya
Is this your first time here?	**Czy jest pan(i) tu po raz pierwszy?**	chi yest pan (pa-nee) too po raz pyerv-shi
Do you like it here?	**Czy się panu (pani) tu podoba?**	chi shye^n pa-noo (nee) too po-do-ba
Are you on your own?	**Czy jest pan(i) sam (-a)?**	chi yest pan (pa-nee) sam (sa-ma)
I am with my husband/wife/ my parents/ my family/ a friend	**Jestem z mężem/żoną/ rodzicami/ rodziną/ przyjacielem (przyjaciółką)**	yes-tem zme^n-zhem/zho-no^n/ ro-dgee-tsa-mee/ ro-dgee-no^n/ pshi-ya-chye-lem (pshi-ya-chyoow-ko^n)
I am travelling alone	**Podróżuję sam(a)**	po-droo-zhoo-ye^n sam (sa-ma)

Where do you come from?	**Skąd pan(i) jest?**	sko^{n}d pan (pa-nee) yest
I come from …	**Jestem z …**	yes-tem z
What do you do?	**Czym się pan(i) zajmuje?**	chim shye^{n} pan (pa-nee) zay-**moo**-ye
What are you studying?	**Co pan(i) studiuje?**	tso pan (pa-nee) stood-**yoo**-ye
I'm on holiday/ a (business) trip	**Jestem na wakacjach/ służbowo**	yes-tem na va-**kats**-yah/ swoozh-**bo**-vo
Are you married? (man)	**Czy pan jest żonaty?**	chi pan yest zho-**na**-ti
(woman)	**Czy pani jest mężatką?**	chi **pa**-nee yest me^{n}-**zhat**-ko^{n}
Do you have children?	**Czy pan(i) ma dzieci?**	chi pan (**pa**-nee) ma **dgye**-chee
Have you been to England/America?	**Czy pan(i) był(a) w Anglii/Ameryce?**	chi pan (**pa**-nee) biw (**bi**-wa) van-glee/a-me-**ri**-tse
I hope to see you again	**Mam nadzieję że się jeszcze zobaczymy**	mam na-**dgye**-ye^{n} zhe shye^{n} **yesh**-che zo-ba-**chi**-mi
Do you smoke?	**Czy pan(i) pali?**	chi pan (**pa**-nee) **pa**-lee
No, I don't, thanks	**Dziękuję, nie palę**	dgye^{n}-**koo**-ye^{n} nye **pa**-le^{n}
I have given it up	**Rzuciłem (-am) palenie**	zhoo-**chee**-wem (wam) pa-**le**-nye
Do you have a light, please?	**Czy mogę prosić o ogień?**	chi **mo**-ge^{n} **pro**-sheech o **o**-gyen
Do you mind if I smoke?	**Czy pan(i) pozwoli ze zapalę?**	chi pan (**pa**-nee) poz-**vo**-lee zhe za-**pa**-le^{n}
Help yourself	**Proszę się poczęstować**	**pro**-she^{n} shye^{n} po-che^{n}-**sto**-vach

Can I get you a drink/ another drink?	**Czy pan(i) się czegoś napije/czy pan(i) się jeszcze czegoś napije?**	chi pan (pa-nee) shye^n che-gosh na-pee-ye/chi pan (pa-nee) shye^n yesh-che che-gosh na-pee-ye
I'd like a … please	**Poproszę o …**	po-pro-she^n o
No thanks, I'm all right	**Nie, dziękuję**	nye, dgye^n-koo-ye^n

INVITATIONS

Would you like to have lunch tomorrow?	**Czy możemy się spotkać jutro na obiad?**	chi mo-zhe-mi shye^n spot-kach yoo-tro na o-byad
Can you come to dinner/for a drink?	**Czy może pan(i) przyjść na kolację/ na wino?**	chi mo-zhe pan (pa-nee) pshiyshch na ko-la-tsye^n/ na vee-no
We're giving/there is a party. Would you like to come?	**Urządzamy/jest przyjęcie. Czy ma pan(i) ochotę przyjść?**	oo-zho^n-dza-mi/yest pshi-ye^n-chye. chi ma pan (pa-nee) o-ho-te^n pshiyshch
Can I bring a (girl) friend?	**Czy mogę przyprowadzić (przyjaciółkę) przyjaciela?**	chi mo-ge^n pshi-pro-va-dgeech (pshi-ya-chyoow-ke^n) pshi-ya-chye-la
Thanks for the invitation	**Dziękuję za zaproszenie**	dgye^n-koo-ye^n za za-pro-she-nye
I'd love to come	**Przyjdę z przyjemnością**	pshiy-de^n z pshi-yem-nosh-chyo^n
I'm sorry, I can't come	**Przepraszam, nie mogę przyjść**	pshe-pra-sham, nye mo-ge^n pshiyshch

Are you doing anything tonight/tomorrow afternoon?	**Czy pan(i) jest zajęty(-a) dziś wieczór/jutro po południu?**	chi pan(pa-nee) yest za-ye^{n}-ti(ta) dgeesh vye-choor/yoo-tro po-po-wood-nyoo
Could we have coffee/a drink somewhere?	**Może wyjdziemy gdzieś na kawę/na wino?**	mo-zhe viy-dgye-mi gdgyesh na ka-ve^{n}/na vee-no
Shall we go to the cinema/theatre/beach?	**Może pójdziemy do kina/do teatru/na plażę?**	mo-zhe pooy-dgye-mi do kee-na/do te-a-troo/na pla-zhe^{n}
Would you like to go dancing/for a drive?	**Czy ma pan(i) ochotę potańczyć/na przejażdżkę?**	chi ma pan (pa-nee) o-ho-te^{n} po-tan-chich/na pshe-yazhj-ke^{n}
Do you know a good disco/restaurant?	**Czy zna pan(i) jakąś dobrą dyskotekę/restaurację?**	chi zna pan (pa-nee) ya-ko^{n}sh do-bro^{n} dis-ko-te-ke^{n}/res-taoo-ra-tsye^{n}
Where shall we meet?	**Gdzie się spotkamy?**	gdye shye^{n} spot-ka-mi
What time shall I/we come?	**O której mam/mamy przyjść?**	o ktoo-rey mam/ma-mi pshiyshch
I could pick you up at (place/time)	**Mogę po pana (panią) przyjść do … o …**	mo-ge^{n} po pana (pa-nyo^{n}) pshiyshch do … o
Could you meet me at (time) outside (place)?	**Czy może pan(i) mnie spotkać o (…) przed (…)?**	chi mo-zhe pan (pa-nee) mnye spot-kach o (…) pshed (…)
What time do you have to be back?	**O której musi pan(i) wrócić?**	o ktoo-rey moo-shee pan (pa-nee) vroo-cheech
May I see you home?	**Czy mogę pana (panią) odprowadzić do domu?**	chi mo-ge^{n} pa-na (nyo^{n}) od-pro-va-dgeech do do-moo

Can we give you a lift home/to your hotel?	**Czy możemy pana (panią) podwieźć do domu/ do hotelu?**	chi mo-zhe-mi pa-na (nyo^n) pod-vyezhch do do-moo/ do ho-te-loo
Can I see you again?	**Czy możemy się jeszcze spotkać?**	chi mo-zhe-mi shye^n yesh-che spot-kach
Where do you live?	**Gdzie pan(i) mieszka?**	gdgye pan (pa-nee) myesh-ka
What is your telephone number?	**Jaki jest pana (pani) numer telefonu?**	ya-kee yest pa-na (nee) noo-mer te-le-fo-noo
Do you live alone?	**Czy pan(i) mieszka sam (-a)?**	chi pan (pa-nee) myesh-ka sam(sa-ma)
Thanks for the evening/ your company	**Dziekuję za miły wieczór/miłe towarzystwo**	dgye^n-koo-ye^n za mee-wi vye-choor/mee-we to-va-zhis-tvo
It was lovely	**Było wspaniale**	bi-wo vspa-nya-le
It's been nice talking to you	**Miło mi było z panem (panią) porozmawiać**	mee-wo mee bi-wo z pa-nem (nyo^n) po-roz-ma-vyach
Hope to see you again soon	**Mam nadzieję że się znowu wkrótce zobaczymy**	mam na-dgye-ye^n zhe shye^n zno-voo fkroot-tse zo-ba-chi-mi
See you soon/later/ tomorrow	**Do zobaczenia wkrótce/później/ jutro**	do zo-ba-che-nya fkroot-tse/poozh-nyey/ yoo-tro

GOING TO A RESTAURANT

Can you suggest a good restaurant/ a cheap restaurant/ a vegetarian restaurant?	**Czy może mi pan(i) polecić dobrą restaurację/tanią restaurację/ restaurację jarską?**	chi mo-zhe mee pan (pa-nee) po-le-cheech dob-ro^n res-taoo-ra-tsye^n/ ta-nyo^n res-taoo-ra-tsye^n/ res-taoo-ra-tsye^n yar-sko^n
I'd like to book a table for four at 1 o'clock	**Chciałbym (-abym) zamówić stolik na cztery osoby na godzinę pierwszą**	hchyaw-bim (hchya-wa-bim) za-moo-veech sto-leek na chte-ri o-so-bi na go-dgee-ne^n pyerv-sho^n
I've reserved a table; my name is …	**Zamówiłem (-am) stolik; moje nazwisko …**	za-moo-vee-wem (wam) sto-leek; mo-ye naz-vees-ko
We did not make a reservation	**Nie mamy zarezerwowanego stolika**	nye ma-mi za-re-zer-vo-va-ne-go sto-lee-ka
Is there a table on the terrace/by the window/ in a corner?	**Czy jest stolik na tarasie/przy oknie/ w rogu?**	chi yest sto-leek na ta-ra-shye/pshi o-knye/ v ro-goo

Is there a non-smoking area?	**Czy jest sekcja dla niepalących?**	chi yest sek-tsya dla nye-pa-lo^{n}-tsih
This way please	***Tędy proszę**	te^{n}-di pro-she^{n}
You would have to wait about … minutes	***Proszę poczekać około … minut**	pro-she^{n} po-che-kach o-ko-wo … mee-noot
We shall have a table free in half an hour	***Będziemy mieć wolny stolik za pół godziny**	be^{n}-dgye-mi myech vol-ni sto-leek za poow go-dgee-ni
We don't serve lunch until 12.30	***Zaczynamy podawać obiad o dwunastej trzydzieści**	za-chi-na-mi po-da-vach o-byad o dvoo-nas-tey tshi-dgyesh-chi
We don't serve dinner until 8 o'clock	***Zaczynamy podawać kolację o ósmej wieczór**	za-chi-na-mi po-da-vach ko-la-tsye^{n} o oos-mey vye-choor
We stop serving at 11	***Kończymy podawać o jedenastej**	kon-chi-mi po-da-vach o ye-de-nas-tey
Last orders at …	***Ostatnie zamówienia o …**	os-tat-nye za-moo-vye-nya o
Sorry, the kitchen is closed	***Przepraszamy, kuchnia jest zamknięta**	pshe-pra-shami, kooh-nya yest zam-knye^{n}-ta
Where is the cloakroom?	**Gdzie jest szatnia?**	gdgye yest shat-nya
It is downstairs	***Na dole**	na do-le
That was an excellent meal	**Jedzenie było doskonałe**	ye-dze-nye bi-wo dos-ko-na-we
We shall come again	**Wrócimy tutaj**	vroo-chee-mi too-tay

ORDERING

Waiter/waitress	**Kelner/kelnerka**[1]	kel-ner/kel-**ner**-ka
May I see the menu/ the wine list, please?	**Proszę o jadłospis/ kartę win?**	pro-she^n o ya-**dwo**-spees/ **kar**-te^n veen
Is there a set menu for lunch?	**Czy mają państwo obiady firmowe?**	chi **ma**-yo^n **pan**-stvo o-**bya**-di feer-**mo**-ve
We are in a hurry	**Spieszymy się**	spye-**shi**-mi shye^n
Do you serve snacks?	**Czy podają państwo przekąski/lekkie posiłki?**	chi po-**da**-yo^n **pan**-stvo pshe-**ko**^{n}s-kee/**lek**-kye po-**sheew**-kee
I want something light	**Proszę o coś lekkiego**	**pro**-she^n o tsosh lek-**kye**-go
Do you have children's helpings?	**Czy są porcje dla dzieci?**	chi so^n **por**-tsye dla **dgye**-chee
What is your dish of the day?	**Co szef kuchni poleca dzisiaj?**	tso shef **kooh**-nee po-**le**-tsa **dgee**-shyay
What do you recommend?	**Co państwo polecają?**	tso **pan**-stvo po-le-**tsa**-yo^n
Can you tell me what this is?	**Czy może mi pan(i) wyjaśnić co to jest?**	chi **mo**-zhe mee pan (**pa**-nee) vi-**yash**-neech tso to yest
What are the specialities of the restaurant/of the region?	**Jakie są specjalności tej restauracji/ miejscowe?**	**ya**-kye so^n spets-yal-**nosh**-chee tey res-taoo-**rats**-yee/ myeys-**tso**-ve
Do you have any local dishes/ vegetarian dishes?	**Czy maja państwo jakieś potrawy regionalne/jarskie?**	chi **ma**-yo^n **pan**-stvo **ya**-kyesh po-**tra**-vi re-gyo-**nal**-ne/**yar**-skye

1. When addressing a waiter/waitress say: 'proszę pana/proszę pani'.

Would you like to try …?	*Czy pan(i) spróbuje …?	chi pan (pa-nee) sproo-boo-ye
There's no more …	*Nie ma …	nye ma
I'd like …	Proszę o …	pro-she^{n} o
May I have peas instead of beans?	Czy mogę prosić o groszek zamiast fasolki?	chi mo-ge^{n} pro-sheech o gro-shek za-myast fa-sol-kee
Is it hot or cold?	Czy to jest na zimno czy na gorąco?	chi to yest na zheem-no chi na go-ro^{n}-tso
I don't want any oil/sauce with it	Proszę mi to podać bez oliwy/bez sosu	pro-she^{n} mee to po-dach bez o-lee-vi/bez so-soo
Some more bread, please	Proszę jeszcze trochę chleba	pro-she^{n} yesh-che tro-he^{n} hle-ba
A little more, please	Proszę jeszcze trochę	pro-she^{n} yesh-che tro-he^{n}

COMPLAINTS

Where are our drinks?	Gdzie są nasze napoje?	gdgye so^{n} na-she na-po-ye
Why is the food taking so long?	Dlaczego tak długo czekamy?	dla-che-go tak dwoo-go che-ka-mi
This isn't what I ordered, I want …	Ja tego nie zamawiałem (-am), prosiłem (-am) o …	ya te-go nye za-ma-vya-wem (wam), pro-shee-wem (wam) o
This isn't fresh	To jest nieświeże	to yest nye-shvye-zhe
This is uncooked/overcooked	To jest niedogotowane/przegotowane	to yest nye-do-go-to-va-ne/pshe-go-to-va-ne
This is stale	To jest nieświeże/czerstwe	to yest nye-shvye-zhe/cher-stve

tough too cold salty	**twarde** **za zimne** **za słone**	tvar-de za zheem-ne za swo-ne
This plate/knife/ spoon/glass is not clean	**Ten talerz/nóż/ ta łyżka/szklanka nie jest czysty (-a)**	ten ta-lezh/noozh/ ta wizh-ka/shklan-ka nye yest chis-ti (a)
I'd like to see the headwaiter	**Czy mogę rozmawiać z kierownikiem sali**	chi mo-ge^{n} roz-ma-vyach z kye-rov-nee-kyem sa-lee

PAYING

The bill, please	**Poproszę rachunek**	po-pro-she^{n} ra-hoo-nek
Is service included?	**Czy obsługa jest włączona?**	chi ob-swoo-ga yest vwo^{n}-cho-na
Please check the bill – I don't think it's correct	**Proszę sprawdzić ten rachunek – wydaje mi się że jest jakaś pomyłka**	pro-she^{n} spraw-dgeech ten ra-hoo-nek vi-da-ye mee shye^{n} zhe yest ya-kash po-miw-ka
What is this amount for?	**Za co jest ta suma?**	za tso yest ta soo-ma
I didn't have soup	**Ja nie zamawiałem (-am) zupy**	ya nye za-ma-vya-wem (wam) zoo-pi
I had chicken, not steak	**Zamawiałem (-am) kurczaka, a nie stek**	za-ma-vya-wem (wam) koor-cha-ka a nye stek
May we have separate bills?	**Czy można prosić o oddzielne rachunki?**	chi mozh-na pro-sheech o od-dgyel-ne ra-hoon-kee
Can I pay with travellers' cheques/ a credit card?	**Czy mogę zapłacić czekami podróżniczymi/ kartą kredytową?**	chi mo-ge^{n} za-pwa-cheech che-ka-mee pod-roozh-nee-chi-mee/ kar-to^{n} kre-di-to-vo^{n}

Keep the change	**Proszę zatrzymać resztę**	pro-she^{n} za-tshi-mach resh-te^{n}
It was very good	**To było bardzo dobre**	to bi-wo bar-dzo do-bre
We enjoyed it, thank you	**Smakowało nam, dziękujemy**	sma-ko-va-wo nam, dgye^{n}-koo-ye-mi

BREAKFAST AND TEA

Breakfast	**Śniadanie**	shnya-da-nye
What time is breakfast served?	**O której jest śniadanie?**	o ktoo-rey yest shnya-da-nye
A large white coffee, please	**Poproszę dużą białą kawę**	po-pro-she^{n} doo-zho^{n} bya-wo^{n} ka-ve^{n}
A black coffee	**Czarną kawę**	char-no^{n} ka-ve^{n}
I would like decaffeinated coffee	**Poproszę o kawę bezkofeinową**	po-pro-she^{n} o ka-ve^{n} bez ka-fe-ee-no-vo^{n}
A cup of tea, please	**Poproszę herbatę**	po-pro-she^{n} her-ba-te^{n}
I'd like tea with milk/lemon	**Poproszę herbatę z mlekiem/z cytryną**	po-pro-she^{n} her-ba-te^{n} zmle-kyem/stsi-tri-no^{n}
I would like a herb tea	**Poproszę herbatę ziołową**	po-pro-she^{n} her-ba-te^{n} zhyo-wo-vo^{n}
Drinking chocolate	**Czekolada na gorąco**	che-ko-la-da na go-ro^{n}-tso
May we have some sugar, please?	**Czy można prosić o cukier?**	chi mozh-na pro-sheech o tsoo-kyer
Do you have artificial sweeteners?	**Czy państwo mają słodzik?**	chi pan-stvo ma-yo^{n} swo-dgeek
Hot/cold milk	**Gorące/zimne mleko**	go-ro^{n}-tse/zheem-ne mle-ko

A roll and butter	**Bułka i masło**	boow-ka ee mas-wo
Toast	**Grzanka**	gzhan-ka
We'd like more butter, please	**Prosimy jeszcze trochę masła**	pro-shee-mi yesh-che tro-he^n mas-wa
Have you some jam/ marmalade?	**Czy jest dżem/ marmelada?**	chi yest jem/ mar-me-la-da
What fruit juices have you?	**Jakie soki owocowe można dostać?**	ya-kye so-kee o-vo-tso-ve mozh-na dos-tach
Orange/ grapefruit/ tomato juice	**Sok pomarańczowy/ grejpfrutowy/ pomidorowy**	sok po-ma-ran-cho-vi/ greyp-froo-to-vi/ po-mee-do-ro-vi
Fresh fruit	**Świeże owoce**	shvye-zhe o-vo-tse
Yogurt	**Jogurt**	yo-goort
Cereal	**Płatki zbożowe**	pwat-kee zbo-zho-ve
Bread	**Chleb**	hleb
I'd like a soft-boiled egg/ a hard-boiled egg/ fried eggs/ scrambled eggs	**Poproszę jajko na miękko/ jajko na twardo/ jajka sadzone/ jajecznicę**	po-pro-she^n yay-ko na mye^{n}k-ko/ yay-ko na tvar-do/ yay-ka sa-dzo-ne/ ya-yech-nee-tse^n
Omelette	**Omlet**	om-let
Help yourself at the buffet	***Proszę się obsłużyć przy stole**	pro-she^n shye^n ob-swoo-zhich pshi sto-le

SNACKS AND PICNICS

Can I have a ... sandwich, please?	**Poproszę kanapkę z ...?**	po-pro-she^n ka-nap-ke^n z

What are those things over there?	**Co to jest?**	tso to yest
What are they made of?	**Z czego one są robione?**	z che-go o-ne so^n ro-byo-ne
What is in them?	**Co jest w środku?**	tso yest fshrod-koo
I'll have one of these, please	**Poproszę jeden (jedną, jedno) z tych**	po-pro-she^n ye-den (yed-no^n, yed-no) stih
It's to take away	**To jest na wynos**	to yest na vi-nos
beefburger	**befsztyk mielony**	bef-shtik mye-lo-ni
biscuits	**herbatniki/ ciasteczka**	her-bat-nee-kee/ chyas-tech-ka
bread	**chleb**	hleb
butter	**masło**	mas-wo
cheese	**ser**	ser
chips	**frytki**	frit-kee
chocolate bar	**tabliczka czekolady**	tab-leech-ka che-ko-la-di
cold cuts	**wędliny/mięsa na zimno**	ve^n-dlee-ni/mye^n-sa na zheem-no
egg(s)	**jajko(-a)**	yay-ko (ka)
ham	**szynka**	shin-ka
ice cream	**lody**	lo-di
pancakes	**naleśniki**	na-lesh-nee-kee
pastries	**ciastka**	chyast-ka
pickles	**marynaty**	ma-ri-na-ti
meat/fruit pie	**pasztecik z mięsem/ ciasto z owocami**	pash-te-cheek z mye^n-sem/ chyas-to z ovo-tsa-mee
milk bar	**bar mleczny**	bar mlech-ni

roast chicken	**kurczak pieczony**	koor-chak pye-cho-ni
roll	**bułeczka/bułka**	boo-wech-ka/boow-ka
salad	**sałata**	sa-wa-ta
snack	**przekąska**	pshe-ko^{n}s-ka
snack bar	**bar garmażeryjny/ bar szybkiej obsługi**	bar gar-ma-zhe-riy-ni/ bar shib-kyey ob-swoo-gee
soup	**zupa**	zoo-pa
tomato	**pomidor**	po-mee-dor

DRINKS[1]

Café	**Kawiarnia**	ka-vyar-nya
Bar	**Bar**	bar
What will you have to drink?	***Co państwo zamówią do picia?**	tso pan-stvo za-moo-vyo^n do-pee-chya
A bottle of wine, please	**Poproszę butelkę wina**	po-pro-she^n boo-tel-ke^n vee-na
Do you serve wine by the glass?	**Czy państwo podają wino na lampki?**	chi pan-stvo po-da-yo^n vee-no na lamp-kee
Carafe/glass	**Karafka/szklanka/ lampka**	ka-raf-ka/shklan-ka/ lamp-ka
Bottle/half bottle	**Butelka/pół butelki**	boo-tel-ka/poow boo-tel-kee
Do you serve cocktails?	**Czy państwo podają koktaile?**	chi pan-stvo po-da-yo^n kok-tay-le
Soft drinks	**Napoje bezalkoholowe**	na-po-ye bez-al-ko-ho-lo-ve

1. For the names of beverages see p. 101.

I'd like a long soft drink	**Poproszę napój bezalkoholowy**	po-p... bez-a...
with ice	**z lodem**	zlo-den...
apple juice	**sok jabłkowy**	sok yabw-...
orange juice	**sok pomarańczowy**	sok po-ma-ra...
fruit juice	**sok owocowy**	sok o-vo-tso-vi
milk shake	**koktail mleczny**	kok-ta-eel mlech-ni
iced coffee	**kawę mrożoną**	ka-ve^n mro-zho-no^n
hot chocolate	**czekoladę na gorąco**	che-ko-la-de^n na go-ro^n-tso
iced tea	**herbatę mrożoną**	her-ba-te^n mro-zho-no^n
tea	**herbatę**	her-ba-te^n
Two glasses of beer, please	**Poproszę dwie szklanki piwa**	po-pro-she^n dvye shklan-kee pee-va
Do you have draught beer?	**Czy jest piwo z beczki?**	chi yest pee-vo z bech-kee
Two more beers	**Poproszę jeszcze dwa piwa**	po-pro-she^n yesh-che dva pee-va
Large/small beer	**Duże/małe piwo**	doo-zhe/ma-we pee-vo
Neat	**Czysty (-a)**	chis-ti (-ta)
On the rocks	**Z lodem**	zlo-dem
With (soda) water	**Z wodą (sodową)**	zvo-do^n (so-do-vo^n)
Ice cubes	**Kostki lodu**	kost-kee lo-doo
Mineral water (with/without gas)	**Woda mineralna (gazowana/niegazowana)**	vo-da mee-ne-ral-na (ga-zo-va-na/nye-ga-zo-va-na)
Cheers!	**Na zdrowie!**	na zdro-vye
I'd like another glass of water, please	**Poproszę jeszcze jedną szklankę wody**	po-pro-she^n yesh-che yed-no^n shklan-ke^n vo-di
The same again, please	**Poproszę jeszcze raz to samo**	po-pro-she^n yesh-che raz to sa-mo

lack coffees and one with cream	Trzy czarne kawy i jedną ze śmietanką	tshi char-ne ka-vi ee yed-na ze shmye-tan-ko^{n}
I want to see the head waiter	Czy mogę rozmawiać z kierownikiem sali	chi mo-ge^{n} roz-ma-vyach z kye-rov-nee-kyem sa-lee
May we have an ashtray?	Czy można prosić o popielniczkę?	chi mozh-na pro-sheech o po-pyel-neech-ke^{n}
May I have a light, please?	Czy można prosić o ogień?	chi mozh-na pro-sheech o o-gyen

RESTAURANT VOCABULARY

ashtray	popielniczka	po-pyel-neech-ka
bill	rachunek	ra-hoo-nek
bowl	miska	mees-ka
cigar	cygaro	tsi-ga-ro
cigarettes	papierosy	pa-pye-ro-si
cloakroom	szatnia/garderoba	shat-nya/gar-de-ro-ba
course/dish	danie	da-nye
cup	filiżanka	fee-lee-zhan-ka
fork	widelec	vee-de-lets
glass	szklanka	shklan-ka
hungry (to be)	być głodnym (-ą)	bich gwod-nim (-o^{n})
jug of water	dzbanek wody	dzba-nek vo-di
knife	nóż	noozh
matches	zapałki	za-paw-kee
mayonnaise	majonez	ma-yo-nez

menu	**karta**	kar-ta
mustard	**musztarda**	moosh-tar-da
napkin	**serwetka**	ser-vet-ka
oil	**olej**	o-ley
olive oil	**oliwa**	o-lee-va
pepper	**pieprz**	pyepsh
plate	**talerz**	ta-lezh
restaurant	**restauracja**	res-taoo-ra-tsya
salt	**sól**	sool
saucer	**spodek**	spo-dek
service	**obsługa**	ob-swoo-ga
spoon	**łyżka**	wizh-ka
table	**stół**	stoow
tablecloth	**obrus**	o-broos
terrace	**taras**	ta-ras
thirsty (to be)	**być spragnionym (-ą)**	bich sprag-nyo-nim (-o^{n})
tip	**napiwek**	na-pee-vek
toothpick	**wykałaczka**	vi-ka-wach-ka
vegetarian	**jarski**	yar-skee
vinegar	**ocet**	o-tset
waiter	**kelner**	kel-ner
waitress	**kelnerka**	kel-ner-ka
water	**woda**	vo-da
wine list	**karta win**	kar-ta veen

THE MENU

ZUPY

Barszcz czerwony	clear beetroot soup	barshch cher-vo-ni
Chłodnik	borscht (served chilled)	**hwod**-neek
Cytrynowa	lemon soup	tsi-tri-**no**-va
Grochowa	pea soup	gro-**ho**-va
Grzybowa	dried mushroom soup	gzhi-**bo**-va
Jarzynowa	vegetable soup	ya-zhi-**no**-va
Kalafiorowa	cauliflower soup	ka-la-fyo-**ro**-va
Kapuśniak	cabbage soup	ka-**poosh**-nyak
Koperkowa	dill soup	ko-per-**ko**-va
Ogórkowa	cucumber soup	o-goor-**ko**-va
Owocowa	fruit soup (usually served cold)	o-vo-**tso**-va

Pomidorowa	tomato soup	po-mee-do-**ro**-va
Rosół	clear soup	**ro**-soow
Szczawiowa	sorrel soup	shcha-**vyo**-va
Szparagowa	asparagus soup	shpa-ra-**go**-va
Ziemniaczana	potato soup	zhyem-mnya-**cha**-na
Żurek	white, slightly sour soup	**zhoo**-rek

PRZEKĄSKI

Jajka mollet z szynką	hard-boiled eggs with ham	**yay**-ka **mo**-le z **shin**-ko^{n}
Jajka w sosie musztardowym/ chrzanowym	hard-boiled eggs in mustard/ horseradish sauce	**yay**-ka **fso**-shye moosh-tar-**do**-vim/ hsha-**no**-vim
Ryba w galarecie	fish in aspic	**ri**-ba vga-la-**re**-chye
Śledź w oliwie/ w śmietanie	herring in olive oil/ cream	shledg vo-**lee**-vye/ fshmye-**ta**-nye
Rolmops	marinated herring with onion and gherkin	**rol**-mops
Sałatka jarzynowa/ śledziowa/mięsna	vegetable/herring/ meat salad with mayonnaise	sa-**wat**-ka ya-zhi-**no**-va/ shle-**dgyo**-va/ **mye**^{n}**s**-na

RYBY

Dorsz	cod	dorsh
Flądra	plaice	**flo**^{n}-dra

Karp	carp	karp
Kawior	caviare	**ka**-vyor
Leszcz	bream	leshch
Lin	tench	leen
Łosoś	salmon	**wo**-sosh
Pstrąg	trout	pstro^{n}g
Rak	crayfish	rak
Sandacz	perch	**san**-dach
Sardynki	sardines	sar-**din**-kee
Szprotki	sprats	**shprot**-kee
Szczupak	pike	**shchoo**-pak
Śledź	herring	shledg
Ryba faszerowana	stuffed fish	**ri**-ba fa-she-ro-**va**-na
Ryba smażona	fried fish	**ri**-ba sma-**zho**-na
Ryba z wody	poached fish	**ri**-ba **zvo**-di

MIĘSO

Wieprzowina:	pork:	vye-psho-**vee**-na
Bigos	stewed pork, sausage and cabbage	**bee**-gos
Golonka	hand of pork	go-**lon**-ka
Cynaderki	kidneys	tsi-na-**der**-kee
Kotlet schabowy	pork chop	**kot**-let s-ha-**bo**-vi
Pieczeń	roast pork	**pye**-chen
Kiełbasa	pork sausage	kyew-**ba**-sa
Żeberka	spare ribs	zhe-**ber**-ka

Wołowina:	beef:	vo-wo-**vee**-na
Brizol	steak	**bree**-zol
Rumsztyk	rump steak	**room**-shtik
Bœuf strogonov	bœuf strogonoff	bef **stro**-go-nof
Zrazy zawijane	beef rolls with filling	**zra**-zi za-vee-**ya**-ne
Cielęcina:	veal:	chye-le^n-**chee**-na
Pieczeń	roast veal	**pye**-chen
Sznycel po wiedeńsku	Wiener schnitzel	**shni**-tsel po-vye-**den**-skoo
Wątróbka	liver	vo^n-**troob**-ka

DRÓB I DZICZYZNA

Kurczak:	chicken:	**koor**-chak
Kotlet de volaille	chicken supreme	**kot**-let de vo-**lay**
Nóżka	leg	**noozh**-ka
Skrzydło	wing	**skshid**-wo
Pierś	breast	**pyersh**
Kaczka	duck	**kach**-ka
Gęś	goose	**ge^{n}sh**
Indyk	turkey	**een**-dik
Kuropatwa	partridge	koo-ro-**pat**-va
Przepiórka	quail	pshe-**pyoor**-ka
Bażant	pheasant	**ba**-zhant
Zając	hare	**za**-yo^{n}ts
Dziczyzna	venison	dgee-**chiz**-na

JARZYNY

Brukiew	turnip	**broo**-kyev
Brukselka	brussels sprouts	brook-**sel**-ka
Cebula	onion	tse-**boo**-la
Cykoria	chicory	tsi-**kor**-ya
Fasola	beans	fa-**so**-la
Groszek	peas	**gro**-shek
Kalafior	cauliflower	ka-**la**-fyor
Kalarepa	kohlrabi	ka-la-**re**-pa
Kapusta	cabbage	ka-**poos**-ta
Marchew	carrots	**mar**-hev
Ogórek	cucumber	o-**goo**-rek
Pietruszka	parsley	pye-**troosh**-ka
Pomidor	tomato	po-**mee**-dor
Sałata	lettuce	sa-**wa**-ta
Seler	celeriac	**se**-ler
Szpinak	spinach	**shpee**-nak
Ziemniaki	potatoes	zhyem-**nya**-kee
Szczaw	sorrel	shchav

KASZA I POTRAWY MĄCZNE

Kasza gryczana	buckwheat	**ka**-sha gri-**cha**-na
Kasza manna	semolina	**ka**-sha **man**-na

Łazanki	macaroni	wa-zan-kee
Makaron	macaroni	ma-ka-ron
Naleśniki	pancakes	na-lesh-nee-kee
z marmeladą	with jam	z mar-me-la-do^{n}
z serem	with curd cheese	z se-rem
Pierogi	dumplings	pye-ro-gee
leniwe	with cottage cheese	le-nee-ve
z jagodami	with blueberries	z ya-go-da-mee
z kapustą	with cabbage	z ka-poos-to^{n}
z mięsem	with meat	z mye^{n}-sem
z wiśniami	with sour cherries	z veesh-nya-mee
Ryż	rice	rizh

DESER

Budyń	milk pudding	boo-din
Ciastka	assorted pastry	chyast-ka
Galaretka	jelly	ga-la-ret-ka
Kisiel	soft jelly	kee-shyel
Kompot	stewed fruit	kom-pot
Lody	ice-cream	lo-di
Tort	tart	tort

OWOCE, JAGODY I ORZECHY

Agrest	gooseberry	a-grest
Ananas	pineapple	a-na-nas

Arbuz	water melon	ar-booz
Banan	banana	ba-nan
Brzoskwinia	peach	bzhos-kvee-nya
Czereśnia	cherry	che-resh-nya
Czernica	bilberry	cher-nee-tsa
Cytryna	lemon	tsi-tri-na
Greipfrut	grapefruit	greyp-froot
Gruszka	pear	groosh-ka
Jabłko	apple	yabw-ko
Jagoda	blueberry	ya-go-da
Malina	raspberry	ma-lee-na
Morela	apricot	mo-re-la
Orzech laskowy	hazelnut	o-zheh las-ko-vi
Orzech włoski	walnut	o-zheh vwos-kee
Pomarańcza	orange	po-ma-ran-cha
Porzeczka	currant	po-zhech-ka
Poziomka	wild strawberry	po-zhyom-ka
Śliwka	plum	shleev-ka
Truskawka	strawberry	troos-kav-ka
Winogrona	grapes	vee-no-gro-na
Wiśnia	sour cherry	veesh-nya
Żurawina	cranberry	zhoo-ra-vee-na

NAPOJE

ALKOHOLOWE

Koniak	brandy	ko-nyak
Piwo	beer	pee-vo
ciemne	dark	chyem-ne
jasne	light	yas-ne
w butelce	bottled	vboo-tel-tse
w puszce	in a can	fpoosh-tse
z beczki	draught	zbech-kee
Wódka	vodka	vood-ka
Wino	wine	vee-no
białe	white	bya-we
czerwone	red	cher-vo-ne
słodkie	sweet	swod-kye
wytrawne	dry	vi-trav-ne

BEZALKOHOLOWE

Czekolada	chocolate	che-ko-la-da
Herbata	tea	her-ba-ta
Herbata ziołowa	herb tea	her-ba-ta zhyo-wo-va
rumiankowa	camomile	roo-myan-ko-va
miętowa	mint	mye^{n}-to-va
lipowa	lime	lee-po-va
głogowa	rose hip	gwo-go-va
Kakao	cocoa	ka-ka-o
Kawa	coffee	ka-va

Koktail mleczny	milk shake	kok-ta-eel mlech-ni
Lemoniada	lemonade	le-mo-nya-da
Mleko	milk	mle-ko
Sok	juice	sok
ananasowy	pineapple	a-na-na-so-vi
grejpfrutowy	grapefruit	greyp-froo-to-vi
jabłkowy	apple	yabw-ko-vi
pomarańczowy	orange	po-ma-ran-cho-vi
pomidorowy	tomato	po-mee-do-ro-vi
winogronowy	grape	vee-no-gro-no-vi
Woda mineralna	mineral water	vo-da mee-ne-ral-na
Woda sodowa (z sokiem)	soda water (with fruit juice)	vo-da so-do-va (z so-kyem)
na czysto/ bez niczego	neat/straight up	na chis-to/ bez nee-che-go
z lodem	on the rocks	zlo-dem

COOKING METHODS

pieczone	baked	pye-cho-ne
z rożna	barbecued	zrozh-na
gotowane	boiled	go-to-va-ne
duszone	braised	doo-sho-ne
siekane	chopped	shye-ka-ne
smażone	fried	sma-zho-ne
tarte	grated	tar-te
z rusztu	grilled	zroosh-too

marynowane	marinated	ma-ri-no-**va**-ne
po angielsku	(meat) rare	po-an-**gyel**-skoo
średnio wysmażone	medium	**shred**-nyo vis-ma-**zho**-ne
mocno wysmażone	well done	**mots**-no vis-ma-**zho**-ne
mielone	minced	mye-**lo**-ne
z wody	poached	**zvo**-di
puree	pureed/creamed	**pyoo**-re
surowe	raw	soo-**ro**-ve
pieczone	roast	pye-**cho**-ne
wędzone	smoked	ve^{n}-**dzo**-ne
gotowane na parze	steamed	go-to-**va**-ne na **pa**-zhe
duszone	stewed	doo-**sho**-ne
faszerowane, nadziewane	stuffed	fa-she-ro-**va**-ne/ na-dgye-**va**-ne
w galarecie	in aspic	vga-la-**re**-chye
gorące/zimne	hot/cold	go-**ro**^{n}-tse/**zheem**-ne
z zieloną pietruszką	with parsley	z zhye-**lo**-no^{n} pyet-**roosh**-ko^{n}
z masłem/oliwą	with butter/oil	**zmas**-wem/o-**lee**-vo^{n}

FOR DRINKS

chłodzone	chilled	hwo-**dzo**-ne
w temperaturze pokojowej	at room temperature	ftem-pe-ra-**too**-zhe po-ko-**yo**-vey

SHOPPING & SERVICES

WHERE TO GO

Which is the best ...?	**Który (-a) jest najlepszy (-a) ...?**	ktoo-ri (ra) yest nay-**lep**-shi (sha)
Where is the nearest ...?	**Gdzie jest najbliższy (-a) ...?**	gdgye yest nay-**bleezh**-shi (sha)
Where is the market?	**Gdzie jest targ?**	gdgye yest targ
Is there a market every day?	**Czy targ jest czynny codziennie?**	chi targ yest **chin**-ni tso-**dgyen**-nye
Where's the nearest chemist?	**Gdzie jest najbliższa apteka/drogeria?**	gdgye yest nay-**bleezh**-sha ap-te-ka/dro-**ger**-ya
Can you recommend a good ...?	**Czy może pan(i) polecić dobry/dobrą/dobrego ...?**	chi **mo**-zhe pan (**pa**-nee) po-le-cheech **dob**-ri (ro^{n}, **re**-go)
Where can I buy ...?	**Gdzie mogę kupić ...?**	gdgye **mo**-ge^{n} **koo**-peech

When do the shops open/close?	**O której godzinie otwierają/ zamykają sklepy?**	o **ktoo**-rey go-**dgee**-nye ot-vye-**ra**-yo^{n}/ za-mi-**ka**-yo^{n} **skle**-pi

SHOPS AND SERVICES

Baker	**Piekarnia**	pye-**kar**-nya
Bank	**Bank**	bank
Barber (see p. 120)	**Fryzjer**	**friz**-yer
Bookshop	**Księgarnia**	kshye^{n}-**gar**-nya
Builder	**Budowniczy**	boo-dov-**nee**-chi
Butcher (see p. 119)	**Sklep mięsny**	sklep **mye^{n}s**-ni
Cake shop	**Cukiernia/Ciastka**	tsoo-**kyer**-nya/**chyast**-ka
Camera shop	**Aparaty fotograficzne**	a-pa-**ra**-ti fo-to-gra-**feech**-ne
Camping equipment	**Sprzęt kampingowy**	spshe^{n}t kam-peen-**go**-vi
Carpenter	**Stolarz**	**sto**-lazh
Chemist (see p. 113)	**Drogeria/Apteka**	dro-**ger**-ya/ap-**te**-ka
Confectioner	**Cukiernia**	tsoo-**kyer**-nya
Dairy	**Mleczarnia**	mle-**char**-nya
Decorator	**Malarz**	**ma**-lazh
Dentist	**Dentysta**	den-**tis**-ta
Department store	**Dom towarowy**	dom to-va-**ro**-vi
Doctor	**Lekarz**	**le**-kazh
Dry cleaner (see p. 123)	**Pralnia chemiczna**	**pral**-nya he-**meech**-na
Electrician	**Elektryk**	e-**lek**-trik

Electrical appliances	**Urządzenia elektryczne**	oo-zho^{n}-dze-nya e-lek-trich-ne
Fishmonger (see p. 119)	**Sklep rybny**	sklep rib-ni
Florist	**Kwiaciarnia**	kvya-char-nya
Gardener	**Ogrodnik**	o-grod-neek
Greengrocer (see p. 118)	**Warzywa i owoce**	va-zhee-va ee o-vo-tse
Grocer (see p. 118)	**Spożywczy**	spo-zhiv-chee
Hairdresser (see p. 120)	**Fryzjer**	friz-yer
Hardware store (see p. 121)	**Sklep z artykułami gospodarstwa domowego**	sklep zar-ti-koo-wa-mee gos-po-dar-stva do-mo-ve-go
Hypermarket	**Megasam**	me-ga sam
Ironmonger	**Artykuły żelazne**	ar-ti-koo-wi zhe-laz-ne
Jeweller	**Jubiler**	yoo-bee-ler
Launderette	**Pralnia samoobsługowa**	pral-nya sa-mo-ob-swoo-go-va
Laundry (see p. 123)	**Pralnia**	pral-nya
Market	**Targ**	targ
Newsagent	**'Ruch'[1]/ Kiosk z gazetami**	rooh/ kyosk zga-ze-ta-mee
Notary	**Notariusz**	no-tar-yoosh
Odd-job man	**Robotnik od drobnych napraw**	ro-bot-neek od drob-nih na-prav
Optician	**Optyk**	op-tik
Pastry shop	**Cukiernia/Ciastka**	tsoo-kyer-nya/chyast-ka
Photographer	**Fotograf**	fo-to-graf

1. Kiosks and shops bearing the name 'Ruch' sell newspapers, cigarettes, stamps, postcards, etc.

Plasterer	**Tynkarz**	tin-kazh
Plumber	**Hydraulik**	hi-dra-oo-leek
Police	**Policja**	po-lee-tsya
Post office	**Poczta**	poch-ta
Shoemaker	**Naprawa obuwia**	na-pra-va o-boo-vya
Shoe shop (see p. 115)	**Obuwie**	o-boo-vye
Sports shop	**Artykuły sportowe**	ar-ti-koo-wi spor-tove
Stationer (see p. 125)	**Artykuły papiernicze**	ar-ti-koo-wi pa-pyer-nee-che
Supermarket	**Supersam**	soo-per-sam
Sweet shop	**Słodycze**	swo-di-che
Tobacconist (see p. 130)	**'Ruch'**	rooh
Toy shop	**Sklep z zabawkami**	sklep z za-bav-ka-mee
Travel agent	**Biuro podróży**	byoo-ro po-droo-zhi
Wine merchant	**Sklep z winami**	sklep zvee-na-mee

IN THE SHOP

Self service	***Samoobsługa**	sa-mo-ob-swoo-ga
Closed for stocktaking	***Remanent**	re-ma-nent
Cash desk	***Kasa**	ka-sa
Shop assistant	**Ekspedient/ ekspedientka**	eks-ped-yent (-ka)
Manager	**Kierownik**	kye-rov-neek
Can I help you?	**Słucham pana (panią)?**	swoo-ham pa-na (nyo^{n})
I want to buy …	**Chcę kupić …**	htse^{n} koo-peech

Do you sell ...?	**Czy państwo sprzedają ...?**	chi pan-stvo spshe-da-yo^n
I just want to look around	**Chcę tylko pooglądać**	htse^n til-ko po-o-glo^n-dach
I don't want to buy anything now	**Nie chcę nic w tej chwili kupować**	nye htse^n neets ftey hvee-lee koo-po-vach
Could you show me ...?	**Czy może mi pan(i) pokazać ...?**	chi mo-zhe mee pan (pa-nee) po-ka-zac
I don't like this	**To mi się nie podoba**	to mee shye^n nye po-do-b
I'll have this	**Wezmę to**	vez-me^n to
We do not have that	***Nie mamy tego**	nye ma-mi te-go
You'll find them at that counter	***Dostanie pan(i) to przy tamtej ladzie/ w tamtym stoisku**	dos-ta-nye pan (pa-nee) t pshi tam-tey la-dgye/ tam-tim sto-ees-koo
We've sold out but we'll have more tomorrow	***Wszystko wysprzedane, ale jutro będzie nowy towar**	fshist-ko vis-pshe-da-n a-le yoot-ro be^n-dgye no-vi to-var
Anything else?	***Czy coś jeszcze?**	chi tsosh yesh-che
That will be all	**To wszystko**	to fshist-ko

CHOOSING

I want something in leather/green	**Chcę coś ze skóry/ w kolorze zielonym**	htse^n tsosh ze skoo-ri/ v ko-lo-zhe zhye-lo-ni
I need it to match this	**Chcę żeby to pasowało do tego**	htse^n zhe-bi to pa-so-va-wo do te-go

I like the one in the window	**Podoba mi się to na wystawie**	po-do-ba mee shye^n to na vis-ta-vye
Could I see that one?	**Czy można zobaczyć tamto?**	chi mozh-na zo-ba-chich tam-to
I like the colour but not the style	**Podoba mi się kolor, ale nie fason**	po-do-ba mee shye^n ko-lor a-le nye fa-son
I want a darker/ lighter shade	**Chcę ciemniejszy/ jaśniejszy odcień**	htse^n chyem-nyey-shi/ yash-nyey-shi od-chyen
I need something warmer/ thinner	**Potrzebuję coś cieplejszego/ cieńszego**	po-tshe-boo-ye^n tsosh chye-pley-she-go/ chyen-she-go
Do you have one in another colour/size?	**Czy ma pan(i) inny kolor/rozmiar?**	chi ma pan (pa-nee) een-ni ko-lor/roz-myar
Have you anything better/cheaper?	**Czy ma pan(i) coś lepszego/tańszego?**	chi ma pan (pa-nee) tsosh lep-she-go/tan-she-go
How much is this?	**Ile to kosztuje?**	ee-le to kosh-too-ye
That is too much for me	**To jest dla mnie za drogo**	to yest dla mnye za dro-go
What is it made of?	**Z czego to jest zrobione?**	zche-go to yest zro-byo-ne
For how long is it guaranteed?	**Na jak długo jest gwarancja?**	na yak dwoo-go yest gwa-ran-tsya
What size is this?	**Jaki to rozmiar?**	ya-kee to roz-myar
Have you a larger/smaller one?	**Czy ma pan(i) większy/mniejszy?**	chi ma pan (pa-nee) vye^{n}k-shi/mnyey-shi
I want size …[1]	**Potrzebuję rozmiar …**	po-tshe-boo-ye^n roz-myar
My chest/waist measurement is …	**Mój obwód klatki piersiowej/ w talii jest …**	mooy ob-vood klat-kee pyer-shyo-vey/ ftal-yee yest

1. See p. 117 for continental sizes.

My collar size is …	**Mój rozmiar kołnierzyka jest …**	mooy **roz**-myar kow-nye-**zhi**-ka yest
Can I try it on?	**Czy mogę przymierzyć?**	chi **mo**-ge^{n} pshi-**mye**-zhich
It doesn't fit me	**Nie leży na mnie dobrze**	nye **le**-zhi na mnye **dob**-zhe
It's too short/long/tight/loose	**To jest za krótkie/długie/ciasne/luźne**	to yest za **kroot**-kye/**dwoo**-gye/**chyas**-ne/**loozh**-ne
Is there a mirror?	**Czy jest tu lustro?**	chi yest too **loos**-tro
Is it colourfast?	**Czy to puszcza w praniu?**	chi to **poosh**-cha **fpra**-nyoo
Is it machine washable?	**Czy to można prać w pralce?**	chi to **mozh**-na prach **fpral**-tse
Will it shrink?	**Czy to się skurczy?**	chi to shye^{n} **skoor**-chi
Is it handmade?	**Czy to jest ręcznie robione?**	chi to yest **re^{n}ch**-nye ro-**byo**-ne

MATERIALS

cotton	**bawełna**	ba-**vew**-na
lace	**koronka**	ko-**ron**-ka
leather	**skóra**	**skoo**-ra
linen	**len**	len
plastic	**plastyk**	**plas**-tik
silk	**jedwab**	**yed**-vab
suede	**zamsz**	zamsh
synthetic	**sztuczne tworzywo**	**shtooch**-ne tvo-**zhi**-vo
wool	**wełna**	**vew**-na

COLOURS

beige	**beżowy**	be-zho-vi
black	**czarny**	char-ni
blue	**niebieski**	nye-byes-kee
brown	**brązowy**	bro^{n}-zo-vi
gold	**złoto, złoty**	zwo-to, zwo-ti
green	**zielony**	zhe-lo-ni
grey	**szary**	sha-ri
mauve	**fiołkoworóżowy**	fyow-ko-vo-roo-zho-vi
orange	**pomarańczowy**	po-ma-ran-cho-vi
pink	**różowy**	roo-zho-vi
purple	**purpurowy**	poor-poo-ro-vi
red	**czerwony**	cher-vo-ni
silver	**srebro, srebrny**	sre-bro, sre-brny
white	**biały**	bya-wi
yellow	**żółty**	zhoow-ti

COMPLAINTS

I want to see the manager	**Chcę rozmawiać z kierownikiem**	htse^{n} roz-ma-vyach skye-rov-nee-kyem
I bought this yesterday	**Kupiłem (-am) to wczoraj**	koo-pee-wem (wam) to fcho-ray
It doesn't work/fit	**Nie działa/pasuje**	nye dgya-wa/pa-soo-ye

I want to return this	**Chcę to zwrócić**	htse^{n} to zvroo-cheech
This is dirty/ stained/ torn/ broken/ cracked	**To jest brudne/ poplamione/ podarte/ rozbite/ pęknięte**	to yest brood-ne/ po-pla-myo-ne/ po-dar-te/ roz-bee-te/ pe^{n}k-nye^{n}-te
Will you change it, please?	**Czy może pan(i) to wymienić?**	chi mo-zhe pan (pa-nee) to vi-mye-neech
Will you refund my money?	**Czy mogę prosić o zwrot pieniędzy?**	chi mo-ge^{n} pro-sheech o zvrot pye-nye^{n}-dzi
Here is the receipt	**Tutaj jest rachunek**	too-tay yest ra-hoo-nek

PAYING

How much does that come to?	**Ile to wynosi?**	ee-le to vi-no-shee
That will be …	***To będzie …**	to be^{n}-dgye
That's 10000 zlotys, please	***To kosztuje dziesięć tysięcy złotych**	to kosh-too-ye dgye-shye^{n}ch ti-shye^{n}-tsi zwo-tih
They are 5000 zlotys each	***One są tysiąc złotych od sztuki**	o-ne so^{n} ti-shyo^{n}ch zwo-tih od shtoo-kee
Will you take travellers' cheques?	**Czy państwo przyjmują czeki podróżnicze?**	chi pan-stvo pshiy-moo-yo^{n} che-kee pod-roozh-nee-che
Please pay the cashier	***Proszę zapłacić w kasie**	pro-she^{n} za-pwa-cheech fka-shye
May I have a receipt, please?	**Czy mogę prosić o rachunek?**	chi mo-ge^{n} pro-sheech o ra-hoo-nek

ou've given me too little/ too much change	**Pan(i) mi wydał(a) za mało/ za dużo**	pan (pa-nee) mee vi-daw(a) za ma-wo/ za doo-zho

CHEMIST[1]

.an you prepare this prescription for me, please?	**Czy może mi pan(i) przygotować to lekarstwo?**	chi mo-zhe mee pan (pa-nee) pshi-go-to-vach to le-kar-stvo
Iave you a small first aid kit?	**Czy ma pan(i) mały komplet środków pierwszej pomocy?**	chi ma pan (pa-nee) ma-wi kom-plet shrod-koov pyerv-shey po-mo-tsi
. bottle of aspirin, please	**Poproszę butelkę aspiryny**	po-pro-she^n boo-tel-ke^n as-pee-ri-ni
tin of adhesive plaster	**Poproszę pudełko plastrów opatrunkowych**	po-pro-she^n poo-dew-ko plast-roov o-pat-roon-ko-vih
want an antiseptic cream	**Poproszę krem dezynfekcyjny**	po-pro-she^n krem de-zin-fek-tsiy-ni
a disinfectant	**dezynfektant**	de-zin-fek-tant
a mouthwash	**płyn do płukania ust**	pwin do pwoo-ka-nya oost
some nose drops	**krople do nosa**	krop-le- do no-sa
throat lozenges	**pastylki na ból gardła**	pas-til-kee na bool gard-wa
stomach pills	**pigułki na ból żołądka**	pee-goow-kee na bool zho-wo^{n}d-ka
lipsalve	**szminkę ochronną**	shmeen-ke^n o-hron-no^n
need something for a hangover/ travel sickness	**Poproszę o coś na kaca/ na chorobę morską**	po-pro-she^n o tsosh na ka-tsa/ na ho-ro-be^n mor-sko^n

An *Apteka* sells medicines, a *Drogeria* only toilet articles, etc.

Can you suggest something for indigestion/ constipation/ diarrhoea?	**Czy może mi pan(i) coś polecić na niestrawność/ obstrukcję/ biegunkę?**	chi mo-zhe mee pan (pa-ne tsosh po-le-cheech na nye-strav-noshch/ ob-strook-tsye^{n}/ bye-goon-ke^{n}
I want something for insect bites	**Poproszę o jakiś środek na pogryzienie przez insekty**	po-pro-she^{n} o ya-keesh shro-dek na po-gri-zhye-nye pshe in-sek-ti
Can you give me something for sunburn?	**Czy ma pan(i) coś na poparzenie słoneczne?**	chi ma pan (pa-nee) tsos na po-pa-zhe-nye swo-nech-ne
Do you sell contraceptives?	**Czy państwo sprzedają środki antykoncepcyjne?**	chi pan-stvo spshe-da-yo^{n} shrod-k an-ti-kon-tsep-tsiy-n
Do you have cotton wool/ sanitary towels/ tampons?	**Czy państwo mają watę/ podpaski higieniczne/ tampony?**	chi pan-stvo ma-yo^{n} va-te^{n}/ pod-pas-kee hee-gye-neech-ne/ tam-poni

TOILET ARTICLES

A packet of razor blades, please	**Poproszę paczkę żyletek**	po-pro-she^{n} pach-ke^{n} zhi-le-tek
Have you an after-shave lotion?	**Czy ma pan(i) wodę po goleniu?**	chi ma pan (pa-nee) vo-d po go-le-nyoo
How much is this lotion?	**Ile ta woda kosztuje?**	ee-le ta vo-da kosh-too-
A tube of toothpaste, please	**Poproszę tubkę pasty do zębów**	po-pro-she^{n} toob-ke^{n} pas-ti do ze^{n}-boov

I want some eau-de-cologne/ perfume	**Chciałbym (-abym) kupić jakąś wodę kolońską/ jakieś perfumy**	hchyaw-bim (hchya-wa-bim) koo-peech ya-ko^{n}sh vo-de^n ko-lon-sko^n/ ya-kyesh per-fu-mi
What kinds of soap have you?	**Jakie państwo mają mydła?**	ya-kye pan-stvo ma-yo^n mi-dwa
A bottle/tube of shampoo, please, for dry/greasy hair	**Poproszę butelkę/ tubkę szamponu na suche/tłuste włosy**	po-pro-she^n boo-tel-ke^n/ toob-ke^n sham-po-noo na soo-he/twoos-te vwo-si
Do you have any suntan oil/cream?	**Czy jest olejek/krem do opalania?**	chi yest o-le-yek/krem do o-pa-la-nya
A box of paper handkerchiefs	**Paczkę papierowych chusteczek do nosa**	pach-ke^n pa-pye-ro-vih hoos-te-chek do no-sa
A roll of toilet paper	**Rolkę papieru toaletowego**	rol-ke^n pa-pye-roo to-a-le-to-ve-go
I'd like some	**Poproszę**	po-pro-she^n
cleansing cream/ lotion	**krem/płyn zmywający/ oczyszczający**	krem/pwin zmi-va-yo^n-tsi/ o-chish-cha-yo^n-tsi
hair conditioner	**odżywkę do włosów**	od-zhiv-ke^n do vwo-soov
hand cream	**krem do rąk**	krem do ro^{n}k
lipsalve	**szminkę ochronną**	shmeen-ke^n o-hron-no^n
moisturizer	**krem/płyn nawilżający**	krem/pwin na-veel-zha-yo^n-tsi

CLOTHES AND SHOES[1]

Where is the underwear/ haberdashery/ coats department?	**Gdzie jest dział z bielizną/ pasmanterią/ płaszczami?**	gdgye yest dgyaw zbye-leez-no^n/ pas-man-ter-yo^n/ pwash-cha-mee

1. See p. 117 for continental sizes.

Where can I find socks/stockings?	**Gdzie są skarpety/ pończochy?**	gdgye so^n skar-pe-ti/ pon-cho-hi
Where are beach clothes?	**Gdzie są ubrania plażowe?**	gdgye so^n oo-bra-nya pla-zho-ve
The men's department is on the second floor	***Odzież męska jest na drugim piętrze**	o-dgyezh me^n-ska yest na droo-geem pye^n-tshe
I am looking for a blouse/ bra/ dress/ jumper	**Chcę kupić bluzkę/ biustonosz/ suknię/ sweter**	htse^n koo-peech blooz-ke^n/ byoo-sto-nosh/ sook-nye^n/ sve-ter
I need a coat/ raincoat/ jacket	**Potrzebny mi jest płaszcz/ deszczowiec/ kurtka**	po-tsheb-ni mee yest pwashch/ desh-cho-vyets/ koort-ka
I want a sunhat	**Potrzebuję kapelusz słoneczny**	po-tshe-boo-ye^n ka-pe-loosh swo-nech-ni
Do you sell buttons/ elastic/ zips?	**Czy sprzedają państwo guziki/ gumki/ suwaki?**	chi spshe-da-yo^n pan-stvo goo-zhee-kee/ goom-kee/ soo-va-kee
I need a pair of walking shoes/ beach sandals	**Potrzebuję parę butów turystycznych/ sandałów plażowych**	po-tshe-boo-ye^n pa-re^n boo-toov too-ris-tich-nih/ san-da-woov pla-zho-vih
This doesn't fit	**To nie pasuje**	to nye pa-soo-ye
I don't know the size	**Nie znam polskiego rozmiaru**	nye znam pol-skye-go roz-mya-roo
Can you measure me?	**Czy może mnie pan(i) zmierzyć?**	chi mo-zhe mnye pan (pa-nee) zmye-zhich
It's for a 3-year-old	**To jest na trzyletnie dziecko**	to yest na tshi-let-nye dgyets-ko

CLOTHING SIZES

WOMEN'S DRESSES, ETC.

British	8	10	12	14	16	18
American	10	12	14	16	18	20
Continental	40	42	44	46	48	50

MEN'S SUITS

British and American	36	38	40	42	44	46
Continental	46	48	50	52	54	56

WAIST, CHEST/BUST AND HIPS

Inches	28	30	32	34	36	38	40
Centimetres	71	76	81	87	92	97	102
Inches	42	44	46	48	50	52	54
Centimetres	107	112	117	122	127	132	137

MEN'S SHIRTS

British and American	14	14½	15	15½	16	16½	17
Continental	36	37	38	39	41	42	43

STOCKINGS

British and American	8	8½	9	9½	10	10½	11
Continental	0	1	2	3	4	5	6

SOCKS

British and American	9½	10	10½	11	11½
Continental	38–39	39–40	40–41	41–42	42–43

SHOES

British	1	2	3	4	5	6	7	8	9	10	11	12
American	2½	3½	4½	5½	6½	7½	8½	9½	10½	11½	12½	13½
Continental	33	34–5	36	37	38	39–40	41	42	43	44	45	46

This table is only intended as a rough guide since sizes may vary from manufacturer to manufacturer.

FOOD[1]

Give me a kilo/ half a kilo of ... please	**Poproszę kilogram/ pół kilograma ...**	po-**pro**-she^{n} kee-lo-gram/ poow kee-lo-**gra**-ma
I want some sweets/ chocolate, please	**Chciałbym (-abym) kupić trochę cukierków/ czekoladę**	**hchyaw**-bim (hchya-**wa**-bim) koo-peech **tro**-he^{n} tsoo-**kyer**-koov/ che-ko-**la**-de^{n}
A bottle of milk	**Butelkę mleka**	boo-**tel**-ke^{n} **mle**-ka
A litre/half a litre	**Litr/pół litra**	leetr/poow **lee**-tra
Is there anything back on the bottle?	**Czy jest zwrot kaucji za butelkę?**	chi yest zvrot **kaoo**-tsyee za boo-**tel**-ke^{n}

1. See also the various MENU sections (p. 94) and WEIGHTS AND MEASURES (p. 189)

I want a jar/tin/ packet of …	**Proszę o słoik/ puszkę/paczkę …**	po-pro-she^{n} o swo-eek/ poosh-ke^{n}/pach-ke^{n}
… slices of ham, please	**proszę … plasterki szynki**	pro-she^{n}… plas-ter-kee shin-kee
Do you sell frozen foods?	**Czy sprzedają państwo mrożonki?**	chi spshe-da-yo^{n} pan-stvo mro-zhon-kee
Is it fresh or frozen?	**Czy to jest świeże czy mrożone?**	chi to yest shvye-zhe chi mro-zho-ne
These pears are too hard/soft	**Te gruszki są za twarde/za miękkie**	te groosh-kee so^{n} za tvar-de/za mye^{n}k-kye
Is it fresh?	**Czy to jest świeże?**	chi to yest shvye-zhe
Are they ripe?	**Czy one są dojrzałe?**	chi o-ne so^{n} doy-zha-we
This is bad/stale	**To jest zepsute/ nieświeże**	to yest ze-psoo-te/ nye-shvye-zhe
A loaf of bread, please	**Poproszę bochenek chleba**	po-pro-she^{n} bo-he-nek hle-ba
How much a kilo/ a litre?	**Ile za kilo/ za litr?**	ee-le za kee-lo/ za leetr
Will you mince it/ bone it?	**Czy może mi pan(i) to zemleć/ obrać z kości?**	chi mo-zhe mee pan (pa-nee) to ze-mlech/ o-brach skosh-chee
Will you clean the fish?	**Czy może pan(i) oczyścić tę rybę?**	chi mo-zhe pan (pa-nee) o-chish-cheech te^{n} ri-be^{n}
Leave/take off the head	**Proszę zostawić/ odciąć głowę**	pro-she^{n} zos-ta-veech/ od-chyo^{n}ch gwo-ve^{n}
Please fillet the fish	**Proszę sfiletować tę rybę**	pro-she^{n} sfee-le-to-vach te^{n} ri-be^{n}
I'll take the bones	**Proszę mi zapakować kości**	pro-she^{n} mee za-pa-ko-vach kosh-chee

Shall I help myself?	**Czy mogę sam(a) wziąć?**	chi mo-ge^n sam (sa-ma) vzhyo^{n}ch

HAIRDRESSER AND BARBER

May I make an appointment for tomorrow/ this afternoon?	**Czy mogę zamówić wizytę na jutro/ dziś po południu?**	chi mo-ge^n za-moo-veech vee-zi-te^n na yoot-ro/ dgeesh po po-wood-nyoo
What time?	***O której godzinie?**	o ktoo-rey go-dgee-nye
I want my hair cut/ trimmed	**Chciałbym (-abym) ściąć/przystrzyc włosy**	hchyaw-bim (hchya-wa-bim) shchyo^{n}ch/pshi-stshits vwo-si
Not too short at the sides	**Nie za krótko z boków**	nye za kroot-ko z bo-koov
I'll have it shorter at the back, please	**Proszę trochę krócej z tyłu**	pro-she^n tro-he^n kroo-tsey sti-woo
Shorter on top	**Krócej na górze**	kroo-tsey na goo-zhe
That's fine	**Tak jest dobrze**	tak yest dob-zhe
No shorter	**Nie krócej**	nye kroo-tsey
I want a shampoo	**Proszę mi umyć włosy**	pro-she^n mee oo-mich vwo-si
Please use conditioner	**Proszę o odżywkę do włosów**	pro-she^n o od-zhiv-ke^n do vwo-soov
I want my hair washed and set	**Proszę mi umyć i ułożyć włosy**	pro-she^n mee oo-mich ee oo-wo-zhich vwo-si
I want my hair blow-dried	**Proszę o wysuszenie suszarką**	pro-she^n o vi-soo-she-nye soo-shar-ko^n

I want a perm	**Proszę o trwałą ondulację**	pro-she^{n} o **trva**-wo^{n} on-doo-**la**-tsye^{n}
I want my hair trimmed just a little	**Proszę mi tylko trochę przystrzyc włosy**	pro-she^{n} mee **til**-ko **tro**-he^{n} **pshi**-stshits **vwo**-si
Please do not use any hairspray	**Proszę nie używać żadnego lakieru do włosów**	pro-she^{n} nye oo-**zhi**-vach zhad-**ne**-go la-**kye**-roo do **vwo**-soov
I'd like it set this way, please	**Proszę je ułożyć w ten sposób**	pro-she^{n} ye oo-**wo**-zhich ften **spo**-soob
The water is too cold	**Woda jest za zimna**	**vo**-da yest za **zheem**-na
The dryer is too hot	**Suszarka jest za gorąca**	soo-**shar**-ka yest za go-**ro**^{n}-tsa
Thank you, I like it very much	**Dziękuję, bardzo mi się to podoba**	dgye^{n}-**koo**-ye^{n} **bar**-dzo mee shye^{n} to po-**do**-ba
I want a shave	**Proszę mnie ogolić**	**pro**-she^{n} mnye o-**go**-leech
I want a manicure	**Proszę mi zrobić manicure**	**pro**-she^{n} mee **zro**-beech ma-**nee**-kyoor
Please trim my beard/ my moustache	**Proszę mi przystrzyc brodę/wąsy**	**pro**-she^{n} mee **pshi**-stshits **bro**-de^{n}/**vo**^{n}-si

HARDWARE[1]

Where is the camping equipment?	**Gdzie jest sprzęt kampingowy?**	gdgye yest spshe^{n}t kam-peen-**go**-vi
Do you have a battery for this?	**Czy mają państwo baterię do tego?**	chi **ma**-yo^{n} **pan**-stvo ba-**ter**-ye^{n} do **te**-go
Where can I get butane gas/paraffin?	**Gdzie dostanę gaz w butli/parafinę?**	gdgye dos-**ta**-ne^{n} gaz **vboo**-tlee/pa-ra-**fee**-ne^{n}

1. See also CAMPING (p. 63) and RENTING OR OWNING A PLACE (p. 67).

I need a bottle opener/ tin opener/ corkscrew/ a small/large srewdriver	**Potrzebuję otwieracz do kapsli/do puszek/korkociąg/ mały/duży śrubokręt**	po-tshe-**boo**-ye^n ot-**vye**-rach do **kap**-slee/do **poo**-shek/ kor-**ko**-chyo^{n}g/ **ma**-wi/**doo**-zhi **shroo**-bo-kre^{n}t
I'd like some candles/ matches	**Proszę o świece/ zapałki**	**pro**-she^n o **shvye**-tse/ za-**paw**-kee
I want a flashlight/ (pen)knife/ pair of scissors	**Potrzebuję latarkę/ scyzoryk/ nożyczki**	po-tshe-**boo**-ye^n la-**tar**-ke^n/ stsi-**zo**-rik/ no-**zhich**-kee
Do you sell string/rope?	**Czy dostanę sznurek/linkę?**	chi dos-**ta**-ne^n **shnoo**-rek/**leen**-ke^n
Where can I find washing-up liquid/ scouring powder?	**Gdzie dostanę płyn do mycia naczyń/ proszek do szorowania?**	gdgye dos-**ta**-ne^n pwin do **mi**-chya **na**-chin/ **pro**-shek do sho-ro-**va**-nya
Do you have a dishcloth/brush?	**Czy dostanę ścierkę/szczotkę?**	chi dos-**ta**-ne^n **shchyer**-ke^n/**shchot**-ke^n
I need a groundsheet/ bucket/ frying pan	**Potrzebuję podłogę namiotową/ wiadro/ patelnię**	po-tshe-**boo**-ye^n po-**dwo**-ge^n na-myo-**to**-vo^n/ **vyad**-ro/ pa-**tel**-nye^n
I want to buy a barbecue	**Chcę kupić rożen**	htse^n **koo**-peech **ro**-zhen
Do you sell charcoal?	**Czy państwo sprzedają węgiel drzewny?**	chi **pan**-stvo spshe-**da**-yo^n **ve^n**-gyel **dzhev**-ni
adapter	**adaptor**	a-**dap**-tor
basket	**koszyk**	**ko**-shik
duster	**ścierka do kurzu**	**shchyer**-ka do **koo**-zhoo
electrical flex	**przewód elektryczny**	**pshe**-vood e-lek-**trich**-ni

extension lead	**przedłużacz**	pshe-**dwoo**-zhach
fuse	**bezpiecznik**	bez-**pyech**-neek
fuse wire	**drut bezpiecznika**	droot bez-pyech-**nee**-ka
insulating tape	**taśma izolacyjna**	**tash**-ma ee-zo-la-**tsiy**-na
light bulb	**żarówka**	zha-**roov**-ka
penknife	**scyzoryk**	stsi-**zo**-rik
plug – bath	**korek do wanny**	**ko**-rek do **van**-ni
– electrical	**wtyczka**	**ftich**-ka

LAUNDRY AND DRY CLEANING

Where is the nearest launderette/ dry cleaner?	**Gdzie jest najbliższa pralnia samoobsługowa/ chemiczna?**	gdgye yest nay-**bleezh**-sha **pral**-nya sa-mo-ob-swoo-**go**-va/ he-**meech**-na
I want to have these things washed/ cleaned	**Chciałbym (-abym) oddać te rzeczy do prania/do czyszczenia**	**hchyaw**-bim (hchya-**wa**-bim) **od**-dach te **zhe**-chi do **pra**-nya/do chish-**che**-nya
These stains won't come out	***Te plamy nie zejdą**	te **pla**-mi nye **zey**-do^n
Can you get this stain out?	**Czy można wywabić tę plamę?**	chi **mozh**-na vi-**va**-beech te^n **pla**-me^n
It is coffee/wine/ grease/blood	**To jest kawa/wino/ tłuszcz/krew**	to yest **ka**-va/**vee**-no/ twooshch/krev
It only needs to be pressed	**To tylko trzeba przeprasować**	to **til**-ko **tshe**-ba pshe-pra-**so**-vach

This is torn; can you mend it?	**To jest podarte; czy może pan(i) to zaszyć/zacerować?**	to yest po-**dar**-te; chi **mo**-zhe pan (**pa**-nee) to za-**shich**/za-tse-**ro**-vach
Do you do invisible mending?	**Czy państwo robią artystyczne cerowanie?**	chi **pan**-stvo **ro**-byo^n ar-tis-**tich**-ne tse-ro-**va**-nye
There's a button missing	**Guzika brakuje**	goo-**zhee**-ka bra-**koo**-ye
Can you sew on a button here, please?	**Czy może pani przyszyć tutaj guzik?**	chi **mo**-zhe pan (**pa**-nee) **pshi**-shich **too**-tay **goo**-zheek
Can you put in a new zip, please?	**Czy może pan(i) przyszyć nowy suwak?**	chi **mo**-zhe pan(**pa**-nee) **pshi**-shich **no**-vi **soo**-vak
When will they be ready?	**Kiedy będą gotowe?**	**kye**-di **be^n**-do^n go-**to**-ve
I need them by this evening/tomorrow	**Będą mi potrzebne na dziś wieczór/ jutro**	**be^n**-do^n mee po-**tsheb**-ne na dgeesh **vye**-choor/ **yoot**-ro
Call back at 5 o'clock	***Proszę przyjść o piątej godzinie**	**pro**-she^n pshiyshch o **pyo^n**-tey go-**dgee**-nye
We can do it by Tuesday	***Możemy to zrobić na wtorek**	mo-**zhe**-mi to **zro**-beech na **fto**-rek
It will take three days	***To zabierze trzy dni**	to za-**bye**-zhe tshi dnee
This isn't mine	**To nie moje**	to nye **mo**-ye
I've lost my ticket	**Zgubiłem (łam) numerek**	zgoo-**bee**-wem (wam) noo-**me**-rek
bath towel	**ręcznik kąpielowy**	**re^{n}ch**-neek ko^n-pye-**lo**-v
blanket	**koc**	kots
duvet cover	**powłoczka na kołdrę**	pov-**woch**-ka na **kow**-dre^n

napkin	**serwetka**	ser-vet-ka
pillow case	**powłoczka na poduszkę**	po-vwoch-ka na po-doosh-ke^{n}
sheet	**prześcieradło**	pshesh-chye-ra-dwo
tablecloth	**obrus**	o-broos
tea towel	**ścierka**	shchyer-ka

NEWSPAPERS, BOOKS AND WRITING MATERIALS

Do you sell English/American newspapers?	**Czy mają państwo angielskie/ amerykańskie gazety?**	chi ma-yo^{n} pan-stvo an-gyel-skye/ a-me-ri-kan-skye ga-ze-ti
Where can I get ...?	**Gdzie dostanę ...?**	gdgye dos-ta-ne^{n}
Can you get me ...?	**Czy mogę prosić o ...?**	chi mo-ge^{n} pro-sheech o
I want a map of the city/ a road map	**Poproszę plan miasta mapę drogową/ samochodową**	po-pro-she^{n} plan myas-ta ma-pe^{n} dro-go-vo^{n}/ sa-mo-ho-do-vo^{n}
Is there an entertainment/ amusement guide?	**Czy jest informator kulturalno/ rozrywkowy?**	chi yest in-for-ma-tor kool-too-ral-no/ roz-riv-ko-vi
Do you have any English books?	**Czy mają państwo jakieś książki w języku angielskim?**	chi ma-yo^{n} pan-stvo ya-kyesh kshyo^{n}zh-kee vye^{n}-zi-koo an-gyel-skim
Have you any novels by ...?	**Czy mają państwo jakieś powieści pisane przez ...?**	chi ma-yo^{n} pan-stvo ya-kyesh po-vyesh-chee pee-sa-ne pshez

I want some colour postcards	**Chciałbym (-abym) kupić widokówki**	hchyaw-bim (hchya-wa-bim) koo-peech vee-do-koov-kee
I want some plain postcards	**Chciałbym (-abym) kupić kilka zwyczajnych kartek pocztowych**	hchyaw-bim (hchya-wa-bim) koo-peech keel-ka zvi-chay-nih kar-tek poch-to-vih
Do you sell souvenirs/toys?	**Czy sprzedają państwo pamiątki/zabawki?**	chi spshe-da-yo^{n} pan-stvo pa-myo^{n}t-kee/za-bav-kee
calculator	**kalkulator**	kal-koo-la-tor
card	**kartka**	kart-ka
dictionary	**słownik**	swov-neek
drawing paper	**papier milimetrowy**	pa-pyer mee-lee-me-tro-vi
felt-tip pen	**flamaster**	fla-ma-ster
guidebook	**przewodnik**	pshe-vod-neek
notebook	**notatnik**	no-tat-neek
paper-clip	**spinacz**	spee-nach
pen	**pióro**	pyoo-ro
pen cartridge	**zbiornik z atramentem**	zbyor-neek za-tra-men-tem
pencil sharpener	**temperówka**	tem-pe-roov-ka
postcard	**pocztówka**	poch-toov-ka
rubber	**gumka**	goom-ka
sellotape	**taśma klejąca**	tash-ma kle-yo^{n}-tsa

OPTICIAN

I have broken my glasses, can you repair them?	**Złamałem (łam) okulary, czy może je pan(i) naprawić**	zwa-**ma**-wem (wam) o-koo-**la**-ri, chi **mo**-zhe ye pan (**pa**-nee) na-**pra**-veech
Can you give me a new pair of glasses to the same prescription?	**Czy mogę dostać nowe okulary na tę receptę?**	chi **mo**-ge^{n} **dos**-tach **no**-ve o-koo-**la**-ri na te^{n} re-**tsep**-te^{n}
I have difficulty with reading/with long-distance vision	**Mam trudności z czytaniem/z patrzeniem na odległość**	mam trood-**nosh**-chee schi-**ta**-nyem/ spa-**tshe**-nyem na **od**-leg-woshch
Please test my eyes	**Proszę mi przeegzaminować oczy**	**pro**-she^{n} mee pshe-e-gza-mee-**no**-vach **o**-chi
I have lost one of my contact lenses	**Zgubiłem (łam) jedno szkło kontaktowe**	zgoo-**bee**-wem (wam) **yed**-no shkwo kon-tak-**to**-ve
I should like to have contact lenses	**Potrzebne mi są szkła kontaktowe**	po-**tsheb**-ne mee so^{n} shkwa kon-tak-**to**-ve
I am short-sighted/ long-sighted	**Jestem krótkowidz/ dalekowidz**	**yes**-tem kroot-**ko**-veedz/ da-le-**ko**-veedz

PHOTOGRAPHY

I want to buy a camera	**Chcę kupić aparat fotograficzny**	htse^{n} **koo**-peech a-**pa**-rat fo-to-gra-**feech**-ni

Have you a film for this camera?	**Czy mają państwo film do tego aparatu?**	chi ma-yo^{n} pan-stvo feelm do te-go a-pa-ra-to
A 100/400/1000 ASA film please	**Poproszę fim o czułości sto/ czterysta/tysiąc**	po-pro-she^{n} feelm o choo-wosh-chyee sto/ chte-ris-ta/ti-shyo^{n}ch
What is the fastest film you have?	**Jaki najczulszy film mogę dostać?**	ya-kee nay-chool-shi feelm mo-ge^{n} dos-tach
Film for slides/prints	**Film do przezroczy (slajdów)/do zdjęć**	feelm do pshe-zro-chi (slay-doov)/do zdye^{n}ch
Can I have a 35-mm film?	**Czy mogę prosić o film na trzydzieści pięć milimetrów?**	chi mo-ge^{n} pro-sheech o feelm na tshi-dgyesh-chi pye^{n}ch mee-lee-met-roov
With 36/24 exposures	**Z wyświetleniem trzydzieści sześć dwadzieścia cztery**	zvish-vyet-le-nyem tshi-dgyesh-chi sheshch dva-dgyesh-chya chte-r
Black-and-white/ colour film	**Film czarno-biały/ kolorowy**	feelm char-no bya-wi/ ko-lo-ro-vi
Would you fit the film in the camera for me, please?	**Czy może pan(i) mi założyć ten film do aparatu?**	chi mo-zhe pan (pa-nee) mee za-wo-zhich ten feelm do a-pa-ra-too
How much is it?	**Ile to kosztuje?**	ee-le to kosh-too-ye
Does the price include processing?	**Czy wywołanie zdjęć jest wliczone w cenę?**	chi vi-vo-wa-nye zdye^{n}ch yest vlee-cho-ne ftse-ne^{n}
I'd like this film developed and printed	**Poproszę o wywołanie tego filmu i zrobienie odbitek**	po-pro-she^{n} o vi-vo-wa-nye te-go feel-moo ee zro-bye-nye od-bee-tek
Can I have … prints/ enlargements of this negative?	**Proszę o odbitki/ powiększenia z tego negatywu?**	pro-she^{n} o od-beet-kee/ po-vye^{n}-kshe-nye ste-go ne-ga-ti-voo
When will they be ready?	**Kiedy będą gotowe?**	kye-di be^{n}-do^{n} go-to-ve

Do you have flash bulbs/ flash cubes?	**Czy są lampy błyskowe/ kwadratowe lampy błyskowe?**	chi so^n lam-pi bwis-ko-ve/ kva-dra-to-ve lam-pi bwis-ko-ve
My camera's not working, can you mend it?	**Mój aparat jest popsuty, czy może pan(i) go naprawić?**	mooy a-pa-rat yest pop-soo-ti, chi mo-zhe pan (pa-nee) go na-pra-veech
The film is jammed	**Film się zaciął**	feelm shye^n za-chyo^{n}w
There is something wrong with the flash/ light meter/shutter/ film winder	**Nie działa flesz/światłomierz/ przesłona/napinacz**	nye dgya-wa flesh/shvya-two-myezh/ pshe-swo-na/na-pee-nach
battery	**bateria**	ba-ter-ya
cine-film	**taśma filmowa**	tash-ma feel-mo-va
filter	**filtr**	feeltr
lens	**obiektyw**	o-byek-tiv
lens cap	**pokrywa obiektywu**	po-kri-va o-byek-ti-voo
video camera	**kamera wideo**	ka-me-ra vee-de-o

RECORDS AND CASSETTES

Do you have any records/cassettes of local music?	**Czy mają państwo jakieś płyty/kasety z muzyką regionalną?**	chi ma-yo^n pan-stvo ya-kyesh pwi-ti/ka-se-ti zmoo-zi-ko^n re-gyo-nal-no^n
Are there any new records by ...?	**Czy są jakieś nowe nagrania ...?**	chi so^n ya-kyesh no-we na-gra-nya
Do you sell compact discs/ video cassettes?	**Czy państwo sprzedają płyty kompaktowe/ kasety wideo?**	chi pan-stvo spshe-da-yo^n pwi-ti kom-pak-to-ve/ ka-se-ti vee-de-o

TOBACCONIST

Do you stock English/American cigarettes?	**Czy pan(i) ma angielskie/ amerykańskie papierosy?**	chi pan(**pa**-nee) ma an-**gyel**-skye/ a-me-ri-**kan**-skye pa-pye-**ro**-si
What English cigarettes have you?	**Jakie pan(i) ma angielskie papierosy?**	**ya**-kye pan(**pa**-nee) ma an-**gyel**-skye pa-pye-**ro**-si
A packet of ... please	**Poproszę paczkę ...**	po-**pro**-she^{n} **pach**-ke^{n}
A box of big/small cigars, please	**Poproszę pudełko dużych/małych cygar**	po-**pro**-she^{n} poo-**dew**-ko **doo**-zhih/**ma**-wih **tsi**-gar
I want some filter tip cigarettes/cigarettes without filter	**Poproszę papierosy z filtrem/bez filtra**	po-**pro**-she^{n} pa-pye-**ro**-si **sfeel**-trem/bez **feel**-tra
A box of matches, please	**Poproszę pudełko zapałek**	po-**pro**-she^{n} poo-**dew**-ko za-**pa**-wek
Do you have cigarette paper/pipe cleaners?	**Czy są bibułki do papierosów/ wyciory do fajki?**	chi so^{n} bee-**boow**-kee do pa-pye-**ro**-soov/ vi-**chyo**-ri do **fay**-kee
I want to buy a lighter	**Chciałbym (-abym) kupić zapalniczkę**	**hchyaw**-bim (hchya-**wa**-bim) **koo**-peech za-pal-**neech**-ke^{n}
Do you sell lighter fuel/flints?	**Czy ma pan(i) benzynę/kamienie do zapalniczki?**	chi ma pan (**pa**-nee) ben-**zi**-ne^{n}/ka-**mye**-nye do za-pal-**neech**-kee
I want a gas refill for this lighter	**Poproszę wkład do tej zapalniczki gazowej**	po-**pro**-she^{n} fkwad do tey za-pal-**neech**-kee ga-**zo**-vey

REPAIRS

This is broken, could somebody mend it?	**To jest zepsute, czy ktoś mógłby to naprawić?**	to yest ze-**psoo**-te, chi ktosh **moogw**-bi to na-**pra**-veech
Could you do it while I wait?	**Czy można to zrobić na poczekaniu?**	chi **mozh**-na to **zro**-beech na po-che-**ka**-nyoo
When should I come back for it?	**Kiedy mogę to odebrać?**	**kye**-di **mo**-ge^n to o-**de**-brach
I want these shoes soled (in leather)	**Proszę o (skórzane) zelówki**	**pro**-she^n o (skoo-**zha**-ne) ze-**loov**-kee
I want these shoes heeled (with rubber)	**Proszę o (gumowe) obcasy**	**pro**-she^n o (goo-**mo**-ve) ob-**tsa**-si
I have broken the glass/strap/spring	**Rozbiłem (-am) szkło/ rozerwałem (-am) pasek/złamałem (-am) sprężynę**	roz-**bee**-wem (wam) **shkwo**/ ro-zer-**va**-wem (wam) **pa**-sek/ zwa-**ma**-wem (wam) spre^n-**zhi**-ne^n
I have broken my glasses/the frame/ the arm	**Rozbiłem (-am) okulary/oprawkę/ złamałem (-am) rączkę**	roz-**bee**-wem (wam) o-koo-**la**-ri/o-**prav**-ke^n/ zwa-**ma**-wem (wam) **ro**^{n}**ch**-ke^n
How much would a new one cost?	**Ile kosztuje nowy (-a)?**	**ee**-le kosh-**too**-ye **no**-vi (va)
The stone/charm/screw has come loose	**Kamień/wisiorek/ śrubka jest obluzowany (-a)**	**ka**-myen/vee-**shyo**-rek/ **shroob**-ka yest ob-loo-zo-**va**-ni (na)

The fastener/clip/ chain is broken	**Zapięcie/klamra/ łańcuszek jest złamane (-a, -y)**	za-**pye**^{n}-chye/**klam**-ra/ wan-**tsoo**-shek yest zwa-**ma**-ne (-a, -i)
How much will it cost?	**Ile to będzie kosztować?**	**ee**-le to **be**^{n}-dgye kosh-**to**-vach
It can't be repaired	***Tego nie da się naprawić**	**te**-go nye da shye^n na-**pra**-veech
You need a new one	***Musi pan(i) kupić nowy**	**moo**-shee pan (**pa**-nee) **koo**-peech **no**-vi

POST OFFICE

Where's the main post office?	Gdzie jest główna poczta?	gdgye yest gwoov-na poch-ta
Where's the nearest post office?	Gdzie jest najbliższa poczta?	gdgye yest nay-bleezh-sha poch-ta
What time does the post office open/close?	O której godzinie otwiera/zamyka się pocztę?	o ktoo-rey go-dgee-nye ot-vye-ra/za-mi-ka shye^{n} poch-te^{n}
Where's the post box?	Gdzie jest skrzynka na listy?	gdgye yest skshin-ka na lis-ti
What window do I go to for stamps/ telegrams/ money orders?	W którym okienku mogę kupić znaczki/ nadać telegram/ zrealizować przekaz pieniężny?	fktoo-rim o-kyen-koo mo-ge^{n} koo-peech znach-kee/na-dach te-le-gram/ zre-a-lee-zo-vach pshe-kaz pye-nye^{n}zh-ni

LETTERS AND TELEGRAMS

How much is a postcard England?	**Ile kosztuje kartka do Anglii?**	ee-le kosh-too-ye to kart-ka do an-glee
How much is a letter to England?	**Ile kosztuje list do Anglii?**	ee-le kosh-too-ye leest do an-glee
What's the rate for airmail/surface mail to the USA?	**Ile kosztuje poczta lotnicza/zwykła do USA?**	ee-le kosh-too-ye poch-ta lot-nee-cha/zvi-kwa do oo-ess-a
It's inland	**Krajowy**	kra-yo-vi
Give me three … stamps, please	**Poproszę trzy … znaczki**	po-pro-she^n tshi znach-kee
I want to send this letter express	**Chciałbym (-abym) wysłać ten list ekspresem**	hchyaw-bim (hchya-wa-bim) vis-wach ten leest eks-pre-sem
I want to register this letter	***Chciałbym (-abym) wysłać ten list pocztą poleconą**	hchyaw-bim (hchya-wa-bim) vis-wach ten leest poch-to^n po-le-tso-no^n
I want to send a parcel	**Chcę nadać paczkę**	htse^n na-dach pach-ke^n
Where is the poste restante section?	**Gdzie jest poste restante?**	gdgye yest po-ste-res-tan-te
Are there any letters for me?	**Czy są do mnie jakieś listy?**	chi so^n do mnye ya-kyesh lees-ti
What is your name?	***Jak się pan(i) nazywa?**	yak shye^n pan (pa-nee) na-zi-va
Have you any means of identification?	***Czy ma pan(i) jakiś dowód osobisty?**	chi ma pan (pa-nee) ya-keesh do-vood o-so-bees-ti

Can I send a telex?	**Czy mogę wysłać telex?**	chi mo-ge^n vis-wach te-leks
I want to send a telegram (reply paid)	**Chciałbym (-abym) wysłać telegram (z opłaconą odpowiedzią)**	hchyaw-bim (hchya-wa-bim) vis-wach te-le-gram (zo-pwa-tso-no^n od-po-vye-dgyo^n)
How much does it cost per word?	**Ile to kosztuje od słowa?**	ee-le to kosh-too-ye od swo-va
Write the message here and your own name and address	***Proszę tutaj napisać tekst oraz pańskie nazwisko i adres**	pro-she^n too-tay na-pee-sach tekst o-raz pan-skye naz-vees-ko ee a-dres

TELEPHONING

Where's the nearest phone box?	**Gdzie jest najbliższa budka telefoniczna?**	gdgye yest nay-bleezh-sha bood-ka te-le-fo-neech-na
I want to make a phone call	**Chcę zatelefonować**	htse^n za-te-le-fo-no-vach
May I use your phone?	**Czy mogę skorzystać z telefonu?**	chi mo-ge^n sko-zhis-tach ste-le-fo-noo
Do you have a telephone directory for …	**Czy ma pan(i) książkę telefoniczną …**	chi ma pan (pa-nee) kshyo^{n}zh-ke^n te-le-fo-neech-no^n
Please get me …	**Proszę mnie połączyć z …**	pro-she^n mnye po-wo^n-chich z
I want to telephone to England	**Chcę zatelefonować do Anglii**	htse^n za-te-le-fo-no-vach do an-glee
What do I dial to get the international operator?	**Jaki numer mam wykręcić do centrali międzynarodowej?**	ya-kee noo-mer mam vi-kre^n-chich do tsen-tra-lee mye^n-dzi-na-ro-do-vey

What is the code for ...?	**Jaki jest numer kierunkowy do ...?**	ya-kee yest noo-mer kye-roon-ko-vi do
Could you give me the cost (time and charges) afterwards?	**Czy może mi pan(i) podać koszt po skończeniu rozmowy?**	chi mo-zhe mee pan (pa-nee) po-dach kosht po skon-che-nyoo roz-mo-vi
I want to make a personal (person-to-person) call	**Chciałbym (-abym) zamówić rozmowę z przywołaniem**	hchyaw-bim (hchya-wa-bim) za-moo-veech roz-mo-ve^n spshi-vo-wa-nyem
I want to reverse the charges/call collect	**Chciałbym (-abym) zamówić rozmowę R (*pron.* air)**	hchyaw-bim (hchya-wa-bim) za-moo-veech roz-mo-ve^n er
I was cut off	**Połączenie zostało przerwane**	po-wo^n-che-nye zos-ta-wo psher-va-ne
Can you reconnect me?	**Czy może mnie pan(i) jeszcze raz połączyć?**	chi mo-zhe mnye pan (pa-nee) yesh-che raz po-wo^n-chich
I want extension ...	**Poproszę wewnętrzny ...**	po-pro-she^n vev-ne^{n}tsh-ni
May I speak to ...	**Czy mogę mówić z ...**	chi mo-ge^n moo-veech z
Who's speaking?	**Kto mówi?**	kto moo-vee
Hold the line, please	***Proszę zaczekać**	pro-she^n za-che-kach
Please, speak slowly	**Proszę mówić powoli**	pro-she^n moo-veech po-vo-lee
Put the receiver down	***Proszę położyć słuchawkę**	pro-she^n po-wo-zhich swoo-hav-ke^n
He's not here	***Nie ma go tutaj**	nye ma go too-tay
He's at ...	***On jest w ...**	on yest v
When will he be back?	**Kiedy wróci?**	kye-di vroo-chee

Will you take a message?	**Czy można zostawić wiadomość?**	chi **mozh**-na zos-**ta**-veech vya-**do**-moshch
Tell him that … phoned	**Proszę mu powiedzieć, że … telefonował**	**pro**-she^{n} moo po-**vye**-dgyech zhe…te-le-fo-**no**-vaw
Please ask him to phone me	**Proszę go poprosić żeby do mnie zatelefonował**	**pro**-she^{n} go po-**pro**-sheech **zhe**-bi do mnye za-te-le-fo-**no**-vaw
What's your number?	***Jaki jest pański numer?**	**ya**-kee yest **pan**-skee **noo**-mer
My number is …	**Mój numer jest …**	mooy **noo**-mer yest
I can't hear you	**Nie słyszę pana (pani)**	nye **swi**-she^{n} **pa**-na (nee)
The line is engaged	***Linia jest zajęta**	**leen**-ya yest za-**ye**^{n}-ta
There's no reply	***Nie ma odpowiedzi**	nye ma od-po-**vye**-dgee
You have the wrong number	***Pomyłka**	po-**miw**-ka
The number is out of order	***Numer jest uszkodzony**	**noo**-mer yest oosh-ko-**dzo**-ni
Telephone directory	**Książka telefoniczna**	**kshyo**^{n}**zh**-ka te-le-fo-**neech**-na
Telephone number	**Numer telefonu**	**noo**-mer te-le-**fo**-noo
Telephone operator	**Telefonista/ telefoniska**	te-le-fo-**nees**-ta/ te-le-fo-**neest**-ka

SIGHTSEEING

Where is the tourist office?	**Gdzie jest biuro obsługi turystycznej?**	gdgye yest byoo-ro ob-swoo-gee too-ris-tich-ney
What should we see here?	**Co powinniśmy tutaj zobaczyć?**	tso po-veen-neesh-mi too-tay zo-ba-cheech
Is there a map/plan of the places to visit?	**Czy jest plan miasta pokazujący miejsca do zwiedzania?**	chi yest plan myas-ta po-ka-zoo-yo^{n}-tsi myeys-tsa do zvye-dza-nya
I want a good guidebook	**Potrzebny mi dobry przewodnik**	po-tshe-bni mee dob-ri pshe-vod-neek
Is there a good sightseeing tour?	**Czy jest ciekawa wycieczka z przewodnikiem?**	chi yest chye-ka-va vi-chyech-ka spshe-vod-nee-kyem
Does the coach stop at … hotel?	**Czy autokar zatrzymuje się przed hotelem …?**	chi a-oo-to-kar za-tshi-moo-ye $shye^{n}$ pshed ho-te-lem
Is there an excursion to …?	**Czy jest wycieczka do …?**	chi yest vi-chyech-ka do

How long does the tour take?	**Jak długo trwa ta wycieczka?**	yak **dwoo**-go trva ta vi-**chyech**-ka
Are there guided tours of the museum?	**Czy w muzeum są tury z przewodnikiem?**	chi vmoo-**ze**-oom so^{n} **too**-ri spshe-vod-**nee**-kyem
Does the guide speak English?	**Czy przewodnik mówi po angielsku?**	chi pshe-**vod**-neek **moo**-vee po an-**gyels**-koo
We don't need a guide	**Nie potrzebujemy przewodnika**	nye po-tshe-boo-**ye**-mi pshe-vod-**nee**-ka
I would prefer to go round alone; is that all right?	**Wolę sam (sa-ma) zwiedzać; czy można?**	**vo**-le^{n} sam (**sa**-ma) **zvye**-dzach; chi **mozh**-na
How much does the tour cost?	**Ile kosztuje ta tura?**	**ee**-le kosh-**too**-ye ta **too**-ra
Are all the admission fees included?	**Czy bilety wstępu są włączone w opłatę?**	chi bee-**le**-ti **fste**^{n}-poo so^{n} vwo^{n}-**cho**-ne vop-**wa**-te^{n}
Does it include lunch?	**Czy obiad jest włączony w opłatę?**	chi **o**-byad yest vwo^{n}-**cho**-ni vop-**wa**-te^{n}

MUSEUMS AND ART GALLERIES

When does the museum open/close?	**Kiedy muzeum jest otwarte/zamknięte?**	**kye**-di moo-**ze**-oom yest ot-**var**-te/zam-**knye**^{n}-te
Is it open every day?	**Czy jest otwarte codziennie?**	chi yest ot-**var**-te tso-**dgyen**-nye
The gallery is closed on Mondays	***Galeria jest zamknięta w poniedziałki**	ga-**ler**-ya yest zam-**knye**^{n}-ta fpo-nye-**dgyaw**-kee

How much does it cost?	**Ile to kosztuje?**	ee-le to kosh-too-ye
Are there reductions for children/students/the elderly?	**Czy są zniżki dla dzieci/studentów/emerytów?**	chi so^{n} zneezh-kee dla dgye-chee/stoo-den-toov/e-me-ri-toov
Are admission fees lower on any special day?	**Czy są specjalne dni ze zniżkowym wstępem?**	chi so^{n} spets-yal-ne dnee ze zneezh-ko-vim fste^{n}-pem
Admission free	***Wstęp bezpłatny**	fste^{n}p bez-pwat-ni
Have you got a ticket?	***Czy ma pan(i) bilet wstępu?**	chi ma pan (pa-nee) bee-let fste^{n}-poo
Where do I buy a ticket?	**Gdzie mam kupić bilet wstępu?**	gdgye mam koo-peech bee-let fste^{n}-poo
Please leave your bag in the cloakroom	***Proszę zostawić torbę w szatni**	pro-she^{n} zos-ta-veech tor-be^{n} fshat-nee
It's over there	***To jest tam**	to yest tam
Where is the … collection/exhibition	**Gdzie jest kolekcja/wystawa …?**	gdgye yest ko-lek-tsya/vis-ta-va
Can I take photographs?	**Czy można fotografować?**	chi mozh-na fo-to-gra-fo-vach
Can I use a tripod?	**Czy można używać statyw?**	chi mozh-na oo-zhi-vach sta-tiv
Photographs are not allowed	***Fotografowanie zabronione/Zabrania się fotografować**	fo-to-gra-fo-va-nye za-bro-nyo-ne/za-bra-nya shye^{n} fo-to-gra-fo-vach
I want to buy a catalogue	**Chcę kupić katalog**	htse^{n} koo-peech ka-ta-log
Will you make photocopies?	**Czy państwo robią fotokopie?**	chi pan-stvo ro-byo^{n} fo-to-ko-pye

Could you make me a transparency of this painting?	Czy mogą mi państwo zrobić przezrocze (slajd) tego obrazu?	chi mo-go^n mee pan-stvo zro-beech pshez-ro-che (slayd) te-go o-bra-zoo
How long will it take?	Jak długo to zajmie?	yak dwoo-go to zay-mye

HISTORICAL SITES

We want to visit … can we get there by car?	Chcemy obejrzeć … czy możemy tam dojechać samochodem?	htse-mi o-bey-zhech … chi mo-zhe-mi tam do-ye-hach sa-mo-ho-dem
Is there far to walk?	Czy trzeba daleko iść?	chi tshe-ba da-le-ko eeshch
Is it an easy walk?	Czy łatwo tam dojść?	chi wat-vo tam doyshch
Is there access for wheelchairs?	Czy jest dostęp dla wózków inwalidzkich?	chi yest do-ste^{n}p dla vooz-koov in-va-leedz-keeh
Is it far to the	Czy jest daleko do	chi yest da-le-ko do
aqueduct?	akweduktu?	a-kve-dook-too
castle?	zamku?	zam-koo
fort?	fortu?	for-too
fortifications?	fortyfikacji?	for-ti-fee-kats-yee
fountain?	fontanny?	fon-tan-ni
gate?	bramy?	bra-mi
walls?	murów?	moo-roov
When was it built?	Kiedy to było zbudowane?	kye-di to bi-wo zboo-do-va-ne
Who built it?	Kto to zbudował?	kto to zboo-do-vaw
Where is the old part of the city?	Gdzie jest stara część miasta?	gdgye yest sta-ra che^{n}shch myas-ta

What is the building?	Co to za budynek?	tso to za boo-di-nek
Where is … house? church? cemetery?	Gdzie jest dom …? kościół …? cmentarz …?	gdgye yest dom kosh-chyoow tsmen-tazh

GARDENS, PARKS AND ZOOS

Where is the botanical garden/zoo?	Gdzie jest ogród botaniczny/zoo?	gdgye yest o-grood bo-ta-neech-ni/zo-o
How do I get to the park?	Jak dojdę do parku?	yak-doy-de^n do par-koo
Can we walk there?	Czy tam można dojść pieszo?	chi tam mozh-na doyshch pye-sho
Can we drive through the park?	Czy można przejechać przez park?	chi mozh-na pshe-ye-hach pshez park
Are the gardens open to the public?	Czy ogrody są otwarte dla publiczności?	chi o-gro-di so^n ot-var-te dla poob-leech-nosh-chee
What time do the gardens close?	O której godzinie zamyka się ogrody?	o ktoo-rey go-dgee-nye za-mi-ka shye^n o-gro-di
Who designed the gardens?	Kto projektował te ogrody?	kto pro-yek-to-vaw te o-gro-di
Where is the tropical plant house/lake?	Gdzie jest oranżeria (palmiarnia)/ jezioro?	gdgye yest o-ran-zher-ya (pal-myar-nya)/ ye-zhyo-ro

EXPLORING

I'd like to walk around the old town	Chcę pochodzić po starym mieście	htse^n po-ho-dgeech po sta-rim myesh-chye

Is there a good street plan showing the buildings?	**Czy jest dobry plan miasta pokazujący budynki?**	chi yest **do**-bri plan **myas**-ta po-ka-zoo-**yo**^{n}-tsi boo-**din**-kee
We want to visit the	**Chcemy zwiedzić**	**htse**-mi **zvye**-dgeech
cathedral	**katedrę**	ka-**ted**-re^{n}
fortress	**fortecę**	for-**te**-tse^{n}
library	**bibliotekę**	bee-blyo-**te**-ke^{n}
monastery	**klasztor**	**klash**-tor
palace	**pałac**	**pa**-wats
ruins	**ruiny**	roo-**ee**-ni
May we walk around the walls/go up the tower?	**Czy można chodzić po murach/wejść na wieżę?**	chi **mozh**-na **ho**-dgeech po **moo**-rah/veyshch na **vye**-zhe^{n}
Where is the antiques market/flea market?	**Gdzie jest rynek z antykami/pchli targ?**	gdgye yest **ri**-nek zan-ti-**ka**-mee/ **p-hlee** targ

GOING TO CHURCH

Is there a	**Czy jest tu kościół**	chi yest too **kosh**-chyoow
Catholic church?	**katolicki?**	ka-to-**leets**-kee
Protestant church?	**protestancki?**	pro-tes-**tants**-kee
mosque?	**meczet?**	**me**-chet
synagogue?	**synagoga?**	si-na-**go**-ga
What time is mass/the service?	**O której godzinie jest msza/nabożeństwo?**	o **ktoo**-rey go-**dgee**-nye yest msha/na-bo-**zhen**-stvo
I'd like to look round the church	**Chcę obejrzeć kościół**	htse^{n} o-**bey**-zhech **kosh**-chyoow
When was the church built?	**Kiedy był zbudowany ten kościół?**	**kye**-di biw zboo-do-**va**-ni ten **kosh**-chyoow

ENTERTAINMENT

What's on at the theatre/cinema?	**Co jest w kinie/w teatrze?**	tso yest fkee-nye/fte-a-tshe
Is there an entertainment guide?	**Czy jest informator kulturalno/ rozrywkowy?**	chi yest infor-ma-tor kool-too-ral-no/ roz-riv-ko-vi
Is there a concert on this evening?	**Czy jest koncert dziś wieczór?**	chi yest kon-tsert dgeesh vye-choor
Can you recommend a good ballet/ film/musical?	**Czy może pan(i) polecić dobry balet/ film/musical**	chi mo-zhe pan (pa-nee) po-le-cheech dob-ri ba-let/ feelm/myoo-zee-kal
Who is directing/ conducting/singing?	**Kto reżyseruje/ dyryguje/śpiewa?**	kto re-zhi-se-roo-ye/ di-ri-goo-ye/shpye-va
I want two seats for tonight/the matinée/ tomorrow	**Poproszę dwa bilety na dziś wieczór/na jutrzejszą/ popołudniówkę**	po-pro-she^{n} dva bee-le-ti na dgeesh vye-choor/na yoo-tshey-sho^{n}/ po-po-wood-nyoov-ke^{n}
I want to book seats for Thursday	**Chcę zamówić bilety na czwartek**	htse^{n} za-moo-veech bee-le-ti na chvar-tek

Is the matinée sold out?	**Czy popołudniowka jest wysprzedana?**	chi po-po-wood-**nyoov**-ka yest vis-pshe-**da**-na
We're sold out (for that performance)	***Bilety wysprzedane (na to przedstawienie)**	**bee**-le-ti vis-pshe-**da**-ne (na to pshed-sta-**vye**-nye)
I'd like seats in the stalls/circle/gallery	**Poproszę miejsca na parterze/pierwszym balkonie/drugim balkonie**	po-**pro**-she^{n} **myey**-stsa na par-**te**-zhe/**pyerv**-shim bal-**ko**-nye/**droo**-geem bal-**ko**-nye
The cheapest seats, please	**Poproszę najtańsze bilety**	po-**pro**-she^{n} nay-**tan**-she bee-**le**-ti
Are they good seats?	**Czy to są dobre miejsca?**	chi to so^{n} **dob**-re **myey**-stsa
Where are these seats?	**Gdzie są te miejsca?**	gdgye so^{n} te **myeys**-tsa
What time does the performance start?	**O której zaczyna się przedstawienie?**	o **ktoo**-rey za-**chi**-na shye^{n} pshed-sta-**vye**-nye
What time does it end?	**O której się kończy?**	o **ktoo**-rey shye^{n} **kon**-chi
Is evening dress necessary?	**Czy strój wieczorowy jest konieczny?**	chi strooy vye-cho-**ro**-vi yest ko-**nyech**-ni
Where is the cloakroom?	**Gdzie jest szatnia?**	gdgye yest **shat**-nya
This is your seat	***To jest pańskie miejsce**	to yest **pan**-skye **myeys**-tse
A programme, please	**Poproszę program**	po-**pro**-she^{n} **pro**-gram
Where are the best nightclubs?	**Gdzie są najlepsze lokale nocne?**	gdgye so^{n} nay-**lep**-she lo-ka-le **nots**-ne
What time is the floorshow?	**O której godzinie jest kabaret?**	o **ktoo**-rey go-**dgee**-nye yest ka-**ba**-ret
Would you like to dance?	**Czy ma pani ochotę potańczyć**	chi ma **pa**-nee o-**ho**-te^{n} po-**tan**-chich

Is there a jazz club here?	**Czy jest tu klub jazzowy?**	chi yest too kloob ja-zo-vi
Where can we go dancing?	**Gdzie możemy pójść potańczyć?**	gdgye mo-zhe-mi pooyshch po-tan-chich
Where is the best disco?	**Gdzie jest najlepsza dyskoteka?**	gdgye yest nay-lep-sha dis-ko-te-ka

SPORTS & GAMES

Where is the nearest tennis court?	**Gdzie są najbliższe korty tenisowe?**	gdgye so^{n} nay-bleezh-she kor-ti te-nee-so-ve
What is the charge per game? hour? day?	**Ile się płaci za grę? godzinę? dzień?**	ee-le shye^{n} pwa-chee za gre^{n} go-dgee-ne^{n} dgyen
Is it a club?	**Czy to jest klub?**	chi to yest kloob
Do I have to be a member?	**Czy muszę być członkiem klubu?**	chi moo-she^{n} bich chwon-kyem kloo-boo
Where can we go swimming/fishing?	**Gdzie możemy pójść popływać/na ryby?**	gdgye mo-zhe-mi pooyshch po-pwi-vach/na ri-bi
Can I hire a racket/fishing tackle?	**Czy mogę wynająć rakietę/sprzęt do łowienia ryb?**	chi mo-ge^{n} vi-na-yo^{n}ch ra-kye-te^{n}/spshe^{n}t do wo-vye-nya rib
Do I need a permit?	**Czy potrzebuję zezwolenie?**	chi po-tshe-boo-ye^{n} zez-vo-le-nye
Where do I get a permit?	**Gdzie dostanę zezwolenie?**	gdgye dos-ta-ne^{n} zez-vo-le-nye

Can we swim in the river?	**Czy możemy pływać w rzece?**	chi mo-zhe-mi pwi-vach vzhe-tse
Is there an open air/indoor swimming pool?	**Czy jest basen na otwartym powietrzu/kryty basen?**	chi yest ba-sen na ot-var-tim po-vye-tshoo/kri-ti ba-sen
Is it heated?	**Czy jest ogrzewany?**	chi yest o-gzhe-va-ni
Is there a skating rink?	**Czy jest lodowisko?**	chi yest lo-do-vees-ko
Can I hire skates/skiing equipment?	**Czy mogę wynająć łyżwy/sprzęt narciarski?**	chi mo-ge^{n} vi-na-yo^{n}ch wizh-vi/spshe^{n}t nar-chyar-skee
Can I take lessons here?	**Czy mogę tu wziąć lekcje?**	chi mo-ge^{n} too vzhyo^{n}ch lek-tsye
I've never skied before	**Nigdy nie jeździłem (łam) na nartach**	neeg-di nye yezh-dgee-wem (wam) na nar-tah
Are there ski runs for beginners/average skiers?	**Czy są trasy dla początkujących/przeciętnych narciarzy?**	chi so^{n} tra-si dla po-cho^{n}t-koo-yo^{n}-tsih/pshe-chye^{n}t-nih nar-chya-zhi
I am interested in cross-country skiing	**Interesuje mnie narciarstwo biegowe (śladowe)**	een-te-re-soo-ye mnye nar-chyar-stvo bye-go-ve (shla-do-ve)
Are there ski lifts?	**Czy są wyciągi narciarskie?**	chi so^{n} vi-chyo^{n}-gee nar-chyar-skye
We want to go to a football match/the tennis tournament	**Chcemy pójść na mecz piłki nożnej/tenisowy**	htse-mi pooyshch na mech peew-kee-nozh-ney/te-nee-so-vi
Can you get us tickets?	**Czy może nam pan(i) załatwić bilety?**	chi mo-zhe nam pan (pa-nee) za-wat-veech bee-le-ti

Are there seats in the grandstand?	**Czy są miejsca na trybunie?**	chi so^n myeys-tsa na tri-boo-nye
How much are the cheapest seats?	**Ile kosztują najtańsze bilety?**	ee-le kosh-too-yo^n nay-tan-she bee-le-ti
Are they in the sun or the shade?	**Czy one są w słońcu czy w cieniu?**	chi one so^n fswon-tsoo chi fchye-nyoo
Who is playing?	**Kto gra?**	kto gra
When does it start?	**O której się zaczyna?**	o ktoo-rey shye^n za-chi-na
Who is winning?	**Kto wygrywa?**	kto vi-gri-va
What is the score?	**Jaki jest stan meczu?**	ya-kee yest stan me-choo
I'd like to ride	**Chcę pojeździć konno**	htse^n po-yezh-dgeech kon-no
Is there a riding stable nearby?	**Czy jest w pobliżu stajnia jeździecka?**	chi yest fpo-blee-zhoo stay-nya yezh-dgyets-ka
Do you give lessons?	**Czy państwo dają lekcje?**	chi pan-stvo da-yo^n lek-tsye
I am an inexperienced rider/a good rider	**Jeżdżę słabo/dobrze**	yezh-je^n swa-bo/ dob-zhe
Can I hire a rowing boat/ motor boat/ surf board?	**Czy mogę wynająć łodzią wiosłową/ motorówkę/ deskę surfingową?**	chi mo-ge^n vi-na-yo^{n}ch wo-dgyo^n vyo-swo-vo^n/ mo-to-roov-ke^n/ des-ke^n ser-feen-go-vo^n
Is there a map of the river?	**Czy jest mapa rzeki?**	chi yest ma-pa zhe-kee
Are there many locks to pass?	**Czy jest dużo śluz po drodze?**	chi yest doo-zho shlooz po dro-dze
Can we get fuel here?	**Czy możemy tu kupić paliwo?**	chi mo-zhe-mi too koo-peech pa-lee-vo
I'd like to try waterskiing	**Chcę spróbować jazdy na nartach wodnych**	htse^n sproo-bo-vach yaz-di na nar-tah vod-nih

I haven't waterskied before	**Nigdy nie jeździłem (łam) na nartach wodnych**	neeg-di nye yezh-**dgee**-wem (wam) na **nar**-tah **vod**-nih
Should I wear a life jacket?	**Czy mam ubrać kurtkę ratowniczą?**	chi mam **oo**-brach **koort**-ke^{n} ra-tov-**nee**-cho^{n}
Where do you go fishing?	**Gdzie tu się chodzi na ryby?**	gdgye too shye^{n} **ho**-dgee na **ri**-bi
What kind of fish can you catch here?	**Jakie ryby się tu łowi?**	ya-kye **ri**-bi shye^{n} too **wo**-vee
Do you play cards?	**Czy gra pan(i) w karty?**	chi gra pan (**pa**-nee) **fkar**-ti
Would you like a game of chess?	**Czy ma pan(i) ochotę na grę w szachy?**	chi ma pan (**pa**-nee) o-**ho**-te^{n} na gre^{n} **fsha**-hi
I'll give you a game of checkers if you like	**Zagram z panem (panią) w szachy jeżeli pan(i) ma ochotę**	za-gram **spa**-nem (nyo^{n}) **fsha**-hi ye-**zhe**-lee pan (**pa**-nee) ma o-**ho**-te^{n}

ON THE BEACH

Where are the best beaches?	**Gdzie są najlepsze plaże?**	gdgye so^{n} nay-**lep**-she **pla**-zhe
Is there a quiet beach near here?	**Czy jest tu gdzieś blisko spokojna plaża?**	chi yest too gdgyesh **blees**-ko spo-**koy**-na **pla**-zha
Can we walk or is it too far?	**Czy możemy tam dojść pieszo, czy jest to za daleko?**	chi mo-**zhe**-mi tam doyshch **pye**-sho chi yest to za da-**le**-ko
Is there a bus to the beach?	**Czy jest autobus na plażę?**	chi yest a-oo-**to**-boos na **pla**-zhe^{n}
Is the beach sand/pebbles/rock?	**Czy to jest plaża piaszczysta/ kamienista/ skalista?**	chi to yest **pla**-zha pyash-**chis**-ta/ ka-mye-**nees**-ta/ ska-**lees**-ta
Is it safe for swimming?	**Czy bezpiecznie tu pływać?**	chi bez-**pyech**-nye too **pwi**-vach
Is there a lifeguard?	**Czy jest ratownik?**	chi yest ra-**tov**-neek

Is it safe for small children?	**Czy tu jest bezpiecznie dla małych dzieci?**	chi too yest bez-pyech-nye dla ma-wih dgye-chee
Does it get very rough?	**Czy są duże fale?**	chi so^{n} doo-zhe fa-le
Bathing prohibited	***Kąpiel wzbroniona**	ko^{n}-pyel vzbro-nyo-na
Diving prohibited	***Nurkowanie wzbronione**	noor-ko-va-nye vzbro-nyo-ne
It's dangerous	***Niebezpiecznie**	nye-bez-pyech-nye
There's a strong current here	***Tutaj jest silny prąd**	too-tay yest sheel-ni pro^{n}d
What time is high/low tide?	**Kiedy jest przypływ/ odpływ?**	kye-di yest pshi-pwiv/ od-pwiv
Are you a strong swimmer?	***Czy jest pan(i) silnym pływakiem/ silną pływaczką?**	chi yest pan (pa-nee) sheel-nim (no^{n}) pwi-va-kyem (chko^{n})
Is it deep?	**Czy tu jest głęboko?**	chi too yest gwe^{n}-bo-ko
Is the water cold/warm?	**Czy woda jest zimna/ ciepła?**	chi vo-da yest zheem-na/ chyep-wa
Can you swim in the lake/river?	**Czy można pływać w jeziorze/rzece?**	chi mozh-na pwi-vach vye-zhyo-zhe/vzhe-tse
Is there an indoor/ outdoor swimming pool?	**Czy jest tu kryty/ otwarty basen?**	chi yest too kri-ti/ ot-var-ti ba-sen
Is it salt or fresh water?	**Czy to jest słona, czy słodka woda?**	chi to yest swo-na chi swod-ka vo-da
Are there showers?	**Czy są prysznice?**	chi so^{n} prish-nee-tse
I want a cabin for the day/for the morning/ for two hours	**Poproszę kabinę na dzień/przed południe/ dwie godziny**	po-pro-she^{n} ka-bee-ne^{n} na dgyen/ pshed-po-wood-nye/ dvye go-dgee-ni

I want to hire a deckchair/sunshade	Chciałbym (-abym) wynająć leżak/ parasol od słońca	hchyaw-bim (hchya-wa-bim) vi-na-yo^{n}ch le-zhak/ pa-ra-sol od swon-tsa
Where can I buy a snorkel/flippers/ a bucket and spade?	Gdzie mogę kupić maskę pływacką/ płetwy/wiaderko i łopatkę?	gdgye mo-ge^{n} koo-peech mas-ke^{n} pwi-vats-ko^{n}/ pwet-vi/vya-der-ko ee wo-pat-ke^{n}
Can we waterski here?	Czy można tu jeździć na nartach wodnych?	chi mozh-na too yezh-dgeech na nar-tah vod-nih
Can we hire the equipment?	Czy możemy wypożyczyć sprzęt?	chi mo-zhe-mi vi-po-zhi-chich spshe^{n}t
Where's the harbour?	Gdzie jest port?	gdgye yest port
Can we go out in a fishing boat?	Czy możemy popłynąć łodzią rybacką?	chi mo-zhe-mi po-pwi-no^{n}ch wo-dgyo^{n} ri-bats-ko^{n}
We want to go fishing	Chcemy pójść na ryby	htse-mi pooyshch na ri-bi
Is there any underwater fishing?	Czy jest tu jakieś łowienie podwodne?	chi yest too ya-kyesh wo-vye-nye pod-vod-ne
Can I hire a boat?	Czy można wynająć łódź?	chi mozh-na vi-na-yo^{n}ch woodg
What does it cost by the hour?	Ile to kosztuje za godzinę?	ee-le to kosh-too-ye za go-dgee-ne^{n}
ball	piłka	peew-ka
beach bag	torba plażowa	tor-ba pla-zho-va
boat	łódź	woodg
sailing/motor/ pedal/rowing boat	żaglowa/motorówka/ rower wodny/ wiosłowa	zha-glo-va/mo-to-roov-ka/ ro-ver vod-ni/ vyo-swo-va
bucket and spade	wiaderko i łopatka	vya-der-ko ee wo-pat-ka
crab	rak	rak

first aid	**pierwsza pomoc**	pyerv-sha po-mots
jellyfish	**meduza**	me-doo-za
lifebelt	**pas ratunkowy**	pas ra-toon-ko-vi
lifebuoy	**pływak ratunkowy**	pwi-vak ra-toon-ko-vi
lighthouse	**latarnia morska**	la-tar-nya mor-ska
rock	**skała**	ska-wa
sand	**piasek**	pya-sek
sandbank	**mielizna**	mye-leez-na
sandcastle	**zamek z piasku**	za-mek spyas-koo
sun	**słońce**	swon-tse
sunglasses	**okulary słoneczne**	o-koo-la-ri swo-nech-ne
sunshade	**parasol od słońca**	pa-ra-sol od swon-tsa
swimming trunks	**spodenki kąpielowe**	spo-den-kee ko^{n}-pye-lo-ve
swimsuit	**kostium kąpielowy**	kos-tyoom ko^{n}-pye-lo-vi
towel	**ręcznik**	re^{n}ch-neek
water wings	**rękawki (skrzydełka) pływackie**	re^{n}-kav-kee (skshi-dew-ka) pwi-vats-kye
waves	**fala**	fa-la

IN THE COUNTRY

Is there a scenic route to …?	**Czy jest trasa wycieczkowa do …?**	chi yest **tra**-sa vee-do-**ko**-va do
Can you give me a lift to …?	**Czy może mnie pan(i) podwieźć do …?**	chi **mo**-zhe mnye pan (**pa**-nee) **pod**-vyezhch do
Is there a footpath to …?	**Czy jest ścieżka do …?**	chi yest **shchyezh**-ka do
Is it possible to go across country?	**Czy można iść na przełaj?**	chi **mozh**-na eeshch na **pshe**-way
Is there a shortcut?	**Czy jest skrót?**	chi yest skroot
Is there a bridge across the stream?	**Czy jest most przez strumień?**	chi yest most pshez **stroo**-myen
Can we walk?	**Czy możemy iść pieszo?**	chi mo-**zhe**-mi eeshch **pye**-sho
How far is the next village?	**Jak daleko jest następna wioska?**	yak da-**le**-ko yest nas-**te^{n}p**-na **vyos**-ka

THE WEATHER

Is it usually as hot as this?	**Czy zwykle jest tak gorąco jak teraz?**	chi zvik-le yest tak go-ro^{n}-tso yak te-raz
It's going to be hot/cold today	**Dziś będzie gorąco/zimno**	dgeesh be^{n}-dgye go-ro^{n}-tso/zheem-no
The mist will clear later	**Mgła się rozwieje później**	mgwa shye^{n} roz-vye-ye poozh-nyey
Will it be fine tomorrow?	**Czy jutro będzie ładnie?**	chi yoot-ro be^{n}-dgye wad-nye
What is the weather forecast?	**Jaka jest prognoza pogody?**	ya-ka yest prog-no-za po-go-di

TRAVELLING WITH CHILDREN

Can you put a child's bed/cot in our room?	**Czy mogą państwo wstawić do pokoju łóżeczko dziecinne?**	chi mo-go^{n} pan-stvo fsta-veech do po-ko-yoo woo-zhech-ko dgye-cheen-ne
Can you give us adjoining rooms?	**Czy możemy dostać pokoje obok siebie?**	chi mo-zhe-mi dos-tach po-ko-ye o-bok shye-bye
Can you find me a baby-sitter?	**Czy mogą mi państwo załatwić opiekunkę do dziecka?**	chi mo-go^{n} mee pan-stvo za-wat-veech o-pye-koon-ke^{n} do dgyets-ka
We shall be out for a couple of hours	**Wychodzimy na parę godzin**	vi-ho-dgee-mi na pa-re^{n} go-dgeen
We shall be back at …	**Wrócimy o …**	vroo-chee-mi o
Is there a children's menu?	**Czy jest karta potraw dla dzieci?**	chi yest kar-ta po-trav dla dgye-chee
Do you have half portions for children?	**Czy są małe porcje dla dzieci?**	chi so^{n} ma-we por-tsye dla dgye-chee

Have you got a high chair?	**Czy mają państwo wysokie krzesło dla dziecka?**	chi **ma**-yo^{n} **pan**-stvo vi-so-kye **kshes**-wo dla **dgyets**-ka
Are there any organized activities for children?	**Czy są jakieś zorganizowane programy dla dzieci?**	chi so^{n} **ya**-kyesh zor-ga-nee-zo-**va**-ne pro-**gra**-mi dla **dgye**-chee
Is there a paddling pool/ children's swimming pool/playground/ games room?	**Czy jest brodzik/ basen dla dzieci/ plac zabaw/pokój do gier?**	chi yest **bro**-dgeek/ **ba**-sen dla **dgye**-chee/ plats **za**-bav/**po**-kooy do gyer
Is there an amusement park nearby/ a zoo/a toyshop?	**Czy jest w pobliżu wesołe miasteczko/ zoo/sklep z zabawkami?**	chi yest fpo-**blee**-zhoo ve-**so**-we myas-**tech**-ko/ **zo**-o/sklep z za-bav-**ka**-mee
I'd like a	**Poproszę**	po-**pro**-she^{n}
beach ball	**piłkę plażową**	**peew**-ke^{n} pla-**zho**-vo^{n}
bucket and spade	**wiaderko i łopatkę**	vya-**der**-ko ee wo-**pat**-ke^{n}
doll	**lalkę**	**lal**-ke^{n}
flippers	**płetwy**	**pwet**-vi
goggles	**gogle**	**gog**-le
playing cards	**karty do gry**	**kar**-ti do gri
roller skates	**wrotki**	**vrot**-kee
snorkel	**maskę pływacką**	**mas**-ke^{n} pwi-**vats**-ko^{n}
Where can I feed/change my baby?	**Gdzie mogę nakarmić/ przewinąć dziecko?**	gdgye **mo**-ge^{n} na-**kar**-meech/ pshe-**vee**-no^{n}ch **dgyets**-ko
Can you heat this bottle for me?	**Czy może mi pan(i) podgrzać tę butelkę?**	chi **mo**-zhe mee pan (**pa**-nee) **pod**-gzhach te^{n} boo-**tel**-ke^{n}

I want some disposable nappies/a feeding bottle/some baby food	**Potrzebuję pieluszki jednorazowe/ butelkę dla niemowląt/ jedzenie dla dzieci**	po-tshe-**boo**-ye^n pye-**loosh**-kee yed-no-ra-**zo**-ve/ boo-**tel**-ke^n dla nye-**mov**-lo^{n}t/ ye-**dze**-nye dla **dgye**-chee
My daughter suffers from travel sickness	**Moja córka cierpi na chorobę lokomocyjną**	mo-ya **tsoor**-ka **chyer**-pee na ho-**ro**-be^n lo-ko-mo-**tsiy**-no^n
She has hurt herself	**Ona się skaleczyła/ uderzyła**	o-na shye^n ska-le-**chi**-wa/ oo-de-**zhi**-wa
My son is ill	**Mój syn jest chory**	mooy sin yest **ho**-ri
He has lost his toy	**On zgubił zabawkę**	on **zgoo**-beew za-**bav**-ke^n
I'm sorry if they have bothered you	**Przepraszam jeżeli przeszkadzały**	pshe-**pra**-sham ye-**zhe**-lee pshesh-ka-**dza**-wi

BUSINESS MATTERS[1]

I would like to make an appointment with …	**Chcę załatwić spotkanie z …**	htse^n za-wat-veech spot-ka-nye z
I have an appointment with …	**Mam umówione spotkanie z …**	mam oo-moo-vyo-ne spot-ka-nye z
My name is …	**Moje nazwisko …**	mo-ye naz-vees-ko
Here is my card	**Moja wizytówka**	mo-ya vee-zi-toov-ka
This is our catalogue	***To jest nasz katalog**	to yest nash ka-ta-log
I would like to see products	**Chciałbym (-abym) zobaczyć pańskie wyroby**	hchyaw-bim your (hchya-wa-bim) zo-ba-chich pan-skye vi-ro-bi
Could you send me some samples?	**Czy mogą mi państwo przysłać parę próbek?**	chi mo-go^n mee pan-stvo pshis-wach pa-re^n proo-bek
Can you provide an	**Czy mogą mi państwo**	chi mo-go^n mee pan-stvo

1. See also TELEPHONING (p. 135).

interpreter/ secretary?	**załatwić tłumacza/ sekretarkę?**	za-wat-veech twoo-ma-cha/ se-kre-tar-ke^{n}
Where can I make some photocopies?	**Gdzie mogę zrobić fotokopie?**	gdgye mo-ge^{n} zro-beech fo-to-ko-pye

AT THE DOCTOR'S

I must see a doctor; can you recommend one?	**Muszę pójść do lekarza; czy może pan(i) kogoś polecić?**	moo-she^n pooyshch do le-ka-zha; chi mo-zhe pan (pa-nee) ko-gosh po-le-cheech
Is there a doctor's surgery near here?	**Czy jest w pobliżu przychodnia lekarska?**	chi yest fpo-blee-zhoo pshi-hod-nya le-kar-ska
Please call a doctor	**Proszę zawołać lekarza**	pro-she^n za-vo-wach le-ka-zha
When can the doctor come?	**Kiedy lekarz przyjdzie?**	kye-di le-kazh pshiy-dgye
Does the doctor speak English?	**Czy lekarz mówi po angielsku?**	chi le-kazh moo-vee po an-gyel-skoo
Can I make an appointment for as soon as possible?	**Czy mogę zamówić wizytę jak najszybciej?**	chi mo-ge^n za-moo-veech vee-zi-te^n yak nay-shib-chyey
I take … can you give me a prescription, please?	**Biorę … czy mogę prosić o receptę?**	byo-re^n … chi mo-ge^n pro-sheech o re-tsep-te^n

AILMENTS

I am ill	**Jestem chory (-a)**	yes-tem ho-ri (a)
I have high/low blood pressure	**Mam wysokie/niskie ciśnienie**	mam vi-so-kye/nees-kye cheesh-nye-nye
I am pregnant	**Jestem w ciąży**	yes-tem fchyo^{n}-zhi
I am allergic to …	**Jestem uczulony(a) na …**	yes-tem oo-choo-lo-ni (a) na
I think it is infected	**Wydaje mi się że jest tu infekcja**	vi-da-ye mee shye^{n} zhe yest too in-fek-tsya
I've a pain in my right arm	**Boli mnie w prawym ramieniu**	bo-lee mnye fpra-vim ra-mye-nyoo
My wrist hurts	**Boli mnie w przegubie**	bo-lee mnye fpshe-goo-bye
I think I've sprained/ broken my ankle	**Wydaje mi się że zwichnąłem (-ęłam)/ złamałem (-am) nogę w kostce**	vi-da-ye mee shye^{n} zhe zveeh-no^{n}-wem (ne^{n}-wam)/ zwa-ma-wem (wam) no-ge^{n} fkost-tse
I fell down and hurt my back	**Upadłem (-am) i potem dostałem (-am) bólu w plecach**	oo-pad-wem (wam) ee po-tem dos-ta-wem (wam) boo-loo fple-tsah
My feet are swollen	**Mam opuchnięte stopy**	mam o-pooh-nye^{n}-te sto-pi
I've burned/cut/ bruised myself	**Sparzyłem (-am) się/ skaleczyłem (-am) się/potłukłem się (-am)**	spa-zhi-wem (wam) shye^{n}/ ska-lechi-wem (wam) shye^{n}/po-twook-wem (wam) shye^{n}

My stomach is upset	**Żołądek mnie boli**	zho-wo^{n}-dek mnye bo-lee
I have indigestion	**Cierpię na niestrawność**	chyer-pye^{n} na nye-strav-noshch
My appetite's gone	**Straciłem (-am) apetyt**	stra-chee-wem (wam) a-pe-tit
I think I've got food poisoning	**Wydaje mi się, że się zatrułem (-am) żywnością**	vi-da-ye mee shye^{n} zhe shye^{n} za-troo-wem (wam) zhiv-nosh-chyo^{n}
I can't eat/sleep	**Nie mogę jeść/ spać**	nye mo-ge^{n} yeshch/spach
I am a diabetic	**Mam cukrzycę**	mam tsoo-kshi-tse^{n}
My nose keeps bleeding	**Nos mi ciągle krwawi**	nos mee chyo^{n}-gle krva-vee
I have earache	**Ucho mnie boli**	oo-ho mnye bo-lee
I have difficulty in breathing	**Mam trudności z oddychaniem**	mam trood-nosh-chee zod-di-ha-nyem
I feel dizzy	**Mam zawroty głowy**	mam za-vro-ti gwo-vi
I feel sick	**Mdli mnie (jest mi niedobrze)**	mdlee mnye (yest mee nye-dob-zhe)
I keep vomiting	**Wciąż wymiotuję**	fchyo^{n}zh vi-myo-too-ye^{n}
I have a temperature/ fever	**Mam temperaturę/ gorączkę**	mam tem-pe-ra-too-re^{n}/ go-ro^{n}ch-ke^{n}
I think I've caught 'flu	**Wydaje mi się, że mam grypę**	vi-da-ye mee shye^{n} zhe mam gri-pe^{n}
I've got a cold	**Jestem przeziębiony (-a)**	yes-tem pshe-zhye^{n}-byo-ni (na)
I've had it since yesterday	**Mam to od wczoraj**	mam to od fcho-ray
I've had it for a few hours	**Mam to od paru godzin**	mam to od pa-roo go-dgeen

abscess	**ropień, wrzód**	ro-pyen, vzhood
ache	**ból**	bool
allergy	**alergia, uczulenie**	a-ler-gya, oo-choo-le-nye
appendicitis	**zapalenie wyrostka robaczkowego**	za-pa-le-nye vi-rost-ka ro-bach-ko-ve-go
asthma	**astma**	ast-ma
back pain	**ból w krzyżu**	bool fkshi-zhoo
blister	**pęcherz**	pe^{n}-hezh
boil	**czyrak**	chi-rak
bruise	**siniec**	shee-nyets
burn	**oparzenie**	o-pa-zhe-nye
cardiac condition	**stan sercowy**	stan ser-tso-vi
chill	**zaziębienie**	za-zhye^{n}-bye-nye
cold	**przeziębienie**	pshe-zhye^{n}-bye-nye
constipation	**obstrukcja**	ob-strook-tsya
cough	**kaszel**	ka-shel
cramp	**skurcz**	skoorch
diabetic	**diabetyk (*m*), diabetyczka (*f*)**	dya-be-tik dya-be-tich-ka
diarrhoea	**biegunka**	bye-goon-ka
earache	**ból ucha**	bool oo-ha
fever	**gorączka**	go-ro^{n}ch-ka
food poisoning	**zatrucie jedzeniem**	za-troo-chye ye-dze-nyem
fracture	**złamanie, pęknięcie**	zwa-ma-nye, pe^{n}k-nye^{n}-chye
hay fever	**katar sienny**	ka-tar shen-ni

headache	**ból głowy**	bool gwo-vi
heart condition	**choroba serca**	ho-ro-ba ser-tsa
high blood pressure	**wysokie ciśnienie**	vi-so-kye cheesh-nye-nye
ill, sick	**chory**	ho-ri
illness	**choroba**	ho-ro-ba
indigestion	**niestrawność**	nye-strav-noshch
infection	**infekcja, zakażenie**	in-fek-tsya, za-ka-zhe-nye
influenza	**grypa**	gri-pa
insect bite	**ukąszenie przez owada**	oo-ko^{n}-she-nye pshez o-va-da
insomnia	**bezsenność**	bez-sen-noshch
itch	**swędzenie**	sfe^{n}-dze-nye
nausea	**mdłości**	mdwosh-chee
nose bleed	**krwawienie z nosa**	krva-vye-nye zno-sa
pain	**ból**	bool
rheumatism	**reumatyzm**	rew-ma-tism
sore throat	**ból gardła**	bool gard-wa
sprain	**zwichnięcie**	zveeh-nye^{n}-chye
sting	**użądlenie**	oo-zho^{n}-dle-nye
stomach ache	**ból brzucha**	bool bzhoo-ha
sunburn	**poparzenie słoneczne**	po-pa-zhe-nye swo-nech-ne
sunstroke	**porażenie słoneczne**	po-ra-zhe-nye swo-nech-ne
swelling	**opuchlizna**	o-pooh-leez-na
tonsillitis	**zapalenie migdałków**	za-pa-le-nye meeg-daw-koov

toothache	**ból zęba**	bool ze^{n}-ba
ulcer	**wrzód**	vzhood
wound	**rana**	ra-na

TREATMENT

Do you have a temperature?	***Czy ma pan(i) temperaturę?**	chi ma pan (pa-nee) tem-pe-ra-too-re^{n}
I have a fever	**Mam gorączkę**	mam go-ro^{n}ch-ke^{n}
I feel better now	**Czuję się teraz lepiej**	choo-ye^{n} shye^{n} te-raz le-pyey
Does that hurt?	***Czy to boli?**	chi to bo-lee
You're hurting me	**Pan(i) zadaje mi ból**	pan (pa-nee) za-da-ye mee bool
A lot?	**Bardzo?**	bar-dzo
A little?	**Trochę?**	tro-he^{n}
Where does it hurt?	***Gdzie pana (panią) boli?**	gdgye pa-na (nyo^{n}) bo-lee
Have you a pain here?	***Czy boli tutaj?**	chi bo-lee too-tay
How long have you had the pain/been suffering from …?	***Od kiedy pana (ią) boli/pan(i) cierpi na …?**	od kye-di pa-na (nyo^{n}) bo-lee/pan (pa-nee) chyer-pee na
Open your mouth	***Proszę otworzyć usta**	pro-she^{n} ot-vo-zhich oos-ta
Put out your tongue	***Proszę pokazać język**	pro-she^{n} po-ka-zach ye^{n}-zik
Breathe in	***Proszę wciągnąć powietrze**	pro-she^{n} fchyo^{n}-gno^{n}ch po-vye-tshe

Hold your breath	***Proszę wstrzymać oddech**	pro-she^n fstshi-mach od-deh
Please lie down	***Proszę się położyć**	pro-she^n shye^n po-wo-zhich
I will need a specimen	***Potrzebna mi będzie próbka**	po-tsheb-na mee be^n-dgye proob-ka
What medicines have you been taking?	***Jakie lekarstwo pan(i) brał (-a)?**	ya-kye le-kar-stva pan(pa-nee) braw (bra-wa)
I take this medicine – could you give me another prescription?	**Biorę to lekarstwo – czy może mi pan(i) wypisać nową receptę?**	byo-re^n to le-kar-stvo chi mo-zhe mee pan (pa-nee) vi-pee-sach no-vo^n re-tsep-te^n
I will give you an antibiotic/a painkiller/a sedative	***Dam panu(i) antybiotyk/środek przeciwbólowy/środek uspokajający**	*dam pa-noo (nee) an-ti-byo-tik/shro-dek pshe-cheev-boo-lo-vi/shro-dek oo-spo-ka-ya-yo^n-tsi
Take these pills/medicine	***Proszę wziąć te pigułki/to lekarstwo**	pro-she^n vzhyo^{n}ch te pee-goow-ki/to le-kar-stvo
Take this prescription to the chemist's	***Proszę wziąć tę receptę do apteki**	pro-she^n vzhyo^{n}ch te^n re-tsep-te^n do ap-te-kee
Take this three times a day	***Proszę to zażywać trzy razy dziennie**	pro-she^n to za-zhi-vach tshi ra-zi dgyen-nye
I'll give you an injection	***Dam panu (pani) zastrzyk**	dam pa-noo (nee) zas-tshik
Roll up your sleeve	***Proszę podwinąć rękaw**	pro-she^n pod-vee-no^{n}ch re^n-kav
You should stay on a diet for a few days	***Powinien pan (powinna pani) przejść na dietę na parę dni**	po-vee-nyen pan (po-veen-na pa-nee) psheyshch na dye-te^n na pa-re^n dnee

Come and see me again in two days' time	***Proszę przyjść ponownie za dwa dni**	pro-she^n pshiyshch po-nov-nye za dva dnee
You must be X-rayed	***Musi pan(i) iść na prześwietlenie**	moo-shee pan (pa-nee) eeshch na pshe-shvyet-le-nye
You must go to hospital	***Musi pan(i) iść do szpitala**	moo-shee pan (pa-nee) eeshch do shpee-ta-la
You must stay in bed for a few days	***Musi pan(i) leżeć w łóżku przez parę dni**	moo-shee pan (pa-nee) le-zhech vwoozh-koo pshez pa-re^n dnee
You should not travel until …	***Nie powinien pan (nie powinna pani) podróżować aż do …**	nye po-vee-nyen pan (nye po-veen-na pa-nee) po-droo-zho-vach azh do
Will you come and see me again?	**Czy przyjdzie pan(i) z nową wizytą?**	chi pshiy-dgye pan (pa-nee) zno-vo^n vee-zi-to^n
Nothing to worry about	***Nie ma powodu do zmartwienia**	nye ma po-vo-doo do zmar-tvye-nya
How much do I owe you?	**Ile jestem winien (winna)?**	ee-le yest-tem vee-nyen (veen-na)
When do you think I can leave?	**Kiedy pan(i) sądzi, że będę mógł (mogła) wyjechać?**	kye-di pan(pa-nee) so^n-dgee zhe be^n-de^n moogw (mo-gwa) vi-ye-hach
I'd like a receipt for the health insurance	**Poproszę o zaświadczenie dla ubezpieczenia**	po-pro-she^n o zash-vyad-che-nye dla oo-bez-pye-che-nya

ambulance	**karetka pogotowia ratunkowego**	ka-ret-ka po-go-to-vya ra-toon-ko-ve-go

anaesthetic	**środek znieczulający**	shro-dek znye-choo-la-yo^{n}-tsi
aspirin	**aspiryna**	as-pee-ri-na
bandage	**bandaż**	ban-dazh
chiropodist	**pedicurzysta (*m*), pedicurzystka (*f*)**	pe-dee-koo-zhis-ta
hospital	**szpital**	shpee-tal
injection	**zastrzyk**	zas-tshik
laxative	**środek przeczyszczający**	shro-dek pshe-chish-cha-yo^{n}-tsi
nurse	**pielęgniarka**	pye-le^{n}g-nyar-ka
operation	**operacja**	o-pe-ra-tsya
optician	**optyk**	op-tik
osteopath	**osteopata**	os-te-o-pa-ta
pill	**pigułka**	pee-goow-ka
(adhesive) plaster	**plaster opatrunkowy**	pla-ster o-pat-roon-ko-vi
prescription	**recepta**	re-tsep-ta
X-ray	**prześwietlenie rentgenowskie**	pshesh-vye-tle-nye rent-ge-nov-skye

PARTS OF THE BODY

ankle	**kostka**	kost-ka
arm	**ramię**	ra-mye^{n}
back	**plecy**	ple-tsi
bladder	**pęcherz**	pe^{n}-hezh

blood	**krew**	krev
body	**ciało**	chya-wo
bone	**kość**	koshch
bowels	**wnętrzności**	vne^{n}-tshnosh-chee
brain	**mózg**	moozg
breast	**pierś**	pyersh
cheek	**policzek**	po-lee-chek
chest	**klatka piersiowa**	klat-ka pyer-sho-va
collar-bone	**obojczyk**	o-boy-chik
ear	**ucho**	oo-ho
elbow	**łokieć**	wo-kyech
eye	**oko**	o-ko
eyelid	**powieka**	po-vye-ka
face	**twarz**	tvazh
finger	**palec**	pa-lets
foot	**stopa**	sto-pa
forehead	**czoło**	cho-wo
gums	**dziąsła**	dgyo^{n}s-wa
hand	**ręka**	re^{n}-ka
head	**głowa**	gwo-va
heart	**serce**	ser-tse
heel	**pięta**	pye^{n}-ta
hip	**biodro**	byo-dro
jaw	**szczęka**	shche^{n}-ka
joint	**staw**	stav

kidney	**nerka**	ner-ka
knee	**kolano**	ko-la-no
knee-cap	**rzepka**	zhep-ka
leg	**noga**	no-ga
lip	**warga**	var-ga
liver	**wątroba**	vo^n-tro-ba
lung	**płuco**	pwoo-tso
mouth	**usta**	oos-ta
muscle	**mięsień**	mye^n-shyen
nail	**paznokieć**	paz-no-kyech
neck	**szyja**	shi-ya
nerve	**nerw**	nerv
nose	**nos**	nos
rib	**żebro**	zhe-bro
shoulder	**ramię**	ra-mye^n
skin	**skóra**	skoo-ra
spine	**kręgosłup**	kre^n-go-swoop
stomach	**żołądek**	zho-wo^n-dek
temple	**skroń**	skron
thigh	**udo**	oo-do
throat	**gardło**	gard-wo
thumb	**kciuk**	kchyook
toe	**palec u nogi**	pa-lets oo no-gee
tongue	**język**	ye^n-zik
tonsils	**migdałki**	meeg-daw-kee

tooth	**ząb**	zo^{n}b
vein	**żyła**	**zhi**-wa
wrist	**przegub**	**pshe**-goob

AT THE DENTIST'S

I must see a dentist	**Muszę iść do dentysty**	moo-she^n eeshch do den-tis-ti
Can I make an appointment with the dentist?	**Czy mogę zamówić wizytę u dentysty?**	chi mo-ge^n za-moo-veech vee-zi-te^n oo den-tis-ti
As soon as possible	**Jak najszybciej**	yak nay-shib-chyey
I have toothache	**Mam ból zęba**	mam bool ze^n-ba
This tooth hurts	**Ten ząb mnie boli**	ten zo^{n}b mnye bo-lee
I have a broken tooth/an abscess	**Mam złamany ząb/ropień**	mam zwa-ma-ni zo^{n}b/ro-pyen
I have lost a filling	**Wypadła mi plomba**	vi-pad-wa mee plom-ba
Can you fill it?	**Czy może pan(i) go zaplombować?**	chi mo-zhe pan (pa-nee) go za-plom-bo-vach
Can you do it now?	**Czy może pan(i) teraz to zrobić?**	chi mo-zhe pan (pa-nee) te-raz to zro-beech
Must you take the tooth out?	**Czy musi pan(i) wyrwać ten ząb?**	chi moo-shee pan (pa-nee) vir-vach ten zo^{n}b

I do not want the tooth taken out	**Proszę mi nie wyrywać zęba**	pro-she^{n} mee nye vi-ri-vach ze^{n}-ba
Please give me an anaesthetic	**Proszę mi dać znieczulenie**	pro-she^{n} mee dach znye-choo-le-nye
My gums are swollen/ keep bleeding	**Dziąsła mi spuchły/krwawią**	dgyo^{n}s-wa mee spooh-wi/krva-vyo^{n}
I have broken/chipped my dentures	**Pękła mi/ wyszczerbiła mi się proteza**	pe^{n}k-wa mee/ vish-cher-bee-wa mee shye^{n} pro-te-za
Can you fix it (temporarily)?	**Czy może pan(i) to naprawić (prowizorycznie)?**	chi mo-zhe pan (pa-nee) to na-pra-veech (pro-vee-zo-rich-nye)
You're hurting me	**Pan(i) mi sprawia ból**	pan (pa-nee) mee spra-vya bool
Please rinse your mouth	***Proszę wypłukać usta**	pro-she^{n} vi-pwoo-kach oos-ta
I will X-ray your teeth	***Prześwietlę panu (pani) zęby**	pshesh-vyet-le^{n} pa-noo (nee) ze^{n}-bi
You have an abscess	***Ma pan(i) ropień**	ma pan (pa-nee) ro-pyen
The nerve is exposed	***Nerw jest odsłonięty**	nerv yest od-swo-nye^{n}-ti
This tooth will have to come out	***Trzeba wyrwać ten ząb**	tshe-ba vir-vach ten zo^{n}b
How much do I owe you?	**Ile jestem winien (winna)?**	ee-le yes-tem vee-nyen (veen-na)
When should I come again?	**Kiedy mam się znowu zgłosić?**	kye-di mam shye^{n} zno-voo zgwo-sheech

PROBLEMS & ACCIDENTS

Where's the police station?	**Gdzie jest posterunek policji?**	gdgye yest po-ste-**roo**-nek po-**leets**-yee
Call the police	**Proszę zawołać policję**	**pro**-she^{n} za-**vo**-wach po-**leets**-ye^{n}
Where is the British/ American consulate?	**Gdzie jest konsulat brytyjski/ amerykański?**	gdgye yest kon-**soo**-lat bri-**tiy**-skee/ a-me-ri-**kan**-skee
Please let the consulate know	**Proszę zawiadomić konsulat**	**pro**-she^{n} za-vya-**do**-meech kon-**soo**-lat
It's urgent	**To jest pilne**	to yest **peel**-ne
There's a fire	**Pali się**	**pa**-lee shye^{n}
Our car has been broken into	**Było włamanie do naszego samochodu**	**bi**-wo vwa-**ma**-nye do na-**she**-go sa-mo-**ho**-doo
I've been robbed/ mugged	**Zostałem (-am) okradziony(a)/ pobity(a)**	zos-**ta**-wem (wam) o-kra-**dgyo**-ni (na)/ po-**bee**-ti (ta)
My son/daughter is lost	**Mój syn/moja córka się zagubił(a)**	**mooy** sin/**mo**-ya **tsoor**-ka shye^{n} za-**goo**-beew (**bee**-wa)

My bag/wallet has been stolen	**Skradziono mi torebkę/portfel**	skra-dgyo-no mee to-reb-ke^{n}/port-fel
I found this in the street	**Znalazłem (-am) to na ulicy**	zna-laz-wem (wam) to na oo-lee-tsi
I have lost my luggage/ passport/travellers' cheques	**Zgubiłem (-am) bagaż/paszport/ czeki podróżnicze**	zgoo-bee-wem (wam) ba-gazh/pash-port/ che-kee po-droozh-nee-che
I have missed my train	**Spoźniłem (-am) się na pociąg**	spoozh-nee-wem (wam) shye^{n} na po-chyo^{n}g
My luggage is on board	**Mój bagaż jest w pociągu**	mooy ba-gazh yest fpo-chyo^{n}-goo
Call a doctor	**Proszę zawołać lekarza**	pro-she^{n} za-vo-wach le-ka-zha
Call an ambulance	**Proszę sprowadzić karetkę pogotowia**	pro-she^{n} spro-va-dgeech ka-ret-ke^{n} po-go-tov-ya
There has been an accident	**Był wypadek**	biw vi-pa-dek
He's/She's badly hurt	**On(a) jest poważnie zraniony (a)**	on (o-na) yest po-vazh-nye zra-nyo-ni (na)
He/She's fainted	**On(a) zemdlał(a)**	on (o-na) zem-dlaw (dla-wa)
He's/She's losing blood	**On(a) krwawi**	on(o-na) krva-vee
Her/His arm is broken	**Ma rękę złamaną**	ma re^{n}-ke^{n} zwa-ma-no^{n}
Please get some water/ a blanket/some bandages	**Proszę przynieść wody/koc/bandaże**	pro-she^{n} pshi-nyeshch vo-di/kots/ban-da-zhe
I've broken my glasses	**Rozbiłem(-am) okulary**	roz-bee-wem (wam) o-koo-la-ri
I can't see	**Nic nie widzę**	neets nye vee-dze^{n}
A child has fallen in the water	**Dziecko wpadło do wody**	dgyets-ko fpad-wo do vo-dee

May I see your insurance certificate?	***Czy mogę zobaczyć pańskie świadectwo ubezpieczeniowe?**	chi mo-ge^{n} zo-ba-chich pan-skye shvya-dets-tvo oo-bez-pye-che-nyo-ve
driving licence	**Prawo jazdy**	pra-vo yaz-di
I didn't understand the sign	**Nie zrozumiałem (-am) tego znaku**	nye zro-zoo-mya-wem (wam) tego zna-koo
How much is the fine?	**Ile wynosi kara?**	ee-le vi-no-shee ka-ra
I want a copy of the police report	**Poproszę o kopię raportu policyjnego**	po-pro-she^{n} o ko-pye^{n} ra-por-too po-lee-tsiy-ne-go
What are the name and address of the owner?	**Jakie jest nazwisko i adres właściciela?**	ya-kye yest naz-vees-ko ee a-dres vwash-chee-chye-la
Are you willing to act as a witness?	**Czy zgodzi się pan(i) na świadka?**	chi zgo-dgee shye^{n} pan (pa-nee) na shvyad-ka
Can I have your name and address, please?	**Czy mogę prosić a nazwisko i adres?**	chi mo-ge^{n} pro-sheech o naz-vees-ko ee a-dres
Can you help me?	**Czy może mi pan(i) pomóc?**	chi mo-zhe mee pan(pa-nee) po-moots
Apply to the insurance company	**Proszę się zwrócić do urzędu ubezpieczeniowego**	pro-she^{n} shye^{n} zvroo-cheech do oo-zhe^{n}-doo oo-bez-pye-che-nyo-ve-go

TIME & DATES

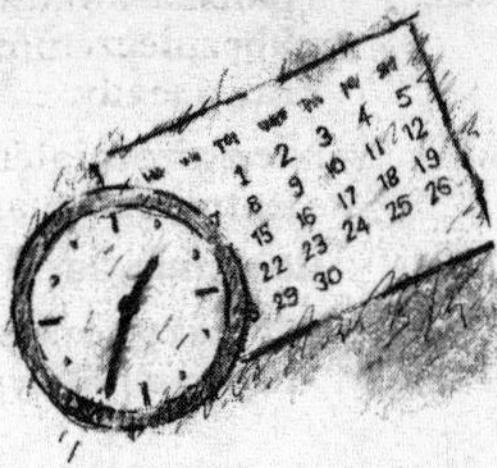

TIME

What time is it?	**Która godzina?**	ktoo-ra go-dgee-na
It's one o'clock	**Pierwsza**	pyerv-sha
two o'clock	**Druga**	droo-ga
five past eight	**Pięć po ósmej**	pye^{n}ch po oos-mey
quarter past five	**Piętnaście po piątej**	pye^{n}t-nash-chye po pyo^{n}-tey
half past four	**Wpół do piątej**	fpoow do pyo^{n}-tey
twenty to three	**Za dwadzieścia trzecia**	za dva-dgyesh-cha tshe-chya
quarter to ten	**Za piętnaście dziesiąta**	za pye^{n}t-nash-chye dgye-shyo^{n}-ta
Second	**sekunda**	se-koon-da
Minute	**minuta**	mee-noo-ta
Hour	**godzina**	go-dzee-na

It's early/late	**Jest wcześnie/ późno**	yest **fchesh**-nye/ **poozh**-no
My watch is slow/fast/ has stopped	**Mój zegarek się spóźnia/śpieszy/ nie chodzi**	mooy ze-**ga**-rek shye^{n} **spoozh**-nya/**shpye**-shi/ nye **ho**-dgee
Sorry I'm late	**Przepraszam za spóźnienie**	pshe-**pra**-sham za spoozh-**nye**-nye

DATE

What's the date?	**Jaka jest dzisiejsza data?**	**ya**-ka yest dgee-**shyey**-sha **da**-ta
It's 9 December	**Dziewiątego grudnia**	dgye-vyo^{n}-**te**-go **grood**-nya
We got here on 27 July	**Przyjechaliśmy tu dwudziestego siódmego lipca**	pshi-ye-ha-**leesh**-mi too dvoo-dgyes-**te**-go shyood-**me**-go **leep**-tsa
We're leaving on 5 January	**Wyjeżdżamy piątego stycznia**	vi-yezh-**ja**-mi pyo^{n}-**te**-go **stich**-nya

DAY

Morning	**rano**	**ra**-no
this morning	**dziś rano**	dgeesh **ra**-no
in the morning	**rano**	**ra**-no
Midday, noon	**południe**	po-**wood**-nye
at noon	**w południe**	fpo-**wood**-nye
Afternoon	**popołudnie**	po-po-**wood**-nye
yesterday afternoon	**wczoraj po południu**	**fcho**-ray po-po-**wood**-nyoo

Evening	**wieczór**	vye-choor
tonight	**dziś wieczór**	dgeesh vye-choor
tomorrow evening	**jutro wieczór**	yoot-ro vye-choor
Midnight	**północ**	poow-nots
Night	**noc**	nots
at night	**wieczorem**	vye-cho-rem
by day	**w dzień**	v dgyen
Sunrise	**wschód słońca**	fs-hood swon-tsa
Dawn	**świt**	shveet
Sunset	**zachód słońca**	za-hood swon-tsa
Dusk, twilight	**zmierzch, półmrok**	zmyezh-h, poow-mrok
Today	**dziś/dzisiaj**	dgeesh, dgee-shyay
Yesterday	**wczoraj**	fcho-ray
day before yesterday	**przedwczoraj**	pshed-fcho-ray
Tomorrow	**jutro**	yoot-ro
day after tomorrow	**pojutrze**	po-yoo-tshe
in ten days' time	**za dziesięć dni**	za dgye-shye^{n}ch dnee

WEEK

Sunday	**niedziela**	nye-dgye-la
Monday	**poniedziałek**	po-nye-dgya-wek
Tuesday	**wtorek**	fto-rek
Wednesday	**środa**	shro-da
Thursday	**czwartek**	chvar-tek
Friday	**piątek**	pyo^{n}-tek
Saturday	**sobota**	so-bo-ta

on Tuesday	**we wtorek**	ve fto-rek
on Sundays	**w niedzielę**	vnye-dgye-le^n
Fortnight	**dwa tygodnie**	dva ti-god-nye

MONTH

January	**styczeń**	sti-chen
February	**luty**	loo-ti
March	**marzec**	ma-zhets
April	**kwiecień**	kfye-chyen
May	**maj**	may
June	**czerwiec**	cher-vyets
July	**lipiec**	lee-pyets
August	**sierpień**	sher-pyen
September	**wrzesień**	vzhe-shen
October	**październik**	pazh-dgyer-neek
November	**listopad**	lee-sto-pad
December	**grudzień**	groo-dgyen

SEASON

Spring	**wiosna**	vyos-na
Summer	**lato**	la-to
Autumn	**jesień**	ye-shyen

Winter	**zima**	zhee-ma
in spring	**na wiosnę**	na vyos-ne^{n}
during the summer	**w lecie**	vle-chye

YEAR

This year	**w tym roku**	ftim ro-koo
Last year	**w zeszłym roku**	vzesh-wim ro-koo
Next year	**w przyszłym roku**	fpshish-wim ro-koo

PUBLIC HOLIDAYS

New Year's Day (1 January)	**Nowy Rok**	no-vi rok
Easter Monday (moveable)	**Poniedziałek Wielkanocny**	po-nye-dgya-wek vyel-ka-nots-ni
Labour Day (1 May)	**Święto Pracy**	shvye^{n}-to pra-tsi
Constitution Day (3 May)	**Konstytucja 3 Maja**	kon-sti-toots-ya tshe-chye-go ma-ya
Pentecost (moveable)	**Zielone Świątki**	zhye-lo-ne shvyo^{n}t-kee
Corpus Christi (moveable)	**Boże Ciało**	bo-zhe chya-wo
Assumption (15 August)	**Wniebowzięcie**	vnye-bo-vzhye^{n}-chye
All Saints' Day (1 November)	**Wszystkich Świętych**	fshist-keeh shvye^{n}-tih

National Independence Day (11 November)	**Narodowe Święto Niepodległości**	na-ro-**do**-ve **shvye**^{n}-to nye-po-dleg-**wosh**-chee
Christmas (25, 26 December)	**Boże Narodzenie**	**bo**-zhe na-ro-**dze**-nye

NUMBERS

CARDINAL

0	**zero**	ze-ro
1	**jeden**	ye-den
2	**dwa**	dva
3	**trzy**	tshi
4	**cztery**	chte-ri
5	**pięć**	pye^{n}ch
6	**sześć**	sheshch
7	**siedem**	shye-dem
8	**osiem**	o-shyem
9	**dziewięć**	dgye-vye^{n}ch
10	**dziesięć**	dgye-shye^{n}ch
11	**jedenaście**	ye-de-nash-chye

12	**dwanaście**	dva-**nash**-chye
13	**trzynaście**	tshi-**nash**-chye
14	**czternaście**	chter-**nash**-chye
15	**piętnaście**	pye^{n}t-**nash**-chye
16	**szesnaście**	shes-**nash**-chye
17	**siedemnaście**	shye-dem-**nash**-chye
18	**osiemnaście**	o-shyem-**nash**-chye
19	**dziewiętnaście**	dgye-vye^{n}t-**nash**-chye
20	**dwadzieścia**	dva-**dgyesh**-chya
21	**dwadzieścia jeden**	dva-**dgyesh**-chya **ye**-den
22	**dwadzieścia dwa**	dva-**dgyesh**-chya **dva**
30	**trzydzieści**	tshi-**dgyesh**-chee
31	**trzydzieści jeden**	tshi-**dgyesh**-chee **ye**-den
40	**czterdzieści**	chter-**dgyesh**-chee
50	**pięćdziesiąt**	pye^{n}ch-**dgye**-shyo^{n}t
60	**sześćdziesiąt**	sheshch-**dgye**-shyo^{n}t
70	**siedemdziesiąt**	shye-dem-**dgye**-shyo^{n}t
80	**osiemdziesiąt**	o-shyem-**dgye**-shyo^{n}t
90	**dziewięćdziesiąt**	dgye-vye^{n}ch-**dgye**-shyo^{n}t
100	**sto**	sto
101	**sto jeden**	**sto ye**-den
200	**dwieście**	**dvyesh**-chye
1,000	**tysiąc**	ti-**shyo**^{n}ts
2,000	**dwa tysiące**	**dva** ti-**shyo**^{n}-tse
1,000,000	**milion**	**mee**-lyon

ORDINAL

1st	**pierwszy**	pyerv-shi
2nd	**drugi**	droo-gee
3rd	**trzeci**	tshe-chee
4th	**czwarty**	chvar-ti
5th	**piąty**	pyo^{n}-ti
6th	**szósty**	shoos-ti
7th	**siódmy**	shyood-mi
8th	**ósmy**	oos-mi
9th	**dziewiąty**	dgye-vyo^{n}-ti
10th	**dziesiąty**	dgye-shyo^{n}-ti
11th	**jedenasty**	ye-de-nas-ti
12th	**dwunasty**	dvoo-nas-ti
13th	**trzynasty**	tshi-nas-ti
14th	**czternasty**	chter-nas-ti
15th	**piętnasty**	pye^{n}t-nas-ti
16th	**szesnasty**	shes-nas-ti
17th	**siedemnasty**	shye-dem-nas-ti
18th	**osiemnasty**	o-shyem-nas-ti
19th	**dziewiętnasty**	dgye-vye^{n}t-nas-ti
20th	**dwudziesty**	dvoo-dgyes-ti
21st	**dwudziesty pierwszy**	dvoo-dgyes-ti pyerv-shi
30th	**trzydziesty**	tshi-dgyes-ti

100th	**setny**	set-ni
half	**pół/połowa**	poow/po-wo-va
quarter	**ćwierć/ćwiartka**	chvyerch/chvyart-ka
three quarters	**trzy czwarte**	tshi chvar-te
a third	**jedna trzecia**	yed-na tshe-chya
two thirds	**dwie trzecie**	dvye tshe-chye

WEIGHTS & MEASURES

DISTANCE

kilometres – miles

km	*miles or km*	miles	km	*miles or km*	miles
1.6	*1*	0.6	14.5	*9*	5.6
3.2	*2*	1.2	16.1	*10*	6.2
4.8	*3*	1.9	32.2	*20*	12.4
6.4	*4*	2.5	40.2	*25*	15.3
8	*5*	3.1	80.5	*50*	31.1
9.7	*6*	3.7	160.9	*100*	62.1
11.3	*7*	4.4	804.7	*500*	310.7
12.9	*8*	5.0			

A rough way to convert from miles to km: divide by 5 and multiply by 8; from km to miles, divide by 8 and multiply by 5.

LENGTH AND HEIGHT

centimetres – inches

cm	*ins or cm*	ins	cm	*ins or cm*	ins
2.5	*1*	0.4	17.8	*7*	2.8
5.1	*2*	0.8	20	*8*	3.2
7.6	*3*	1.2	22.9	*9*	3.5
10.2	*4*	1.6	25.4	*10*	3.9
12.7	*5*	2.0	50.8	*20*	7.9
15.2	*6*	2.4	127	*50*	19.7

A rough way to convert from inches to cm: divide by 2 and multiply by 5; from cm to inches, divide by 5 and multiply by 2.

metres – feet

m	*ft or m*	ft	m	*ft or m*	ft
0.3	*1*	3.3	2.4	*8*	26.3
0.6	*2*	6.6	2.7	*9*	29.5
0.9	*3*	9.8	3	*10*	32.8
1.2	*4*	13.1	6.1	*20*	65.6
1.5	*5*	16.4	15.2	*50*	164
1.8	*6*	19.7	30.5	*100*	328.1
2.1	*7*	23			

A rough way to convert from ft to m: divide by 10 and multiply by 3; from m to ft, divide by 3 and multiply by 10.

metres – yards

m	*yds or m*	yds	m	*yds or m*	yds
0.9	*1*	1.1	7.3	*8*	8.8
1.8	*2*	2.2	8.2	*9*	9.8
2.7	*3*	3.3	9.1	*10*	10.9
3.7	*4*	4.4	18.3	*20*	21.9
4.6	*5*	5.5	45.7	*50*	54.7
5.5	*6*	6.6	91.4	*100*	109.4
6.4	*7*	7.7	457.2	*500*	546.8

A rough way to convert from yds to m: subtract 10 per cent from the number of yds; from m to yds, add 10 per cent to the number of metres.

LIQUID MEASURES

litres – gallons

litres	*galls or litres*	galls	litres	*galls or litres*	galls
4.6	*1*	0.2	36.4	*8*	1.8
9.1	*2*	0.4	40.9	*9*	2.0
13.6	*3*	0.7	45.5	*10*	2.2
18.2	*4*	0.9	90.9	*20*	4.4
22.7	*5*	1.1	136.4	*30*	6.6
27.3	*6*	1.3	181.8	*40*	8.8
31.8	*7*	1.5	227.3	*50*	11

1 pint = 0.6 litre   1 litre = 1.8 pint

A rough way to convert from galls to litres: divide by 2 and multiply by 9; from litres to galls, divide by 9 and multiply by 2.

WEIGHT

kilogrammes – pounds

kg	*lb or kg*	lb	kg	*lb or kg*	lb
0.5	*1*	2.2	3.2	*7*	15.4
0.9	*2*	4.4	3.6	*8*	17.6
1.4	*3*	6.6	4.1	*9*	19.8
1.8	*4*	8.8	4.5	*10*	22.1
2.3	*5*	11.0	9.1	*20*	44.1
2.7	*6*	13.2	22.7	*50*	110.2

A rough way to convert from lb to kg: divide by 11 and multiply by 5; from kg to lb, divide by 5 and multiply by 11.

grammes – ounces

grammes	oz	oz	grammes
100	3.5	2	57.1
250	8.8	4	114.3
500	17.6	8	228.6
1,000(1 kg)	35	16(1 lb)	457.2

TEMPERATURE

centigrade (°C)	fahrenheit (°F)
°C	°F
–10	14
–5	23
0	32
5	41
10	50
15	59
20	68
25	77
30	86
35	95
37	98.4
40	104

To convert from °F to °C: deduct 32, divide by 9 and multiply by 5; to convert °C to °F: divide by 5, multiply by 9 and add 32.

BASIC GRAMMAR

VERBS

The Polish verb has only three tenses: present, past and future. The two main aspects of Polish verbs are imperfective (*impf.*) and perfective (*pf.*). The former denotes a continued, incomplete action, the latter a completed action. In the vocabulary both aspects are given for some important verbs.

Polish verbs are divided into four conjugations and the basis of this division is the form of the first and third person singular; these are indicated in the vocabulary. The following are the most usual conjugation patterns:

Present tense

pisać – to write	widzieć – to see	czytać – to read	wiedzieć – to know
ja piszę I write	widzę I see	czytam I read	wiem I know
ty piszesz	widzisz	czytasz	wiesz
on/ona pisze	widzi	czyta	wie
my piszemy	widzimy	czytamy	wiemy

wy piszecie	widzicie	czytacie	wiecie
oni/one piszą	widzą	czytają	wiedzą

Two commonly used verbs, **iść** – to go (on foot) and **jechać** – to go (by any means of transport) fall into the same category as the verb pisać – to write.

iść – to go	jechać – to go
idę – I go	jadę – I go
idziesz	jedziesz
idzie	jedzie
idziemy	jedziemy
idziecie	jedziecie
idą	jadą

As the verb changes its form in the process of conjugation, the personal pronoun is usually left out.

Past tense

This is formed by adding to the past participle the past tense endings of the verb **być** – to be, which vary according to number and gender.

The endings are as follows:

Singular

m	*f*	*n*
-łem, -łeś, -ł	-łam, -łaś, -ła	-ło

Plural

m	*f*	*n*
-liśmy, -liście, -li,	-łyśmy, -łyście, -ły	-ły

The past participle is formed by replacing the infinitive ending **-ć** with the suffix **-ł** for masculine gender, **-ła** for feminine, **-ło** for neuter.

robić – to do; robił (*m*), robiła (*f*), robiło (*n*)

The plural is formed by adding the suffix **-li** for masculine personal subjects and **-ły** for all other subjects.

pisać – to write; pisali (*m personal*), pisały (*others*)

The past tense of the verb **pić** – to drink, illustrates the pattern of conjugation for the three genders in the singular and plural.

	m	*f*	*n*
I drank, etc.	ja piłem	ja piłam	—
	ty piłeś	ty piłaś	—
	on pił	ona piła	ono piło
	my piliśmy	my piłyśmy	—
	wy piliście	wy piłyście	—
	oni pili	one piły	one piły

Future tense

The simple future tense is formed by adding the perfective aspect to the present tense of the verb, i.e. czytać, *impf.*, **przeczytać**, *pf.* – to read; ja czytam, *present tense* – I am reading; ja przeczytam, *future tense* – I shall read.

Singular		***Plural***
I shall read, etc.	ja przeczytam	my przeczytamy
	ty przeczytasz	wy przeczytacie
	on/ona przeczyta	oni/one przeczytają

REFLEXIVE VERBS

The reflexive verbs consist of the verb followed immediately by the reflexive pronoun **się**. They are conjugated according to the normal patterns with **się** remaining unchanged throughout.

myć się – to wash (oneself): ja myję się – I wash
ty myjesz się – you wash
on myje się – he washes, etc.

All the reflexive verbs are indicated in the vocabulary.

Polish has only one auxiliary verb **być** – to be. Its conjugation is irregular.

być – to be

Present tense

Positive		*Negative*	
I am	ja jestem	I am not	ja nie jestem
you are	ty jesteś	you are not	ty nie jesteś
he is	on jest	he is not	on nie jest
she is	ona jest	she is not	ona nie jest
it is	ono jest	it is not	ono nie jest
we are	my jesteśmy	we are not	my nie jesteśmy
you are	wy jesteście	you are not	wy nie jesteście
they are	oni są ***m***	they are not	oni nie są ***m***
	one są ***f&n***		one nie są ***f&n***

Past tense

	m	*f*	*n*
I was, have been, etc	byłem	byłam	—
	byłeś	byłaś	—
	był	była	było
	byliśmy	byłyśmy	—
	byliście	byłyście	—
	byli	były	były

Future tense

I shall be, etc.	ja będę
	ty będziesz
	on będzie
	ona będzie
	ono będzie
	my będziemy
	wy będziecie
	oni będą *m*
	one będą *f&n*

NEGATIVES

To form negative sentences **nie** is placed before the verb, even if there are other negative words in the sentence.

ona **nie** wiedziała	she didn't know
ja **nie** mam **nic** do oclenta	I have nothing to declare

INTERROGATIVES

A question, the answer to which may be only yes or no, begins with the interrogative **czy**. The position of the subject and the verb may remain the same as in the affirmative sentence, or they may be reversed. When the inverted order is used, **czy** is frequently omitted, particularly in colloquial Polish.

czy pan ma zapałki? ma pan zapałki?	have you a match?

When the sentence begins with an interrogative pronoun the normal affirmative sentence order is used.

gdzie pani była wczoraj?	where were you yesterday?
co pan zamówił?	what did you order?

YOU

The second person singular and plural (**ty** and **wy**) are only used when addressing relatives, friends and children. The polite form of address is **pan** (sir, Mr) for men and **pani** (madam, Mrs) for women with the third person of the verb. When addressing a group of people, a collective form **państwo** is used with the third person plural of the verb.

czy pan jest zmęczony?	are you tired?
gdzie pani była?	where have you been?
czy państwo mają pokój na jedną noc?	have you a room for the night?

The polite forms are used throughout this book and where necessary the alternative feminine endings of the verbs are given in brackets.

NOUNS[1]

There are three genders in Polish: masculine, feminine and neuter. The gender of a noun is usually indicated by its ending.

Most masculine nouns end in a consonant, e.g. **stół** – table, **talerz** – plate; but there are a few that end in **-a,** e.g. **mężczyzna** – man, **artysta** – artist.

Most feminine nouns end in **-a,** or **-i,** e.g. **herbata** – tea, **pani** – lady; but a few end in a consonant, e.g. **noc** – night, **wieś** – village.

Neuter nouns end in **-o** or **-e,** e.g. **lato** – summer, **pole** – field.

Declension of nouns

Masculine nouns ending in a consonant

	Singular	
nom.	pan – gentleman, Mr	dom – house
gen.	pana	domu
dat.	panu	domowi
acc.	pana	dom
instr.	panem	domem
loc.	panu	domu
	Plural	
nom.	panowie	domy
gen.	panów	domów
dat.	panom	domom
acc.	panów	domy
instr.	panami	domami
loc.	panach	domach

1. The definite and indefinite articles (the, a) do not exist in Polish, but the sense is usually quite clear from the context.

Note that the accusative is the same as the nominative if the noun is inanimate, but as the genitive if the noun is animate.

Most masculine nouns form the plural by adding **-i**, **-e** or **-y**; the ending **-owie** is found with nouns denoting status, profession or family relationship.

Masculine nouns ending in **-a** are declined in the singular as feminine nouns ending in **-a** and in the plural as the masculine nouns ending in a consonant.

Feminine nouns

	Singular		
	-a	-i	*Consonant*
nom.	woda – water	pani – lady, madam	noc – night
gen.	wody	pani	nocy
dat.	wodzie	pani	nocy
acc.	wodę	panią	nocą
instr.	wodą	panią	nocą
loc.	wodzie	pani	nocy

	Plural		
	-a	-i	*Consonant*
nom.	wody	panie	noce
gen.	wód	pań	nocy
dat.	wodom	paniom	nocom
acc.	wody	panie	noce
instr.	wodami	paniami	nocami
loc.	wodach	paniach	nocach

Neuter nouns

	Singular	*Plural*
nom.	lato – summer	lata
gen.	lata	lat
dat.	latu	latom
acc.	lato	lata
instr.	latem	latami
loc.	lecie	latach

PERSONAL PRONOUNS

	Singular				
nom.	ja – I	ty – you	on – he	ona – she	ono – it
gen.	mnie	ciebie	jego, niego	jej, niej	niego, go
dat.	mnie, mi	tobie, ci	jemu, mu	jej, niej	jemu, mu
acc.	mnie	ciebie, cię	jego, go	ja, nią	je
instr.	mną	tobą	nim	nią	nim
loc.	mnie	tobie	nim	niej	nim

	Plural				
nom.	my – we	wy – you	oni – they *m*	one – they *f*	one – they *n*
gen.	nas	was	ich, nich	ich, nich	ich, nich
dat.	nam	wam	im, nim	im, nim	im, nim

acc.	nas	was	ich, nich	je, nie	je, nie
instr.	nami	wami	nimi	nimi	nimi
loc.	nas	was	nich	nich	nich

In both the singular and the plural more than one form occurs in the genitive, dative and accusative. The forms beginning with **n-** are used after preposi-tions, and the remaining forms are used in all other cases. The short forms, **ci, cię, go, mi, mu** do not have independent stress.

REFLEXIVE PRONOUNS

gen.	siebie, się
dat.	sobie
acc.	siebie, się
instr.	sobą
loc.	sobie

Reflexive pronouns can be applied to any of the three genders in the singular or the plural.

e.g. ja widzę siebie w lustrze – I can see myself in the mirror
ona nalała sobie herbaty – she poured herself some tea
oni są zawsze z siebie zadowoleni – they are always pleased with themselves

ADJECTIVES

Adjectives are placed before nouns and agree in gender, case and number with the noun to which they refer. The singular endings are as follows: **-y** for masculine, **-a** for feminine, **-e** for neuter.

In the plural there are only two forms, masculine personal for men only and general for women, children, animals and things of all three genders.

pełny – full

Singular

	m	*f*	*n*
nom.	pełny	pełna	pełne
gen.	pełnego	pełnej	pełnego
dat.	pełnemu	pełnej	pełnemu
acc.	pełnego, pełny	pełna	pełne
instr.	pełnym	pełną	pełnym
loc.	pełnym	pełnej	pełnym

The masculine and neuter declensions are identical except for the nominative and the accusative where the respective gender endings are shown. In the case of masculine nouns there are two alternative endings in the accusative, the first form is used for the animate subject and the second one for the inanimate subject.

Plural – masculine personal		*Plural – all other*
nom.	pełni	pełne
gen.	pełnych	pełnych
dat.	pełnym	pełnym
acc.	pełnych	pełne
instr.	pełnymi	pełnymi
loc.	pełnych	pełnych

POSSESSIVE PRONOUNS AND ADJECTIVES

Possessive pronouns and adjectives have the same form in Polish. The adjectives agree in gender and number with the thing possessed.

m	*f*	*n*	
mój	moja	moje	my, mine
twój	twoja	twoje	your, yours
jego	jego	jego	his
jej	jej	jej	her, hers
nasz	nasza	nasze	our, ours
wasz	wasza	wasze	your, yours
ich	ich	ich	their, theirs

The possessive adjectives decline as follows:

my, mine

Singular

	m	*f*	*n*
nom.	mój	moja	moje
gen.	mojego	mojej	mojego
dat.	mojemu	mojej	mojemu
acc.	mojego, mój	moją	moje
instr.	moim	moją	moim
loc.	moim	mojej	moim

Plural – masculine personal		*Plural – all other*
nom.	moi	moje
gen.	moich	moich
dat.	moim	moim
acc.	moich	moje
instr.	moimi	moimi
loc.	moich	moich

In Polish there is a specific personal adjective. It has roughly the same meaning as 'my, your, etc., own' and is used when the thing possessed belongs to the subject of the sentence.

e.g. ona bierze swoją książkę – she is taking her book
on zostawił swój adres – he left his address
oni zgubili swoje bilety – they lost their tickets

In Polish possessive adjectives are not used as frequently as in English and are often omitted.

e.g. czuję ból w ramieniu – I feel pain in my arm (*my* is omitted)

DEMONSTRATIVE PRONOUNS AND ADJECTIVES

Singular	*Plural*
ten, ta, to – this	ci, te – these
tamten, tamta, tamto – that	tamci, tamte – those
taki, taka, takie – such	tacy, takie – such

INDEFINITE PRONOUNS AND ADJECTIVES

niektóry, niektóra, niektóre – some

każdy, każda, każde – every

inny, inna, inne – other

wielu, wiele, wiele – many

żaden, żadna, żadne – none

INTERROGATIVE AND RELATIVE PRONOUNS

który, która, które – which?

kto? – who?

co? – what?

VOCABULARY

Various groups of specialized words are given elsewhere in this book and these words are not usually repeated in this vocabulary.

Throughout the vocabulary first and third person singular of all verbs are given as well as the infinitive.

A

abbey	**opactwo**	o-pats-tvo
able (to be)	**móc, potrafić (mogę, może, potrafię, -i)**	moots, po-tra-feech
about	**o (+*loc.*)**	o
above	**nad (+*instr.*)**	nad
abroad	**za granicą**	za gra-nee-tso^n
accept (to)	**przyjąć (przyjmuję, -e)**	pshi-yo^{n}ch
accident	**wypadek**	vi-pa-dek
accommodation	**pomieszczenie**	po-myesh-che-nye
account	**rachunek/konto**	ra-hoo-nek/kon-to
ache (to)	**boleć (boli)**	bo-lech
acquaintance	**znajomy**	zna-yo-mi
across	**przez (+*acc.*)**	pshez
act (to)	**zachowywać się *impf.*, zachować się *pf.* (zachowuję się, -e się)**	za-ho-vi-vach shye^n za-ho-vach shye^n
add (to)	**dodawać *impf.*, dodać *pf.* (dodaję, -e)**	do-da-vach, do-dach
address	**adres**	ad-res
admire (to)	**podziwiać (podziwiam, podziwia)**	po-dgee-vyach
admission	**wstęp**	fste^{n}p
adventure	**przygoda**	pshi-go-da
advertisement	**ogłoszenie**	o-gwo-she-nye

advice	**rada**	ra-da
aeroplane	**samolot**	sa-mo-lot
afford (to)	**pozwolić sobie na ...**	poz-vo-leech so-bye na
afraid (to be)	**bać się (+*gen.*) (boję się, -i)**	bach shye^{n}
after	**po (+*loc.*)**	po
afternoon	**popołudnie**	po-po-wood-nye
again	**znowu**	zno-voo
against	**przeciw, wbrew (+*dat.*)**	pshe-cheev, vbrev
age	**wiek**	vyek
ago	**...temu**	te-moo
agree (to)	**zgadzać się *impf.* zgodzić się *pf.* (zgadzam się, -a)**	zga-dzach shye^{n} zgo-dgeech shye^{n}
ahead	**z przodu**	spsho-doo
air	**powietrze**	po-vye-tshe
air-conditioning	**klimatyzacja**	klee-ma-ti-za-tsya
alarm clock	**budzik**	boo-dgeek
alcoholic (drink)	**alkoholowy (napój)**	al-ko-ho-lo-vi (na-pooy)
alike	**podobnie**	po-dob-nye
alive	**żywy**	zhi-vi
all	**wszystko *n*, wszystkie *f*, wszyscy *f&m, pl.***	fshist-ko
allow (to)	**pozwalać *impf.*, pozwolić *pf.* (pozwalam, -a)**	poz-va-lach, poz-vo-leech
all right	**w porządku**	fpo-zho^{n}d-koo

almost	prawie	pra-vye
alone	sam *m*, sama *f*, samo *n*	sam
along	wzdłuż	vzdwoozh
already	już	yoozh
alter (to)	zmieniać, przerabiać *impf.*, zmienić, przerobić *pf.* (zmieniam, -a, przerabiam, -a)	zmye-nyach, pshe-ra-byach
alternative *adj.*	alternatywny	al-ter-na-tiv-ni
noun	alternatywa	al-ter-na-ti-va
although	chociaż	ho-chyazh
always	zawsze	zaf-sze
ambulance	karetka pogotowia ratunkowego	ka-ret-ka po-go-to-vya ra-toon-ko-ve-go
America	Ameryka	a-me-ri-ka
American *noun*	Amerykanin *m*, Amerykanka *f*	a-me-ri-ka-nin a-me-ri-kan-ka
adj.	amerykański	a-me-ri-kan-skee
among	między, wśród	mye^{n}-dzi, fshrood
amuse (to)	zabawiać, rozweselać *impf.* (zabawiam, -a), zabawić, rozweselić *pf.*	za-ba-vyach, roz-ve-se-lach
amusement park	wesołe miasteczko	ve-so-we myas-tech-ko
amusing	zabawny	za-bav-ni
ancient	starożytny	sta-ro-zhit-ni
and	i	ee
angry	zły	zwi

animal	**zwierzę**	zvye-zhe^{n}
anniversary	**rocznica**	roch-nee-tsa
annoy (to)	**dokuczać** *impf.*, **dokuczyć** *pf.* **(dokuczam, -a)**	do-koo-chach, do-koo-chich
another	**inny**	een-ni
answer	**odpowiedź**	ot-po-vyedg
answer (to)	**odpowiadać** *impf.*, **odpowiedzieć** *pf.* **(odpowiadam, -a)**	ot-po-vya-dach, ot-po-vye-dgyech
antique	**antyk**	an-tik
any	**jakikolwiek**	ya-kee-kol-vyek
anyone	**ktokolwiek**	kto-kol-vyek
anything	**cokolwiek**	tso-kol-vyek
anyway	**w każdym razie**	fkazh-dim ra-zhye
anywhere	**gdziekolwiek**	gdgye-kol-vyek
apartment	**apartament**	a-par-ta-ment
apologize (to)	**przepraszać** *impf.*, **przeprosić** *pf.* **(przepraszam, -a)**	pshe-pra-shach, pshe-pro-sheech
appetite	**apetyt**	a-pe-tit
appointment	**umówiony termin**	oo-moo-vyo-ni ter-meen
architect	**architekt**	ar-hee-tekt
architecture	**architektura**	ar-hee-tek-too-ra
area	**obszar, teren**	ob-shar, te-ren
area code	**numer kierunkowy**	noo-mer kye-roon-ko-vi
arm	**ramię**	ra-mye^{n}

armchair	**fotel**	fo-tel
army	**armia, wojsko**	ar-mya, voy-sko
around	**naokoło, około**	na-o-ko-wo, o-ko-wo
arrange (to)	**załatwiać** *impf.*, **załatwić** *pf.* **(załatwiam, -a)**	za-wat-fyach, za-wat-feech
arrival	**przybycie, przyjazd**	pshi-bi-che, pshi-yazd
arrive (to)	**przybywać, przyjeżdżać** *impf.* **(przyjeżdżam, -a), przybyć, przyjechać** *pf.*	pshi-bi-vach, pshi-yezh-jach, pshi-bich, pshi-ye-hach
art	**sztuka**	shtoo-ka
art gallery	**galeria sztuki**	ga-le-rya shtoo-kee
artist	**artysta** *m*, **artystka** *f*	ar-tis-ta, ar-tist-ka
as *conj.*	**skoro, kiedy, jak**	sko-ro, kye-di, yak
adv.	**równie, jak, jako**	roov-nye, yak, ya-ko
as much as	**tyle ile**	ti-le ee-le
as soon as	**jak tylko**	yak-til-ko
as well	**równie dobrze**	roov-nye dob-zhe
ashtray	**popielniczka**	po-pyel-neech-ka
ask (to)	**pytać się** *impf.*, **zapytać się** *pf.* **(pytam się, -a)**	pi-tach shye^{n} za-pi-tach shye^{n}
asleep	**we śnie**	ve-shnye
at	**w (+*loc.*), przy (+*loc.*), u (+*gen.*)**	v, pzhi, oo
at last	**nareszcie**	na-resh-chye

at once	**natychmiast**	na-tih-myast
atmosphere	**atmosfera**	at-mos-fe-ra
attention	**uwaga**	oo-va-ga
attractive	**atrakcyjny**	a-trak-tsiy-ni
auction	**licytacja**	lee-tsi-tats-ya
audience	**publiczność**	poob-leech-noshch
aunt	**ciocia**	chyo-chya
Australia	**Australia**	a-oos-tra-lya
Australian *adj.*	**australijski (-a)**	a-oo-stra-leey-skee
noun	**Australijczyk** *m*, **Australijka** *f*	a-oo-stra-leey-chik, a-oo-stra-leey-ka
author	**autor**	a-oo-tor
autumn	**jesień**	ye-shyen
available	**do nabycia, do dyspozycji**	do na-bi-cha, do di-spo-zits-yee
avalanche	**lawina**	la-vee-na
avenue	**aleja**	a-le-ya
average	**przeciętny, średni**	pshe-chye^{n}t-ni, shred-nee
avoid (to)	**unikać**	oo-nee-kach
awake	**przebudzony**	pshe-boo-dzo-ni
away	**z dala, w oddaleniu**	z da-la, v od-da-le-nee-oo
awful	**okropny, straszny**	o-krop-ni, strash-ni

B

baby	**niemowlę, dziecko**	nye-mov-le^{n}, dgyets-ko
baby food	**jedzenie dla dzieci**	ye-dze-nye dla dgye-chee

baby sitter	**opiekunka do dziecka**	o-pye-koon-ka do dgyets-ka
bachelor	**kawaler**	ka-va-ler
back *adv.*	**do tyłu, z powrotem**	do ti-woo, s pov-ro-tem
bad *food*	**zły, bolesny** **zepsuty, nieświeży**	zwi, bo-les-ni ze-psoo-ti, nye-shvye-zhi
bag	**torba**	tor-ba
baggage	**bagaż**	ba-gazh
baggage cart	**wózek bagażowy**	voo-zek ba-ga-zho-vi
baggage check		
bait	**przynęta**	pshi-ne^n-ta
balcony	**balkon**	bal-kon
ball *sport*	**piłka**	peew-ka
ballet	**balet**	ba-let
balloon	**balon**	ba-lon
band *music*	**orkiestra**	or-kyes-tra
bank	**bank**	bank
bank account	**konto bankowe**	kon-to ban-ko-ve
bare	**nagi, ogołocony**	na-gee, o-go-wo-tso-ni
barn	**stodoła**	sto-do-wa
basket	**koszyk**	ko-shik
bath	**wanna**	van-na
bathe (to)	**kąpać się** *impf.*, **wy-** *pf.* **(kąpię się, -e)**	ko^n-pach shye^n
bathing cap	**czepek kąpielowy**	che-pek ko^n-pye-lo-vi
bathing costume	**kostium kąpielowy**	kos-tyoom ko^n-pye-lo-vi
bathing trunks	**spodenki kąpielowe**	spo-den-kee ko^n-pye-lo-ve

bathroom	łazienka	wa-zhyen-ka
battery	bateria	ba-ter-ya
bay	zatoka	za-to-ka
be (to)	być (jestem, jest)	bich
beach	plaża	pla-zha
beard	broda	bro-da
beautiful	piękny	pye^{n}-kni
because	ponieważ	po-nye-vazh
become (to)	stawać się *impf.*, stać się *pf.* (staję, -e)	sta-vach shye^{n} stach shye^{n}
bed	łóżko	woozh-ko
bedroom	sypialnia	si-pyal-nya
before (in time)	przed	pshed
begin (to)	zaczynać	za-chi-nach
beginning	początek	po-cho^{n}-tek
behind	za (+*instr.*), z tyłu (+*gen.*)	za, sti-woo
believe (to)	wierzyć *impf.*, uwierzyć *pf.* (wierzę, -y)	vye-zhich, oo-vye-zhich
bell	dzwon, dzwonek	dzvon, dzvo-nek
belong (to)	należeć (należę, -y)	na-le-zhech
below	pod (+*instr.*)	pod
belt	pasek	pa-sek
bench	ławka	wav-ka
bend	zakręt	za-kre^{n}t
beneath	poniżej	po-nee-zhey
berth	miejsce do spania	myey-stse do spa-nya

beside	**obok, przy**	o-bok, pshi
best	**najlepszy**	nay-lep-shi
bet	**zakład**	za-kwad
better	**lepszy**	lep-shi
between	**między** (+*instr.* or *acc.*)	mye^n-dsi
bicycle	**rower**	ro-ver
big	**duży**	doo-zhi
bill	**rachunek**	ra-hoo-nek
binoculars	**lornetka**	lor-net-ka
bird	**ptak**	ptak
birthday	**urodziny**	oo-ro-dgee-ni
bit	**kawałek, odrobina**	ka-va-wek, o-dro-bee-na
bite (to)	**gryźć** *impf.*, **ugryźć** *pf.* **(gryzę, -ie)**	grizhch, oo-grizhch
bitter	**gorzki**	gozh-ki
blanket	**koc**	kots
bleed (to)	**krwawić (krwawię, -i)**	krva-veech
blind	**ślepy, niewidomy**	shle-pi, nye-vee-do-mi
blister	**pęcherz**	pe^n-hezh
blond	**blond, blondyn**	blond, blon-din
blood	**krew**	krev
blouse	**bluzka**	blooz-ka
blow	**cios, uderzenie**	chyos, oo-de-zhe-nye
blow (to)	**dmuchać** *impf.* **(dmucham, -a), dmuchnąć** *pf.*	dmoo-hach, dmooh-no^{n}ch

on board	**na pokładzie**	po-kwa-dgye
boarding house	**pensjonat**	pen-syo-nat
boat	**łódź**	woodg
body	**ciało**	chya-wo
bolt	**zasuwa**	zo-soo-va
bone	**kość**	koshch
bonfire	**ognisko**	o-gnees-ko
book	**książka**	kshyo^{n}zh-ka
book (to)	**rezerwować** *impf.*, **za-** *pf.* **(rezerwuję, -e)**	re-zer-vo-vach
boot	**but, bagażnik**	boot, ba-gazh-neek
border	**granica, brzeg, skraj**	gra-nee-tsa, bzheg, skray
bored	**znudzony**	znoo-dzo-ni
boring	**nudny**	nood-ni
borrow (to)	**pożyczać od** *impf.* **(+***gen.***), pożyczyć** *pf.* **(pożyczam, -a)**	po-zhi-chach, po-zhi-chich
both	**obaj** *m*, **obie** *f*, **oba** *n*	o-bay, o-bye, o-ba
bother (to) *annoy*	**przeszkadzać**	pshesh-ka-dzach
bottle	**butelka**	boo-tel-ka
bottle opener	**otwieracz do kapsli**	o-tfye-rach do kap-slee
bottom	**dno**	dno
bowl	**misa, miseczka**	mee-sa, mee-sech-ka
bow tie	**muszka**	moosh-ka
box *container*	**pudełko**	poo-dew-ko
theatre	**loża**	lo-zha

box office	**kasa biletowa**	ka-sa bi-le-to-wa
boy	**chłopiec**	hwo-pyets
bracelet	**bransoletka**	bran-so-let-ka
braces	**szelki**	shel-kee
brain	**mózg**	moozg
branch *veg. & office*	**gałąź, filia**	ga-wo^{n}zh, fee-lya
brand	**gatunek, znak firmowy**	ga-too-nek, znak feer-mo-vi
brassière	**biustonosz**	byoo-sto-nosh
break (to)	**łamać, rozbijać** *impf.*, **z-, rozbić** *pf.* **(łamię, -e, rozbijam, -a)**	wa-mach, roz-bee-yach, roz-beech
breakfast	**śniadanie**	shnya-da-nye
breathe (to)	**oddychać (oddycham, -a)**	od-di-hach
brick	**cegła**	tseg-wa
bridge	**most**	most
briefs	**kalesony**	ka-le-so-ni
bright	**jasny**	yas-ni
bring (to)	**przynosić** *impf.*, **przynieść** *pf.* **(przynoszę, -si)**	pshi-no-sheech, pshi-nyeshch
British	**brytyjski (-a)**	bri-tiy-skee
broken	**złamany, rozbity**	zwa-ma-ni, roz-bee-ti
brooch	**broszka**	brosh-ka
brother	**brat**	brat
bruise (to)	**posiniaczyć**	po-shee-nya-chich

brush	**szczotka**	shchot-ka
brush (to)	**szczotkować** *impf.*, **wy-** *pf.* **(szczotkuję, -e)**	shchot-ko-vach, vi-shchot-ko-vach
bucket	**wiaderko**	vya-der-ko
buckle	**sprzączka, klamra**	spsho^{n}ch-ka, klam-ra
build (to)	**budować** *impf.*, **z-** *pf.* **(buduję, -e)**	boo-do-vach
building	**budynek**	boo-di-nek
bunch *flowers*	**bukiet**	boo-kyet
grapes	**kiść**	kishch
keys	**pęk**	pe^{n}k
buoy	**boja**	bo-ya
burn (to)	**palić** *impf.*, **spalić** *pf.* **(palę, -i) parzyć** *impf.*, **s-** *pf.* **(parzę, -y)**	pa-leech, spa-leech pa-zhich
burst (to)	**rozrywać, wybuchać** *impf.*, **rozerwać, wybuchnąć** *pf.* **(rozrywam, -a)**	roz-ri-vach, vi-boo-hach ro-zer-vach, vi-booh-no^{n}ch
bus	**autobus**	a-oo-to-boos
bus stop	**przystanek autobusowy**	pshi-sta-nek a-oo-to-boo-soo-vi
business	**sprawa, interes**	spra-va, in-te-res
busy	**zajęty**	za-ye^{n}-ti
but	**ale**	a-le
butterfly	**motyl**	mo-til
button	**guzik**	goo-zheek

buy (to)	**kupować** *impf.*, **kupić** *pf.* **(kupuję -e)**	koo-po-vach, koo-peech
by	**przy (+***instr.***), przez (+***acc.***)**	pshi, pshez

C

cabin	**kabina, kajuta**	ka-bee-na, ka-yoo-ta
calculator	**kalkulator**	kal-koo-la-tor
calendar	**kalendarz**	ka-len-dazh
call *visit*	**wizyta, odwiedziny**	vee-zi-ta, od-vye-dgee-ni
call (to) *summon*	**wołać** *impf.*, **za-** *pf.* **(wołam, -a)**	vo-wach
telephone	**telefonować** *impf.*, **za-** *pf.* **(telefonuję, -e)**	te-le-fo-no-vach
visit	**odwiedzać** *impf.*, **odwiedzić** *pf.* **(odwiedzam, -a)**	od-vye-dzach, od-vye-dgeech
calm	**spokojny, opanowany**	spo-koy-ni, o-pa-no-va-ni
camp (to)	**rozbijać obóz (rozbijam, -a)**	roz-bee-yach o-booz
camp site	**miejsce kampingowe**	myeys-tse kam-peen-go-ve
can *to be able*	**móc (mogę, może)**	moots
tin	**puszka**	poosh-ka
can opener	**otwieracz do puszek**	o-tvye-rach do poo-shek
Canada	**Kanada**	ka-na-da
Canadian *adj.*	**kanadyjski (-a)**	ka-na-diy-skee
noun	**Kanadyjczyk** *m*, **Kanadyjka** *f*	ka-na-diy-chik, ka-na-diy-ka

cancel (to)	unieważniać *impf.*, unieważnić *pf.* (unieważniam, -a)	oo-nye-vazh-nyach, oo-nye-vazh-neech
candle	świeca	shvye-tsa
canoe	kajak	ka-yak
cap	czapka	chap-ka
capable of	zdolny do	zdol-ni do
capital city	stolica	sto-lee-tsa
car	samochód, wóz	sa-mo-hood, vooz
car park	parking	par-king
carafe	karafka	ka-raf-ka
caravan	przyczepa kampingowa	pshi-che-pa kam-peen-go-va
card	karta	kar-ta
care	opieka, troska	o-pye-ka, tros-ka
careful	ostrożny	os-trozh-ni
careless	niedbały, nieostrożny	nyed-ba-wi, nye-o-strozh-ni
caretaker	dozorca	do-zor-tsa
carpet	dywan	di-van
carry (to)	nieść *impf.*, przy- *pf.* (niosę -e)	nyeshch, pshi-
cash	gotówka	go-toov-ka
cash (to)	spieniężać *impf.*, spieniężyć *pf.* (spieniężam, -a)	spye-nye^{n}-zhach, spye-nye^{n}-zhich
cashier	kasjer	kas-yer
casino	kasyno	ka-si-no

cassette	**kaseta**	ka-se-ta
cassette player	**magnetofon kasetowy**	ma-gne-to-fon ka-se-to-vi
castle	**zamek**	za-mek
cat	**kot**	kot
catalogue	**katalog**	ka-ta-log
catch (to)	**łapać,** *impf.*, **z-** *pf.* **(łapię, -e)**	wa-pach
cathedral	**katedra**	ka-ted-ra
Catholic	**Katolik**	ka-to-leek
cause	**powód, sprawa**	po-vood, spra-va
cave	**jaskinia, grota**	yas-kee-nya, gro-ta
cement	**cement**	tse-ment
central	**centralny, środkowy**	tsen-tral-ni, shrod-ko-vi
centre	**centrum**	tsen-troom
century	**wiek**	vyek
ceremony	**ceremonia**	tse-re-mo-nya
certain	**pewny**	pev-ni
certainly	**na pewno**	na pev-no
chair	**krzesło**	kshe-swo
chambermaid	**pokojowa**	po-ko-yo-va
(small) change	**drobne**	drob-ne
change (to)	**zmieniać, przesiadać, się** *impf.*, **zmienić, przesiąść się** *pf.* **(zmieniam, -a przesiadam się -a)**	zmye-nyach, pshe-shya-dach shye^{n}, zmye-neech pshe-shyo^{n}shch shye^{n}
chapel	**kaplica**	ka-plee-tsa

charge	**opłata**	o-pwa-ta
charge (to)	**liczyć, pobierać** *impf.*, **po-, pobrać** *pf.* **(liczę, -y, pobieram, -a)**	lee-chich, po-bye-rach, po-brach
cheap	**tani**	ta-nee
check (to)	**sprawdzać** *impf.*, **sprawdzić** *pf.*, **(sprawdzam, -a)**	sprav-dzach, sprav-dgeech
chef	**kucharz**	koo-hazh
cheque	**czek**	chek
chess	**szachy**	sha-hi
chess set	**komplet szachowy**	kom-plet sha-ho-vi
child	**dziecko**	dgyets-ko
chill (to)	**ochłodzić**	o-hwo-dgeech
china	**porcelana**	por-tse-la-na
choice	**wybór**	vi-boor
choose (to)	**wybierać** *impf.*, **wybrać** *pf.* **(wybieram, -a)**	vi-bye-rach, vi-brach
church	**kościół**	kosh-chyoow
cigarette case	**papierośnica**	pa-pye-rosh-nee-tsa
cinema	**kino**	kee-no
circle *theatre*	**balkon**	bal-kon
circus	**cyrk**	tsirk
city	**miasto**	mya-sto
class	**klasa**	kla-sa

clean	**czysty**	chi-sti
clean (to)	**czyścić** *impf.*, **wy-** *pf.* **(czyszczę, -ści)**	chi-shcheech, vi-
cleansing cream	**krem zmywający**	krem zmi-va-yo^{n}-tsi
clear *reason*	**jasny**	yas-ni
substance	**klarowny**	kla-rov-ni
clerk	**urzędnik**	oo-zhe^{n}d-neek
cliff	**urwisko**	oor-vees-ko
climb (to)	**wspinać się** *impf.*, **wspiąć się** *pf.* **(wspinam się, -a się)**	fspee-nach shye^{n} fspyo^{n}ch shye^{n}
cloakroom	**szatnia, garderoba**	shat-nya, gar-de-ro-ba
clock	**zegar**	ze-gar
close (to)	**zamykać** *impf.*, **zamknąć** *pf.* **(zamykam, -a)**	za-mi-kach, zam-kno^{n}ch
closed	**zamknięty**	zam-knye^{n}-ti
cloth	**materiał**	ma-ter-yaw
clothes	**ubranie**	oo-bra-nye
cloud	**chmura**	hmoo-ra
coach	**autokar**	a-oo-to-kar
coast	**wybrzeże**	vi-bzhe-zhe
coat	**płaszcz**	pwashch
coat hanger	**wieszak**	vye-shak
coin	**moneta**	mo-ne-ta
cold *adj.*	**zimny**	zheem-ni
collar	**kołnierz, kołnierzyk**	kow-nyezh, kow-nye-zhik

collect (to)	**zbierać** *impf.*, **zebrać** *pf.* (**zbieram, -a**)	zbye-rach, ze-brach
colour	**kolor**	ko-lor
comb	**grzebień**	gzhe-byen
come (to)	**przychodzić** *impf.*, **przyjść** *pf.* (**przychodzę, -i**)	pshi-ho-dgeech, pshiyshch
come in!	**proszę!**	pro-she^n
comfortable	**wygodny**	vi-god-ni
common	**powszechny, pospolity**	pov-sheh-ni, pos-po-lee-ti
compact disc	**płyta kompaktowa**	pwi-ta kom-pak-to-va
company	**towarzystwo**	to-va-zhist-vo
compartment *train*	**przedział**	pshe-dgyaw
compass	**kompas**	kom-pas
compensation	**kompensacja**	kom-pen-sats-ya
complain (to)	**składać zażalenie** *impf.*, **złożyć** *pf.* (**składam ..., -a**)	skwa-dach za-zha-le-nye, zwo-zhich
complaint	**skarga, zażalenie**	skar-ga, za-zha-le-nye
complete	**całkowity**	tsaw-ko-vee-ti
computer	**komputer**	kom-poo-ter
concert	**koncert**	kon-tsert
concert hall	**sala koncertowa**	sa-la kon-tser-to-va
concrete	**konkretny**	kon-kret-ni
condition	**warunek, stan**	va-roo-nek, stan
conductor *bus*	**konduktor**	kon-dook-tor
orchestra	**dyrygent**	di-ri-gent

congratulations	**gratulacje**	gra-too-la-tsye
connect (to)	**łączyć** *impf.*, **po-** *pf.* **(łączę, -y)**	wo^{n}chich, po-wo^{n}-chich
connection *train, etc.*	**połączenie**	po-wo^{n}-che-nye
consul	**konsul**	kon-sool
consulate	**konsulat**	kon-soo-lat
contact lens	**szkło kontaktowe**	shkwo kon-tak-to-ve
contain (to)	**zawierać (zawieram, -a)**	za-vye-rach
contraceptive	**środek antykoncepcyjny**	shro-dek anti-kon-tsep-tsiy-ni
contrast	**kontrast**	kont-rast
convenient	**dogodny**	do-god-ni
conversation	**rozmowa**	roz-mo-va
cook	**kucharz, kucharka**	koo-hazh, koo-har-ka
cook (to)	**gotować** *impf.*, **u-** *pf.* **(gotuję, -e)**	go-to-vach, oo-
cool	**chłodny**	hwod-ni
copper	**miedź**	myedg
copy *object*	**zeszyt**	ze-shit
duplicate	**kopia**	ko-pya
copy (to)	**kopiować** *impf.*, **s-** *pf.* **(kopiuję, -e)**	ko-pyo-vach
cork	**korek**	ko-rek
corkscrew	**korkociąg**	kor-ko-chyo^{n}g
corner	**róg**	roog
correct	**prawidłowy**	pra-veed-wo-vi
corridor	**korytarz**	ko-ri-tazh

cosmetics	**kosmetyki**	kos-me-ti-kee
cost	**koszt**	kosht
cost (to)	**kosztować (kosztuję, -e)**	kosh-to-vach
costume jewellery	**sztuczna biżuteria**	shtooch-na bee-zhoo-ter-ya
cot	**dziecinne łóżeczko**	dgye-cheen-ne woo-zhech-ko
cottage	**domek, chata**	do-mek, ha-ta
cotton	**bawełna**	ba-vew-na
cotton wool	**wata**	va-ta
couchette	**kuszetka**	koo-shet-ka
count (to)	**liczyć** *impf.*, **po-** *pf.* **(liczę, -y)**	lee-chich, po-
country *nation*	**kraj**	kray
country (side)	**wieś**	vyesh
couple	**para**	pa-ra
course *dish*	**danie**	da-nye
courtyard	**dziedziniec, podwórze**	dgye-dgee-nyets, pod-voo-zhe
cousin	**kuzyn** *m*, **kuzynka** *f*	koo-zin, koo-zin-ka
cover	**przykrycie, okładka**	pshi-kri-chye, o-kwad-ka
cover (to)	**przy-, na-krywać** *impf.*, **przy-, na-kryć** *pf.* **(przykrywam, -a)**	pshi-kri-vach, na-krich
cow	**krowa**	kro-va
crash *collision*	**zderzenie**	zde-zhe-nye
credit	**kredyt**	kre-dit
credit card	**karta kredytowa**	kar-ta kre-di-to-va

crew	**załoga**	za-wo-ga
cross	**krzyż**	kzhizh
cross (to)	**przechodzić przez (+***acc.***)** *impf.*, **przejść** *pf.* **(przechodzę, -i)**	pshe-ho-dgeech pshez, psheyshch
cross country skiing	**narciarstwo biegowe (śladowe)**	nar-chyar-stvo bye-go-ve (shla-do-ve)
crossroads	**skrzyżowanie**	skzhi-zho-va-nye
crowd	**tłum**	twoom
crowded	**zatłoczony**	za-two-cho-ni
cry (to) *shout*	**wołać** *impf.*, **za-** *pf.* **(wołam, -a)**	vo-wach
weep	**płakać (płaczę, -e)**	pwa-kach
crystal	**kryształ**	krish-taw
cufflinks	**spinki do mankietów**	speen-kee do man-kye-toov
cup	**filiżanka**	fee-lee-zhan-ka
cupboard	**kredens, szafa**	kre-dens, sha-fa
cure (to)	**leczyć** *impf.*, **wy-** *pf.* **(leczę, -y)**	le-chich, vi-
curious	**ciekawy**	chye-ka-vi
curl	**lok**	lok
current	**aktualny**	ak-too-al-ni
curtain	**kurtyna, firanka**	koor-ti-na, fee-ran-ka
curve	**zagięcie, zakręt**	za-gye^{n}-chye, za-kre^{n}t
cushion	**poduszka**	po-doosh-ka

customs	**cło, urząd celny**	tswo, oo-zho^{n}d tsel-ni
customs officer	**celnik**	tsel-neek
cut	**skaleczenie**	ska-le-che-nye
cut (to)	**kaleczyć się; krajać** *impf.*, **s-, ukroić** *pf.* **(kroję, -i)**	ka-le-chich shye^{n}; kra-yac oo-kro-eech
cycling	**jazda na rowerze**	yaz-da na ro-ve-rze
cyclist	**rowerzysta**	ro-ve-zhis-ta

D

daily	**codzienny**	tso-dgyen-ni
damaged	**uszkodzony**	oo-shko-dzo-ni
damp	**wilgotny**	veel-got-ni
dance	**taniec**	ta-nyets
dance (to)	**tańczyć** *impf.* **(tańczę, -y), za-** *pf.*	tan-chich
danger	**niebezpieczeństwo**	nye-bez-pye-chen-stvo
dangerous	**niebezpieczny**	nye-bez-pyech-ni
dark	**ciemny**	chyem-ni
date *appointment*	**(umówione) spotkanie**	oo-moo-vyo-ne spot-ka-nye
calendar	**data**	da-ta
daughter	**córka**	tsoor-ka
day	**dzień**	dgyen
dead	**nieżywy, martwy**	nye-zhi-vi, mar-tvi
deaf	**głuchy**	gwoo-hi
dealer	**pośrednik, ajent**	posh-red-neek, a-yent

dear	**drogi**	dro-gee
deckchair	**leżak**	le-zhak
declare (to)	**deklarować** *impf.*, **za-** *pf.*, **zgłaszać** *impf.*, **zgłosić** *pf.* (**zgłaszam, -a**)	de-kla-ro-vach, zgwa-shach, zgwo-sheech
deep	**głęboki**	gwe^{n}-bo-kee
delay	**opóźnienie**	o-poozh-nye-nye
deliver (to)	**dostarczać** *impf.*, **dostarczyć** *pf.* (**dostarczam, -a**)	dos-tar-chach, dos-tar-chich
delivery	**doręczenie, dostawa**	do-re^{n}-che-nye, dos-ta-va
demi-pension	**częściowe utrzymanie**	che^{n}-shchyo-ve oo-tshi-ma-nye
dentures	**sztuczna szczęka, proteza**	shtooch-na shche^{n}-ka, pro-te-za
deodorant	**krem dezodoro**	krem de-zo-do-ro
depart (to)	**odchodzić, odjeżdżać** *impf.*, **odejść, odjechać** *pf.* (**odchodzę, -i, odjeżdżam, -a**)	od-ho-dgeech, od-yezh-jach o-deyshch, od-ye-hach
department	**oddział**	od-dgyaw
departure	**odjazd**	od-yazd
dessert	**deser**	de-ser
detour	**objazd**	ob-yazd
dial (to)	**nakręcać** *impf.*, **nakręcić** *pf.* (**nakręcam, -a**)	na-kre^{n}-tsach, na-kre^{n}-chich

dialling code	**numer**	noo-mer
diamond	**diament, brylant**	dya-ment, bri-lant
dictionary	**słownik**	swov-neek
diet	**dieta**	dye-ta
diet (to)	**być na diecie**	bich na dye-chye
different	**inny**	een-ni
difficult	**trudny**	trood-ni
dine (to)	**jeść obiad** ***impf.*****, z-** ***pf.*** **(jem, je obiad)**	yeshch o-byad
dining room	**jadalnia**	ya-dal-nya
dinner	**obiad**	o-byad
dinner jacket	**smoking**	smo-keeng
direct	**bezpośredni, prosty**	bez-posh-red-nee, pros-ti
direction	**kierunek**	kye-roo-nek
dirty	**brudny**	brood-ni
disappointed	**rozczarowany**	roz-cha-ro-va-ni
discotheque	**dyskoteka**	dis-ko-te-ka
discount	**rabat**	ra-bat
dish	**potrawa**	po-tra-va
disinfectant	**środek dezynfekujący**	shro-dek de-zin-fe-koo-yo^{n}-tsi
distance	**odległość**	od-leg-woshch
disturb (to)	**przeszkadzać** ***impf.*****,** **przeszkodzić** ***pf.*** **(przeszkadzam, -a)**	pshe-shka-dzach, pshe-shko-dgeech
ditch	**rów**	roov

dive (to)	**nurkować (nurkuję, -e)**	noor-ko-vach
diving board	**trampolina**	tram-po-lee-na
divorced	**rozwiedziony**	roz-vye-dgyo-ni
do (to)	**robić** *impf.*, **z-** *pf.* **(robię, -i)**	ro-beech
dock (to)	**dokować** *impf.*, **za-** *pf.* **(dokuję -e)**	do-ko-vach
doctor	**doktor, lekarz**	dok-tor, le-kazh
dog	**pies**	pyes
doll	**lalka**	lal-ka
door	**drzwi**	dzhvee
double	**podwójny, dwuosobowy**	pod-vooy-ni, dvoo-o-so-bo-vi
double bed	**łóżko dwuosobowe**	woozh-ko dvoo-o-so-bo-ve
double room	**pokój dwuosobowy**	po-kooy dvoo-o-so-bo-vi
down (stairs)	**na dole**	na do-le
dozen	**tuzin**	too-zheen
draughty		
draw (to)	**rysować/kreślić**	ri-so-vach/kre-shleech
drawer	**szuflada**	shoof-la-da
drawing	**rysunek**	ri-soo-nek
dream	**sen, marzenie**	sen, ma-zhe-nye
dress	**suknia**	sook-nya
dressing gown	**szlafrok**	shla-frok
dressmaker	**krawcowa**	kraf-tso-va
drink (to)	**pić** *impf.*, **wy-** *pf.* **(piję, -e)**	peech, vi-

drinking water	**woda do picia**	vo-da do pee-cha
drive (to)	**prowadzić samochód (prowadzę …, -i)**	pro-va-dgeech sa-mo-hood
driver	**kierowca**	kye-rof-tsa
driving licence	**prawo jazdy**	pra-vo yaz-di
drop (to)	**u-, s-, wy-padać** *impf.*, **u-, s-, wy-paść** *pf.* **(upadam, -a)**	oo-, s-, vi-pa-dach, vi-pashch
drunk *noun*	**pijak**	pee-yak
adj.	**pijany**	pee-ya-ni
dry	**suchy, wytrawny**	soo-hi, vi-trav-ni
during	**podczas (+*gen.*)**	pod-chas
duvet	**kołdra**	kow-dra
dye	**farba**	far-ba

E

each	**każdy**	kazh-di
early	**wcześnie**	fchesh-nye
earrings	**kolczyki**	kol-chi-kee
east	**wschód**	fs-hood
Easter	**Wielkanoc**	vyel-ka-nots
easy	**łatwy**	wat-vi
eat (to)	**jeść** *impf.*, **z-** *pf.* **(jem, je)**	yeshch
edge	**ostrze, krawędź, skraj**	os-tzhe, kra-ve^{n}dg, skray
EC	**EWG**	e-voo-gye

eiderdown	kołdra puchowa, pierzyna	kow-dra poo-ho-va, pye-zhi-na
elastic	elastyczny	e-las-tich-ni
electric light bulb	żarówka	zha-roof-ka
electric point	kontakt	kon-takt
electricity	elektryczność	e-lek-trich-noshch
elevator	winda	veen-da
embarrassed	skrępowany	skre^n-po-va-ni
embassy	ambasada	am-ba-sa-da
emergency exit	wyjście (drzwi) zapasowe	viy-shchye (dzhvee) za-pa-so-ve
empty	pusty	poos-ti
end	koniec	ko-nyets
engaged *people*	zaręczony	za-re^n-cho-ni
phone, toilet	zajęty	za-ye^n-ti
engine	motor, silnik	mo-tor, sheel-neek
England	Anglia	an-glya
English *adj.*	angielski (-a)	an-gyel-skee
noun	Anglik *m*, Angielka *f*	an-gleek, an-gyel-ka
enjoy (to)	cieszyć się *impf.*, u- *pf.* (cieszę się, -y się)	chye-shich shye^n
enjoy oneself (to)	dobrze się bawić *impf.*, ...za- *pf.* (bawię się)	dob-zhe shye^n ba-veech
enough	dosyć, wystarczająco	do-sich, vis-tar-cha-yo^n-tso
enquiries	informacja	in-for-ma-tsya
enter (to)	wchodzić *impf.*, wejść *pf.* (wchodzę, -i)	fho-dgeech, veyshch

entrance	**wejście**	vey-shchye
entrance fee	**opłata za wstęp**	o-pwa-ta za fste^{n}p
envelope	**koperta**	ko-per-ta
equipment	**wyposażenie**	vi-po-sa-zhe-nye
escalator	**schody ruchome**	s-ho-di roo-ho-me
escape (to)	**unikać** *impf.*, **uniknąć** *pf.* **(unikam, -a)**	oo-nee-kach, oo-neek-no^{n}ch
estate agent	**pośrednik sprzedaży nieruchomości**	posh-red-neek spshe-da-zhi nye-roo-ho-mosh-chee
Europe	**Europa**	e-oo-ro-pa
even *not odd*	**parzysty**	pa-zhis-ti
evening	**wieczór**	vye-choor
event	**wydarzenie**	vi-da-zhe-nye
every	**każdy**	kazh-di
everybody	**każdy**	kazh-di
everything	**wszystko**	vshist-ko
everywhere	**wszędzie**	vshe^n-dgye
example	**przykład**	pshi-kwad
excellent	**doskonały**	dos-ko-na-wi
except	**oprócz (+*gen.*)**	o-prooch
excess	**nadmiar, nadwaga**	nad-myar, nad-va-ga
exchange (bureau)	**wymiana waluty**	vi-mya-na va-loo-ti
exchange rate	**kurs**	koors
excursion	**wycieczka**	vi-chyech-ka
excuse	**wymówka, pretekst**	vi-moov-ka, pre-tekst

exhausted	**wyczerpany**	vi-cher-pa-ni
exhibition	**wystawa**	vi-sta-va
exit	**wyjście**	viy-shchye
expect (to)	**oczekiwać, spodziewać się (oczekuję, -e, spodziewam się, -a)**	o-che-kee-vach, spo-dgye-vach shye^n
expensive	**drogi**	dro-gee
explain (to)	**wyjaśniać** *impf.*, **wyjaśnić** *pf.* **(wyjaśniam, -a)**	vi-yash-nyach, vi-yash-neech
express	**ekspres**	eks-pres
express train	**pociąg ekspresowy**	po-chyo^{n}g eks-pre-so-vi
extra	**dodatkowy**	do-dat-ko-vi
eye shadow	**puder/krem do oczu**	poo-der/krem do o-choo

F

fabric	**materiał**	ma-ter-yaw
face	**twarz**	tvazh
face cream	**krem do twarzy**	krem do tva-zhi
face powder	**puder**	poo-der
fact	**fakt**	fakt
factory	**fabryka**	fa-bri-ka
fade (to)	**płowieć** *impf.*, **wy-** *pf.* **(płowieje)**	pwo-vyech, vi-pwo-vyech
faint (to)	**mdleć** *impf.*, **ze-** *pf.* **(mdleję, -e)**	mdlech
fair *colour*	**jasny**	yas-ni
fête	**jarmark**	yar-mark

fall (to)	upadać *impf.*, upaść *pf.* (upadam, -a)	oo-pa-dach, oo-pashch
family	rodzina	ro-dgee-na
far	daleko	da-le-ko
fare	opłata	o-pwa-ta
farm	gospodarstwo rolne	gos-po-dar-stvo rol-ne
farmer	rolnik	rol-neek
farmhouse	dom na wsi	dom na fshee
farther	dalej	da-ley
fashion	moda	mo-da
fast	szybki	ship-kee
fat	tłusty	twoos-ti
father	ojciec	oy-chyets
fault	błąd	bwo^{n}d
fear	strach, obawa	strah, o-ba-va
feed (to)	karmić *impf.*, na- *pf.* (karmię, -i)	kar-meech, na-kar-meech
feeding bottle	butelka dla niemowląt	boo-tel-ka dla nye-mo-vla^{n}t
feel (to)	czuć	chooch
felt-tip pen	flamastra	fla-mas-tra
female *adj.*	żeński	zhen-skee
fetch (to)	przynosić, przyprowadzać *impf.* (przynoszę, -si), przynieść, przyprowadzić *pf.* (przyprowadzam, -a)	pshi-no-sheech, pshi-pro-va-dzach pshi-nyeshch pshi-pro-va-dgeech

(a) few	kilka	keel-ka
fiancé(e)	narzeczony, -a	na-zhe-cho-ni
field	pole	po-le
field glasses	lornetka polowa	lor-net-ka po-lo-va
fight (to)	walczyć, bić się (walczę, bije się, -y, -e)	val-chich, beech shye^{n}
fill (to)	wypełniać *impf.*, wypełnić *pf.* (wypełniam, -a)	vi-pew-nyach, vi-pew-neech
fill in (to)	wypełnić	vi-pew-neech
film	film	feelm
find (to)	znajdywać *impf.*, znaleźć *pf.* (znajduję, -e)	znay-di-vach, zna-lezhch
fine *adj.*	wspaniały	fspa-nya-wi
noun	grzywna, mandat	gzhi-vna, man-dat
finish (to)	kończyć *impf.*, s- *pf.* (kończę, -y)	kon-chich
finished	skończony	skon-cho-ni
fire	ogień, pożar	o-gyen, po-zhar
fire escape	wyjście (drzwi, schody) zapasowe	viy-shchye (dzhvee, s-ho-di) za-pa-so-ve
fire extinguisher	gaśnica	gash-nee-tsa
fireworks	ognie sztuczne	og-nye shtooch-ne
first	pierwszy	pyerf-shi
first aid	pierwsza pomoc	pyerf-sha po-mots
first class	pierwsza klasa	pyerf-sha kla-sa

fish	**ryba**	ri-ba
fish (to)	**łowić ryby**	wo-veech ri-bi
fisherman	**rybak**	ri-bak
fit	**nadający się (do …, na …)**	na-da-yo^{n}-tsi shye^{n}
fit (to)	**pasować (pasuję, -e)**	pas-so-vach
flag	**flaga**	fla-ga
flat *noun*	**mieszkanie**	myesh-ka-nye
adj.	**płaski**	pwas-kee
flavour	**smak**	smak
flea market	**pchli targ**	p-hlee targ
flight	**lot**	lot
flood	**powódź**	po-voodg
floor	**podłoga**	po-dwo-ga
storey	**piętro**	pye^{n}-tro
floorshow	**kabaret**	ka-ba-ret
flower	**kwiat**	kfyat
fly	**mucha**	moo-ha
fly (to)	**lecieć** *impf.*, **po-** *pf.* **(lecę, -i)**	le-chyech, po-
fog	**mgła**	mgwa
fold (to)	**składać** *impf.*, **złożyć** *pf.* **(składam, -a)**	skwa-dach, zwo-zhich
follow (to)	**iść, jechać za** *impf.*, **pójść, po-** *pf.* **(+***instr.***)** **(idę, idzie, jadę, jedzie)**	eeshch, ye-hach za, pooyshch
food	**żywność**	zhiv-noshch
foot	**stopa**	sto-pa

football	**piłka nożna**	**peew-ka nozh-na**
footpath	**ścieżka**	**shchyezh-ka**
for	**dla** (+*gen.*), **na** (+*acc.*)	dla, na
forbid (to)	**zabronić**	za-**bro**-neech
foreign	**obcy, zagraniczny**	**ob**-tsi, za-gra-**neech**-ni
forest	**las, puszcza**	las, **poosh**-cha
forget (to)	**zapominać** *impf.*, **zapomnieć** *pf.* (**zapominam, -a**)	za-po-**mee**-nach, za-**pom**-nyech
fork	**widelec**	vee-**de**-lets
forward	**naprzód**	**na**-pshood
forward (to)	**przesyłać** *impf.*, **przesłać** *pf.* (**przesyłam, -a**)	pshe-**si**-wach, **pshe**-swach
fountain	**fontanna**	fon-**tan**-na
fragile	**delikatny**	de-lee-**kat**-ni
free	**wolny**	**vol**-ni
freight	**przewóz, fracht**	**pshe**-vooz, fraht
fresh	**świeży**	**shvye**-zhi
fresh water	**słodka woda**	**swot**-ka **vo**-da
friend	**przyjaciel**	pshi-**ya**-chyel
friendly	**przyjacielski, życzliwy**	pshi-ya-**chyel**-skee, zhich-**lee**-vi
from	**od** (+*gen.*), **z** (+*gen.*)	od, z
front	**przód, front**	pshood, front
frontier	**granica**	gra-**nee**-tsa

frost	**mróz**	mrooz
frozen	**zamarznięty**	za-mar-znye^{n}-ti
fruit	**owoce**	o-vo-tse
full	**pełny**	pew-ni
full board	**pełne utrzymanie**	pew-ne oo-tshi-ma-nye
fun	**zabawa, uciecha**	za-ba-va, oo-chye-ha
funny	**śmieszny**	shmyesh-ni
fur	**futro**	foo-tro
furniture	**meble**	me-ble
further	**dalej (*adv.*), dalszy (*adj.*)**	da-ley, dal-shi

G

gallery	**galeria**	ga-ler-ya
gamble (to)	**uprawiać hazard (uprawiam, -a)**	oo-pra-vyach ha-zard
game	**gra**	gra
garage	**garaż**	ga-razh
garbage	**śmieci, odpadki**	shmye-chee, od-pad-kee
garden	**ogród**	o-grood
gas	**gaz**	gaz
gate	**brama**	bra-ma
gentlemen	**panowie**	pa-no-vye
genuine	**prawdziwy**	prav-dgee-vi
get (to)	**dostawać *impf.*, dostać *pf.* (dostaję, -e)**	dos-ta-vach, dos-tach

get off (to)	**wysiadać** *impf.*, **wysiąść** *pf.* **(wysiadam, -a)**	vi-sha-dach, vi-shyo^{n}shch
get on (to)	**wsiadać** *impf.*, **wsiąść** *pf.* **(wsiadam, -a)**	fsha-dach, fshyo^{n}shch
gift	**podarunek**	po-da-roo-nek
girdle	**gorset**	gor-set
girl	**dziewczyna**	dgyev-chi-na
give (to)	**dawać** *impf.*, **dać** *pf.* **(daję, -e)**	da-vach, dach
glad	**zadowolony**	za-do-vo-lo-ni
glass	**szkło, szklanka**	shkwo, shklan-ka
glasses	**okulary**	o-koo-la-ri
gloomy	**ponury**	po-noo-ri
glorious	**wspaniały, przepiękny**	fspa-nya-wi, pshe-pye^{n}k-ni
glove	**rękawiczka**	re^{n}-ka-veech-ka
go (to)	**iść** *impf.*, **pójść** *pf.* **(idę, idzie)**	eeshch, pooyshch
goal	**gol**	gol
god	**bóg**	boog
gold	**złoto, złoty** *adj.*	zwo-to, zwo-ti
gold plated	**pozłacany**	po-zwa-tsa-ni
golf course	**pole golfowe**	po-le gol-fo-ve
good	**dobry**	do-bri
government	**rząd**	zho^{n}d
granddaughter	**wnuczka**	vnoo-chka

grandfather	**dziadek**	dgya-dek
grandmother	**babcia**	bab-chya
grandson	**wnuk**	vnook
grass	**trawa**	tra-va
grateful	**wdzięczny**	vdge^{n}-chni
gravel	**żwir**	zhveer
great	**wielki**	vyel-kee
groceries	**artykuły spożywcze**	ar-ti-koo-wi spo-zhiv-che
ground	**ziemia**	zhye-mya
grow (to)	**rosnąć** *impf.* **(rosnę, -ie)**	ros-no^{n}ch
guarantee	**gwarancja**	gva-ran-tsya
guard	**wartownik**	var-tov-nik
guest	**gość**	goshch
guest house	**kwatera prywatna**	kva-te-ra pri-vat-na
guide (book)	**przewodnik (książka)**	pshe-vod-neek (kshyo^{n}zh-ka)
guided tour	**wycieczka z przewodnikiem**	vi-chyech-ka spshe-vod-nee-kyem

H

hail	**grad**	grad
hair	**włosy**	vwo-si
hair brush	**szczotka do włosów**	shchot-ka do vwo-soov
hair dryer	**suszarka do włosów**	soo-shar-ka do vwo-soov
hairpin	**szpilka do włosów**	shpeel-ka do vwo-soov
hair spray	**lakier do włosów**	la-kyer do vwo-soov
half	**połowa**	po-wo-va

half board	częściowe utrzymanie	che^{n}sh-chyo-ve oo-tshi-ma-nye
half fare	pół biletu	poow bee-le-too
hammer	młotek	mwo-tek
hand	ręka	re^{n}-ka
handbag	torebka	to-rep-ka
handkerchief	chusteczka do nosa	hoos-tech-ka do no-sa
handmade	ręcznie robiony	re^{n}ch-nye ro-byo-ni
hang (to)	wieszać *impf.*, powiesić *pf.* (wieszam, -a)	vye-shach, po-vye-sheech
hanger	wieszak	vye-shak
happen (to) *impersonal*	zdarzyć się (zdarza się – *3rd sing.*)	zda-zhich shye^{n}
happy	szczęśliwy	shche^{n}-shlee-vi
happy birthday	wszystkiego najlepszego	fshist-kye-go nay-lep-she-go
harbour	port	port
hard	ciężki, twardy	che^{n}-zhkee, tvar-di
hardly	ledwo, z trudem	led-vo, stroo-dem
harmful	szkodliwy	shkod-lee-vi
harmless	nieszkodliwy	nye-shkod-lee-vi
hat	kapelusz	ka-pe-loosh
have (to)	mieć (mam, ma)	myech
he	on	on
head	głowa	gwo-va
health	zdrowie	zdro-vye

hear (to)	**słyszeć** *impf.*, **u-** *pf.* **(słyszę, -y)**	swi-shech oo-
heart	**serce**	ser-tse
heat	**gorąco, upał**	go-ro^{n}-tso, oo-paw
heating	**ogrzewanie**	o-gzhe-va-nye
heavy	**ciężki**	chye^{n}zh-kee
hedge	**żywopłot**	zhi-vo-pwot
heel *shoe*	**obcas**	ob-tsas
help	**pomoc**	po-mots
help (to)	**pomagać** *impf.*, **pomóc** *pf.* **(pomagam, -a)**	po-ma-gach, po-moots
hem	**kraj**	kray
her	**jej**	yey
here	**tutaj**	too-tay
high	**wysoki**	vi-so-kee
hike (to)	**wędrować**	ve^{n}-dro-vach
helicopter	**helikopter**	he-lee-kop-ter
hill	**wzgórze**	vzgoo-zhe
him	**jego –** *acc.*, **jemu –** *dat.*	ye-go, ye-moo
hip	**biodro**	byo-dro
hire (to)	**wynająć** *pf.* **(wynajmuję, -e)**	vi-na-yo^{n}ch
his	**jego**	ye-go
history	**historia**	hees-tor-ya
hitchhike (to)	**jechać autostopem**	ye-hach a-oo-to-sto-pem
hobby	**hobby, konik, pasja**	ho-bee, ko-neek, pas-ya

hold (to)	**trzymać**	tshi-mach
hole	**dziura**	dgyoo-ra
holiday	**święto**	shvye^{n}-to
holidays	**wakacje, urlop**	va-kats-ye, oor-lop
hollow	**wydrążony, pusty**	vi-dro^{n}-zho-ni, poos-ti
(at) home	**w domu**	v do-moo
honeymoon	**miodowy miesiąc**	myo-do-vi mye-sho^{n}ch
hope	**nadzieja**	na-dgye-ya
hope (to)	**mieć nadzieję (mam, ma nadzieję)**	myech na-dgye-ye^{n}
horse	**koń**	kon
horse races	**wyścigi konne**	vi-shchee-gee kon-ne
horse riding	**konna jazda**	kon-na yaz-da
hose	**wąż gumowy**	va^{n}zh goo-mo-vi
hospital	**szpital**	shpee-tal
host	**gospodarz (pan domu)**	gos-po-dazh, pan do-moo
hostel	**schronisko**	s-hro-nees-ko
hostess	**gospodyni (pani domu)**	gos-po-di-nee, pa-nee do-moo
hot	**gorący**	go-ro^{n}-tsi
hotel	**hotel**	ho-tel
hotel keeper	**kierownik hotelu**	kye-rov-neek ho-te-lu
hot water bottle	**termofor**	ter-mo-for
hour	**godzina**	go-dgee-na
house	**dom**	dom
hovercraft	**poduszkowiec**	po-doosh-ko-vyets

how?	**jak?**	yak
how much, many?	**ile?**	ee-le
hungry (to be)	**być głodnym**	bich gwo-dnim
hunt (to)	**polować**	po-lo-vach
hurry (to)	**śpieszyć się (śpieszę się, -y)**	shpye-shich shye^{n}
hurt (to)	**boleć**	bo-lech
husband	**mąż**	mo^{n}zh
hydrofoil	**wodolot**	vo-do-lot

I

I	**ja**	ya
ice	**lód**	lood
ice cream	**lody**	lo-di
identify (to)	**zidentyfikować**	zee-den-ti-fee-ko-vach
if	**jeżeli**	ye-zhe-lee
imagine (to)	**wyobrazić sobie**	vi-o-bra-zheech so-bye
immediately	**natychmiast**	na-tih-myast
immersion heater	**terma**	ter-ma
important	**ważny**	vazh-ni
in	**w (+*instr.*)**	v
include (to)	**włączać, wliczać *impf.*, włączyć, wliczyć *pf.* (włączam, wliczam, -a)**	vwo^{n}-chach, vlee-chach, vwo^{n}-chich, vlee-chich
included	**wliczony**	vlee-cho-ni
inconvenient	**niewygodny, kłopotliwy**	nye-vi-god-ni, kwo-pot-lee-vi

incorrect	**błędny**	bwe^{n}d-ni
indeed	**naprawdę**	na-prav-de^{n}
independent	**niezależny**	nye-za-lezh-ni
indoors	**wewnątrz**	vev-na^{n}tsh
industry	**przemysł**	pshe-misw
inexpensive	**niedrogi**	nye-dro-gee
inflammable	**łatwopalny**	wat-vo-pal-ni
inflatable	**nadmuchiwany**	na-dmoo-hee-va-ni
inflation	**inflacja**	een-flats-ya
ink	**atrament**	a-tra-ment
inn	**gospoda**	gos-po-da
insect	**insekt, owad**	een-sekt, o-vad
insect bite	**pokąszenie przez insekty**	po-ko^{n}-she-nye pshez in-sek-ti
insect repellent	**płyn przeciw komarom**	pwin pshe-chiv ko-ma-rom
inside	**wewnątrz, w środku**	vev-no^{n}ch, f shrot-koo
instead	**zamiast**	za-myast
instructor	**instruktor**	een-strook-tor
insurance	**ubezpieczenie**	oo-bes-pye-che-nye
insure (to)	**ubezpieczać** *impf.*, **ubezpieczyć** *pf.* **(ubezpieczam, -a)**	oo-bes-pye-chach, oo-bes-pye-chich
insured	**ubezpieczony**	oo-bez-pye-cho-ni
interest	**zainteresowanie, procent**	za-een-te-re-so-va-nye pro-tsent
interested	**zainteresowany**	za-in-te-re-so-va-ni

interesting	ciekawy	chye-ka-vi
interpreter	tłumacz	twoo-mach
into	do (+*gen.*)	do
introduce (to)	przedstawiać *impf.*, przedstawić *pf.* (przedstawiam, -a)	pshet-sta-vyach, pshet-sta-veech
invitation	zaproszenie	za-pro-she-nye
invite (to)	zapraszać *impf.*, zaprosić *pf.* (zapraszam, -a)	za-pra-shach, za-pro-sheech
Ireland	Irlandia	eer-lan-dya
Irish *adj.*	irlandzki (-a)	eer-landz-kee
noun	Irlandczyk *m*, Irlandka *f*	eer-land-chik, eer-land-ka
iron (to)	prasować *impf.*, u- *pf.* (prasuję, -e)	pra-so-vach, oo-
island	wyspa	vis-pa
it	to, ono	to, o-no

J

jacket	żakiet, marynarka	zha-kyet, ma-ri-nar-ka
jar	słoik	swo-eek
jelly fish	meduza	me-doo-za
Jew	Żyd	zhid
jewellery	biżuteria	bee-zhoo-ter-ya
Jewish	żydowski	zhi-dov-skee

K

keep (to)	**trzymać** *impf.*, **za-** *pf.* **(trzymam, -a, zatrzymuję, -e)**	tshi-mach, za-
key	**klucz**	klooch
kick (to)	**kopać** *impf.*, **kopnąć** *pf.* **(kopię, -e)**	ko-pach, kop-no^{n}ch
kind *adj.*	**dobry, uprzejmy**	dob-ri, oop-shey-mi
king	**król**	krool
kiss (to)	**całować** *impf.*, **po-** *pf.* **(całuję, -e)**	tsa-wo-vach
kitchen	**kuchnia**	kooh-nya
knickers/briefs	**majtki, reformy**	mayt-kee, re-for-mi
knife	**nóż**	noozh
knock (to)	**pukać** *impf.*, **za-** *pf.* **(pukam, -a); stukać** *impf.*, **za-** *pf.*	poo-kach, za-poo-kach; stoo-kach, za-stoo-kach
know (to) *fact*	**wiedzieć (wiem, wie)**	vye-dgyech
person	**znać (znam, zna)**	znach

L

label	**etykieta, nalepka**	e-ti-kye-ta, na-lep-ka
lace	**koronka**	ko-ron-ka
ladies	**damski, dla kobiet, dla pań**	dam-skee, dla ko-byet, dla pan
lady	**pani**	pa-nee
lake	**jezioro**	ye-zhyo-ro

lamp	**lampa**	lam-pa
land	**ląd, ziemia**	lo^{n}d, zhye-mya
landing *plane*	**lądowanie**	lo^{n}-do-va-nye
stairs	**półpiętrze**	poow-pye^{n}t-she
landlady/lord	**właścicielka/właściciel**	vwash-chee-chyel-ka/ vwash-chee-chyel
landmark *area*	**punkt orientacyjny**	poonkt o-ryen-ta-tsiy-ni
history	**zwrotny**	zvrot-ni
landscape	**krajobraz**	kra-yo-braz
lane	**pas ruchu**	pas roo-hoo
language	**język**	ye^{n}-zik
large	**duży**	doo-zhi
last	**ostatni**	os-tat-nee
late	**późny**	poozh-ni
laugh (to)	**śmiać się (śmieję się, -e)**	shmyach shye^{n}
launderette	**pralnia samoobsługowa**	pral-nya sa-mo-ob-swoo-go-va
lavatory	**ubikacja, ustęp, klozet, toaleta**	oo-bee-ka-tsya, oo-ste^{n}p, klo-zet, to-a-le-ta
lavatory paper	**papier toaletowy**	pa-pyer to-a-le-to-vi
law	**prawo**	pra-vo
lawn	**trawnik**	trav-neek
lawyer	**prawnik**	prav-neek
lead (to)	**prowadzić**	pro-va-dgeech
leaf	**liść**	leeshch
leak (to) *liquid*	**przeciekać**	pshe-che-kach
gas	**ulatniać**	oo-lat-nyach

learn (to)	**uczyć się** *impf.*, **na-** *pf.* (**uczę się, -y**)	oo-chich shye^{n}, na-
least	**najmniejszy**	nay-mnyey-shi
at least	**przynajmniej**	pshi-nay-mnyey
leather	**skóra**	skoo-ra
leave (to) *abandon*	**zostawiać** *impf.*, **zostawić** *pf.* (**zostawiam, -a**)	zos-ta-vyach, zos-ta-veech
go away	**odchodzić** *impf.*, **odejść** *pf.* (**odchodzę, -i**)	ot-ho-dgeech, o-deyshch
left	**lewy, na lewo**	le-vi, na le-vo
left luggage	**przechowalnia bagażu**	pshe-ho-val-nya ba-ga-zhoo
leg	**noga**	no-ga
lend (to)	**pożyczać** *impf.*, **pożyczyć** *pf.* (+*dat.*) (**pożyczam, -a**)	po-zhi-chach, po-zhi-chich
length	**długość**	dwoo-goshch
less	**mniej**	mnyey
lesson	**lekcja**	lek-tsya
let (to) *rent*	**wynajmować** *impf.*, **wynająć** *pf.* (**wynajmuję, -e**)	vi-nay-mo-vach, vi-na-yo^{n}ch
allow	**pozwalać** *impf.*, **pozwolić** *pf.* (**pozwalam, -a**)	poz-va-lach, poz-vo-leech
letter	**list**	leest
level crossing	**przejazd przez tory kolejowe**	pshe-yazd pshez to-ri ko-le-yo-ve

library	**biblioteka**	bee-bleeo-te-ka
licence	**pozwolenie**	poz-vo-le-nye
life	**życie**	zhi-chye
lifebelt	**pas ratunkowy**	pas ra-toon-ko-vi
lifeboat	**łódź ratunkowa**	woodg ra-toon-ko-va
lifeguard	**ratownik**	ra-tov-neek
lift	**winda**	vin-da
light	**światło**	shvyat-wo
light	**lekki**	lek-kee
colour	**jasny**	yas-ni
lighter fuel	**benzyna do zapalniczek**	ben-zi-na do za-pal-nee-chek
lighthouse	**latarnia morska**	la-tar-nya mor-ska
lightning	**błyskawica**	bwis-ka-vee-tsa
like (to)	**lubić (lubię, -i)**	loo-bich
wish	**chcieć (chcę, -e)**	hchyech
line	**lina**	lee-na
linen	**bielizna**	bye-leez-na
lingerie	**bielizna damska**	bye-leez-na dam-ska
lipsalve	**szminka ochronna**	shmeen-ka o-hron-na
lipstick	**szminka**	shmeen-ka
liquid *adj.*	**płynny**	pwin-ni
noun	**płyn**	pwin
listen (to)	**słuchać (słucham, -a)**	swoo-hach
little *amount*	**mało, trochę**	ma-wo, tro-he^n
size	**mały**	ma-wi

live (to)	żyć, mieszkać (żyję, -e, mieszkam, -a)	zhich, myesh-kach
local	miejscowy	myey-stso-vi
lock	zamek	za-mek
lock (to)	zamykać na klucz *impf.*, zamknąć... *pf.* (zamykam..., -a,...)	za-mi-kach na klooch, zam-kno^{n}ch
long	długi	dwoo-gee
look (to) *at*	patrzeć (patrzę, -y)	pa-tshech
like	wyglądać (wyglądam, -a)	vi-glo^{n}-dach
for	szukać (szukam, -a)	shoo-kach
loose	luźny	loozh-ni
lorry	ciężarówka	chye^{n}-zha-roov-ka
lose (to)	gubić *impf.*, z- *pf.* (gubię, -i)	goo-bich
lost property office	biuro rzeczy znalezionych	byoo-ro zhe-chi zna-le-zhyo-nih
(a) lot	dużo	doo-zho
loud	głośny	gwosh-ni
love (to)	kochać (kocham, -a)	ko-hach
lovely	śliczny	shleech-ni
low	niski	nees-kee
luggage	bagaż	ba-gazh
lunch	obiad	o-byad

M

mad	obłąkany, wściekły	o-bwo^{n}-ka-ni, fshchyek-wi

magazine	**czasopismo**	cha-so-**pees**-mo
maid	**pokojowa**	po-ko-**yo**-va
mail	**poczta**	**poch**-ta
main street	**główna ulica**	**gwoov**-na oo-**lee**-tsa
make (to)	**robić** *impf.*, **z-** *pf.* (**robię, -i**)	**ro**-bich
make-up	**makijaż**	ma-**kee**-yazh
male *adj.*	**męski**	**me**ⁿs-kee
man	**mężczyzna**	meⁿzh-**chiz**-na
man-made	**sztuczny**	**shtooch**-ni
manage (to)	**zarządzać** (**zarządzam, -a**)	za-**zho**ⁿ-dzach
manager	**kierownik**	kye-**rov**-neek
manicure	**manicure**	ma-**nee**-kyoor
many	**dużo**	**doo**-zho
map	**mapa**	**ma**-pa
marble	**marmur**	**mar**-moor
market	**rynek**	**ri**-nek
married	**żonaty** *m*, **mężatka** *f*	zho-**na**-ti, meⁿ-**zhat**-ka
marsh	**bagno, moczary**	**bag**-no, mo-**cha**-ri
Mass	**msza**	msha
massage	**masaż**	**ma**-sazh
match *light*	**zapałka**	za-**paw**-ka
sport	**mecz**	mech
material	**materiał**	ma-**ter**-yaw
matinée	**poranek**	po-**ra**-nek
mattress	**materac**	ma-**te**-rats

maybe	**być może**	bich mo-zhe
me	**mnie, mi**	mnye, mee
meal	**posiłek**	po-shee-wek
mean (to)	**zamierzać**	za-mye-zhach
measurements	**wymiary**	vi-myar-i
meet (to)	**spotykać** *impf.*, **spotkać** *pf.* **(spotykam, -a)**	spo-ti-kach, spot-kach
mend (to)	**naprawiać** *impf.*, **naprawić** *pf.* **(naprawiam, -a)**	na-pra-vyach, na-pra-veech
menstruation	**menstruacja**	men-stroo-a-tsya
mess	**nieporządek**	nye-po-zho^{n}-dek
message	**wiadomość**	vya-do-moshch
messenger	**posłaniec**	pos-wa-nyets
metal	**metal**	me-tal
midday	**południe**	po-wood-nye
middle	**środek**	shro-dek
middle-aged	**w średnim wieku**	fshred-neem vye-koo
midnight	**północ**	poow-nots
mild	**łagodny**	wa-god-ni
mill	**młyn**	mwin
mine	**mój** *m*, **moja** *f*, **moje** *n*	mooy, mo-ya, mo-ye
minute	**minuta**	mee-noo-ta
mirror	**lustro**	loos-tro
Miss	**panna**	pan-na

miss (to) *train*	**spóźniać się** ***impf.***, **spoźnić się** ***pf.*** **(na +** ***acc.*****)**	**spoozh-nyach shye^{n} spoozh-neech shye^{n}**
mistake	**pomyłka**	**po-miw-ka**
mix (to)	**mieszać** ***impf.*****, z-** ***pf.*** **(mieszam, miesza)**	**mye-shach, zmye-shach**
mixed	**mieszany**	**mye-sha-ni**
modern	**nowoczesny**	**no-vo-ches-ni**
moisturizer	**nawilżacz**	**na-veel-zhach**
moment	**moment**	**mo-ment**
monastery	**klasztor**	**klash-tor**
money	**pieniądze**	**pye-nyo^{n}-dze**
monk	**zakonnik**	**za-kon-neek**
month	**miesiąc**	**mye-shyo^{n}ts**
monument	**pomnik**	**pom-neek**
moon	**księżyc**	**kshye^{n}-zhits**
moorland	**wrzosowisko**	**vzho-so-vees-ko**
more	**więcej**	**vye^{n}-tsey**
morning	**rano/poranek**	**ra-no/po-ra-nek**
mortgage	**hipoteka**	**hee-po-te-ka**
mosque	**meczet**	**me-chet**
mosquito	**komar**	**ko-mar**
most	**najwięcej**	**nay-vye-tsey**
mother	**matka**	**mat-ka**
motor	**motor, silnik**	**mo-tor, sheel-neek**
motor bike	**motocykl**	**mo-to-tsikl**

motor boat	**motorówka**	mo-to-roof-ka
motor cycle	**motocykl**	mo-to-tsikl
motor racing	**wyścigi samochodowe**	vish-chee-gee sa-mo-ho-do-ve
motorway	**autostrada**	a-oo-to-stra-da
mountain	**góra**	goo-ra
mouse	**mysz**	mish
mouth	**usta**	oos-ta
move (to)	**ruszać** *impf.*, **ruszyć** *pf.* **(ruszam, rusza)**	roo-shach, roo-shich
Mr	**pan**	pan
Mrs	**pani**	pa-nee
much	**dużo**	doo-zho
museum	**muzeum**	moo-ze-oom
music	**muzyka**	moo-zi-ka
must *to have to*	**musieć (muszę, musi)**	moo-shyech, moo-she^{n}, moo-shee
my, mine	**mój** *m*, **moja** *f*, **moje** *n*	mooy, mo-ya, mo-ye
myself	**siebie; sam, -a**	shye-bye, sam (a)

N

nail *pin*	**gwóźdź**	gvoozhdg
nailbrush	**szczotka do paznokci**	shchot-ka do paz-nok-chee
nailfile	**pilnik do paznokci**	peel-neek do paz-nok-chee
nail polish	**lakier do paznokci**	la-kyer do paz-nok-chee
name	**imię**	ee-mye^{n}
napkin	**serwetka**	ser-vet-ka

nappy	**pieluszka**	pye-loosh-ka
narrow	**wąski**	vo^{n}s-kee
natural	**naturalny**	na-too-ral-ni
near	**bliski**	blees-kee
nearly	**prawie**	pra-vye
necessary	**potrzebny**	po-tsheb-ni
necklace	**naszyjnik**	na-shiy-neek
need (to)	**potrzebować (potrzebuję, -e)**	po-tshe-bo-vach
needle	**igła**	ee-gwa
nephew[1]	**siostrzeniec/bratanek**	shyo-stshe-nyets/bra-ta-nek
net	**siatka, sieć**	shyat-ka, shyech
never	**nigdy**	neeg-di
new	**nowy**	no-vi
New Zealand	**Nowa Zelandia**	no-va ze-lan-dya
news	**wiadomości**	vya-do-mosh-chee
newspaper	**gazeta**	ga-ze-ta
next	**następny**	nas-te^{n}p-ni
nice	**miły**	mee-wi
niece	**siostrzenica/bratanica**	shyo-stshe-nee-tsa/ bra-ta-nee-tsa
night	**noc**	nots
nightclub	**lokal nocny**	lo-kal nots-ni
nightdress	**koszula nocna**	ko-shoo-la nots-na
no one	**nikt**	neekt

1. Siostrzeniec means sister's son; bratanek means brother's son. The same principle applies to niece.

nobody	**nikt**	neekt
noisy	**hałaśliwy**	ha-wash-lee-vi
non-alcoholic	**bezalkoholowy**	bez-al-ko-ho-lo-vi
none	**żaden** *m*, **żadna** *f*, **żadne** *n*	zha-den, zhad-na, zhad-ne
normal	**normalny**	nor-mal-ni
north	**północ**	poow-nots
nosebleed	**krwawienie z nosa**	krva-vye-nye zno-sa
not	**nie**	nye
note	**notatka**	no-tat-ka
notebook	**notes**	no-tes
nothing	**nic**	neets
notice	**zawiadomienie, ostrzeżenie**	za-vya-do-mye-nye, os-tshe-zhe-nye
notice (to)	**zauważyć** *pf.* **(zauważam, -a)**	za-oo-va-zhich
novel	**powieść**	po-vyeshch
now	**teraz**	te-raz
number	**numer**	noo-mer
nylon	**nylon**	ni-lon

O

obtain (to)	**zdobyć**	zdo-bich
occasion	**sposobność, okazja**	spo-sob-noshch, o-kaz-ya
occupation	**zawód**	za-vood
occupied	**zajęty**	za-ye^{n}-ti
ocean	**ocean**	o-tse-an

odd *strange*	**dziwny**	dgeev-ni
not even	**nieparzysty**	nye-pa-zhis-ti
of course	**oczywiście**	o-chi-veesh-chye
offer	**oferta, propozycja**	o-fer-ta, pro-po-zits-ya
offer (to)	**proponować** *impf.*, **za-** *pf.* **(proponuję, -e)**	pro-po-no-vach, za-pro-po-no-vach
office	**biuro**	byoo-ro
officer	**funkcjonariusz/ (*milit.*) oficer**	foonk-tsyo-nar-yoosh, o-fee-tser
official	**urzędnik**	oo-zhe^{n}d-neek
often	**często**	che^{n}s-to
ointment	**maść**	mashch
OK	**w porządku**	fpo-zho^{n}d-koo
old	**stary**	sta-ri
on	**na (+*instr.*)**	na
on foot	**na piechotę**	na pye-ho-te^{n}
on time	**na czas**	na chas
once	**raz**	raz
only	**tylko**	til-ko
open *adj.*	**otwarte**	ot-far-te
open (to)	**otwierać** *impf.*, **otworzyć** *pf.* **(otwieram, -a)**	ot-fye-rach, ot-fo-zhich
open-air	**otwarte powietrze**	o-tvar-te po-vye-tshe
opening	**otwarcie, otwór**	ot-var-chye, ot-voor
opera	**opera**	o-pe-ra
opportunity	**sposobność**	spo-sob-noshch

opposite *adj.*	**przeciwny**	pshe-chiv-ni
adv.	**naprzeciwko**	na-pshe-chiv-ko
optician	**optyk**	o-ptik
or	**albo**	al-bo
orchard	**sad**	sad
orchestra	**orkiestra**	or-kyest-ra
order (to)	**zamawiać** *impf.*, **zamówić** *pf.* **(zamawiam, -a)**	za-ma-vyach, za-moo-veech
ordinary	**zwyczajny**	zvi-chay-ni
other	**inny**	een-ni
otherwise	**w przeciwnym razie/ skądinąd**	fpshe-cheev-nim ra-zhye, sko^{n}d-in-o^{n}d
ought	**powinien** *m*, **powinna** *f*, **powinno** *n*	po-vee-nyen, po-veen-na, po-veen-no
our, ours	**nasz** *m*, **nasza** *f*, **nasze** *n*	nash, na-sha, na-she
out(side)	**na zewnątrz**	na zev-no^{n}tsh
out of order	**nieczynny**	nye-chin-ni
out of stock	**wysprzedany**	vis-pshe-da-ni
over	**nad (+*instr.*)**	nad
overcoat	**płaszcz**	pwashch
over night	**na noc, przez noc**	na noch, pshez noch
over there	**tam**	tam
owe (to)	**być winnym**	bich veen-nim
owner	**właściciel**	vwash-chee-chyel

P

pack (to)	**pakować** ***impf.*****, s-** ***pf.*** **(pakuję, -e)**	pa-ko-vach
packet	**paczka**	pach-ka
paddle	**brodzić**	bro-dgeech
paddling pool	**brodzik**	bro-dgeek
page	**strona**	stro-na
paid	**opłacony**	o-pwa-tso-ni
pain	**ból**	bool
painkiller	**środek przeciwbólowy**	shro-dek pshe-cheev-boo-lo-vi
paint (to)	**malować** ***impf.*****, po-** ***pf.*** **(maluję, -e)**	ma-lo-vach, po-
painting	**obraz**	o-braz
pair	**para**	pa-ra
palace	**pałac**	pa-wats
pale	**blady**	bla-di
paper	**papier**	pa-pyer
parcel	**paczka**	pach-ka
park	**park**	park
parking meter	**parkometr**	par-ko-metr
parking ticket	**mandat**	man-dat
parliament	**parlament, sejm**	par-la-ment, seym
park (to)	**parkować** ***impf.*****, za-** ***pf.*** **(parkuję, -e)**	par-ko-vach, za-
part	**część**	che^{n}shch

party *fête*	**przyjęcie, zabawa**	pshi-ye^{n}-chye, za-ba-va
political	**partia**	par-tya
pass (to)	**mijać** *impf.*, **minąć** *pf.* **(mijam, -a)**	mee-yach, mee-no^{n}ch
passenger	**pasażer**	pa-sa-zher
passport	**paszport**	pash-port
past *adj.*	**przeszły, dawny**	pshesh-wi, dav-ni
noun	**przeszłość**	pshesh-woshch
path	**ścieżka**	shchyezh-ka
patient	**pacjent**	pats-yent
pavement	**chodnik**	hod-neek
pay (to)	**płacić** *impf.*, **za-** *pf.* **(płacę, -i)**	pwa-cheech, za-
payment	**opłata**	o-pwa-ta
peace	**pokój**	po-kooy
peak	**szczyt, wierzchołek**	shcit, vyezh-ho-wek
pearl	**perła**	per-wa
pebble	**kamyk**	ka-mik
pedal	**pedał**	pe-daw
pedestrian	**pieszy**	pye-shi
pedestrian crossing	**przejście dla pieszych**	pshey-shchye dla pye-shih
pedestrian precinct	**strefa piesza**	stre-fa pye-sha
(fountain) pen	**(wieczne) pióro**	vyech-ne pyoo-ro
pencil	**ołówek**	o-woo-vek
penknife	**scyzoryk**	stsi-zo-rik
pensioner	**emeryt**	e-me-rit

people	**ludzie**	loo-dgye
perfect	**doskonały**	dos-ko-na-wi
performance	**przedstawienie**	pshed-sta-vye-nye
perfume	**perfumy**	per-foo-mi
perhaps	**być może**	bich mo-zhe
perishable	**psujący się**	psoo-yo^{n}-tsi she^{n}
permit	**pozwolenie**	poz-vo-le-nye
permit (to)	**pozwalać** *impf.*, **pozwolić** *pf.* **(pozwalam, -a)**	poz-va-lach, poz-vo-lich
person	**osoba**	o-so-ba
per person	**od osoby**	od o-so-bi
personal	**osobisty**	o-so-bees-ti
petticoat	**halka**	hal-ka
photograph	**fotografia**	fo-to-gra-fya
photographer	**fotograf**	fo-to-graf
piano	**pianino**	pya-nee-no
pick (to)	**obierać** *impf.*, **obrać** *pf.* **(obieram, obiera)**	o-bye-rach, o-brach
choose	**zrywać** *impf.*, **zerwać** *pf.* **(zrywam, zrywa)**	zri-vach, zer-vach
picnic	**majówka, posiłek na świeżym powietrzu, picnic**	ma-yoof-ka, po-shee-wek na shvye-zhim po-vye-tshoo, peek-neek
piece	**kawałek**	ka-va-wek
pier	**molo**	mo-lo
pillow	**poduszka**	po-doosh-ka

pin	**szpilka**	shpeel-ka
(safety) pin	**agrafka**	a-graf-ka
pipe	**fajka**	fay-ka
place	**miejsce**	myeys-tse
plain	**prosty, jednolity**	pros-ti, ye-dno-lee-ti
plan	**plan**	plan
plant	**roślina**	rosh-lee-na
plastic	**plastikowy**	plas-tee-ko-vi
plate	**talerz**	ta-lezh
play	**sztuka**	shtoo-ka
play (to)	**bawić się (bawię się, -i)**	ba-vich shye^n
player	**gracz**	grach
please	**proszę**	pro-she^n
pleased	**zadowolony**	za-do-vo-lo-ni
plenty	**mnóstwo**	mnoos-tvo
pliers	**obcążki**	ob-tso^{n}zh-kee
plimsoll	**tenisówka**	te-nee-soov-ka
plug *electric*	**wtyczka**	ftich-ka
bath	**korek**	ko-rek
pocket	**kieszeń**	kye-shen
point	**punkt**	poonkt
poisonous	**trujący**	troo-yo^n-tsi
Poland	**Polska**	pol-ska
Pole	**Polak *m*, Polka *f***	po-lak, pol-ka
policeman	**policjant**	po-leets-yant
police station	**komisariat, posterunek**	ko-mee-sar-yat, pos-te-roo-nek

Polish *adj.*	**polski**	pol-skee
political	**polityczny**	po-lee-tich-ni
politician	**polityk**	po-lee-tik
politics	**polityka**	po-lee-ti-ka
pollution	**zanieczyszczenie**	za-nye-chish-che-nye
pond	**staw**	stav
poor	**biedny**	byed-ni
pope	**papież**	pa-pyezh
popular	**popularny**	po-poo-lar-ni
porcelain	**porcelana**	por-tse-la-na
port	**port**	port
porter	**bagażowy**	ba-ga-zho-vi
possible	**możliwy**	mozh-lee-vi
post (to)	**wysyłać pocztą** *impf.*, **wysłać pocztą** *pf.* **(wysyłam, -a)**	vi-si-wach poch-to^n vi-swach
post box	**skrzynka na listy**	skshin-ka na lees-ti
postcard	**pocztówka**	poch-toof-ka
postman	**listonosz**	lees-to-nosh
post office	**poczta**	poch-ta
postpone (to)	**odkładać** *impf.*, **odłożyć** *pf.* **(odkładam, odkłada)**	od-kwa-dach, od-wo-zhich
pound	**funt**	foont
powder	**puder**	poo-der
prefer (to)	**woleć (wolę, -i)**	vo-lech

pregnant	w ciąży	fchyo^{n}-zhi
prepare (to)	przygotowywać *impf.*, przygotować *pf.* (przygotowuję, -e)	pshi-go-to-vi-vach, pshi-go-to-vach
present *gift*	prezent	pre-zent
president	prezydent	pre-zi-dent
press (to)	naciskać *impf.*, nacisnąć *pf.* (naciskam, -a)	na-chees-kach, na-chees-no^{n}ch
pretty	ładny	wad-ni
price	cena	tse-na
priest	ksiądz	kshyo^{n}dz
prime minister	premier	pre-myer
print	rycina/(photo) odbitka	ri-chee-na, od-beet-ka
print (to)	drukować *impf.*, wy- *pf.* (drukuję, -e)	droo-ko-vach, vi-droo-ko-vach
photographs	robić odbitkę *impf.*, z- *pf.* (robię ..., robi ...)	ro-beech od-beet-ke^{n}, zro-beech
private	prywatny	pri-vat-ni
problem	problem	prob-lem
profession	zawód	za-vood
programme	program	pro-gram
promise	obietnica	o-byet-nee-tsa
promise (to)	obiecywać *impf.*, obiecać *pf.* (obiecuję, -e)	obye-tsi-vach, obye-tsach
prompt	szybki, bezzwłoczny	shib-kee, bez-zvwoch-ni

protestant	protestant *m*, -ka *f*	pro-tes-tant, pro-tes-tant-ka
provide (to)	zaopatrywać *impf.*, zaopatrzyć *pf.* (zaopatruję, -e)	za-o-pa-tri-vach, za-o-pa-chich
public *adj.*	publiczny	poo-bleech-ni
public holiday	święto państwowe	shvye^{n}-to pan-stvo-ve
pull (to)	ciagnąć *impf.*, po- *pf.* (ciagnę, -ie)	chyo^{n}g-no^{n}ch
pump	pompa	pom-pa
pure	czysty, bez domieszki	chis-ti, bez do-myesh-kee
purse	portmonetka	port-mo-net-ka
push (to)	pchać *impf.*, popchnąć *pf.* (pcham, -a)	phach, pop-hno^{n}ch
put (to)	kłaść *impf.*, położyć *pf.* (kładę, -dzie)	kwashch, po-wo-zhich
pyjamas	pidżama	pee-ja-ma

Q

quality	jakość	ya-koshch
quantity	ilość	ee-loshch
queen	królowa	kroo-lo-va
question	pytanie	pi-ta-nye
queue	kolejka	ko-ley-ka
queue (to)	stać w kolejce (stoję ..., stoi ...)	stach fko-ley-tse (sto-ye^{n}, sto-ee)
quick	szybki	shib-kee
quiet	spokojny	spo-koy-ni

uite	**całkowicie, zupełnie**	tsaw-ko-vee-che, zoo-pew-nye

ace	**wyścig**	vish-cheeg
acecourse	**tor wyścigowy**	tor vi-shchee-go-vi
adiator	**kaloryfer**	ka-lo-ri-fer
adio	**radio**	ra-dyo
ailway	**kolej**	ko-ley
ain	**deszcz**	deshch
t is) raining	**pada deszcz**	pa-da deshch
aincoat	**płaszcz nieprzemakalny**	pwashch nye-pshe-ma-kal-ni
are	**rzadki**	zhad-kee
ash	**wysypka** *n*	vi-syp-ka
ate	**stawka**	stav-ka
ather *more or less*	**dość, nieco**	doshch, nye-tso
preference	**raczej**	ra-chey
aw	**surowy**	soo-ro-vi
azor	**brzytwa**	bzhit-fa
azor blade	**żyletka**	zhi-let-ka
each (to)	**dosięgać** *impf.*, **dosięgnąć** *pf.* **(dosięgam, dosięga)**	do-shye^{n}-gach, do-shye^{n}g-no^{n}ch
ead (to)	**czytać** *impf.*, **prze-** *pf.* **(czytam, -a)**	chi-tach, pshe-
eady	**gotowy**	go-to-vi

real	**prawdziwy**	prav-dgeevi
really	**naprawdę**	na-prav-de^n
reason	**przyczyna**	pshi-chi-na
receipt	**pokwitowanie**	po-kfee-to-va-nye
receive (to)	**otrzymywać** *impf.*, **otrzymać** *pf.* **(otrzymuję, -e)**	o-tshi-mi-vach, o-tshi-mach
recent	**ostatni, niedawny**	os-tat-nee, nye-dav-ni
recipe	**przepis**	pshe-pees
recognize (to)	**rozpoznawać** *impf.*, **rozpoznać** *pf.* **(rozpoznaję, -e)**	roz-poz-na-vach, roz-poz-nach
recommend (to)	**polecać,** *impf.*, **polecić** *pf.* **(polecam, -a)**	po-le-tsach, po-le-cheech
record	**płyta**	pwi-ta
sport	**rekord**	re-kord
refill (to)	**napełnić na nowo**	na-pew-neech na no-vo
refrigerator	**lodówka**	lo-doov-ka
refund	**zwrot**	zvrot
regards	**pozdrowienia, ukłony**	poz-dro-vye-nya, oo-kwo-
register (to)	**meldować** *impf.*, **za-** *pf.* **(melduję, -e)**	mel-do-vach, za-
relatives	**krewni**	krev-nee
religion	**religia**	re-lee-gya
remember (to)	**pamiętać** *impf.*, **za-** *pf.* **(pamiętam, -a)**	pa-mye^n-tach, za-
rent	**czynsz**	chinsh

rent (to)	**wynajmować** *impf.*, **wynająć** *pf.* **(wynajmuję, -e)**	vi-nay-mo-vach, vi-na-yo^{n}ch
repair (to)	**naprawiać** *impf.*, **naprawić** *pf.* **(naprawiam, -a)**	na-pra-vyach, na-pra-veech
repeat (to)	**powtarzać** *impf.*, **powtórzyć** *pf.* **(powtarzam, -a)**	pof-ta-zhach, pof-too-zhich
reply (to)	**odpowiadać** *impf.*, **odpowiedzieć** *pf.* **(odpowiadam, -a)**	ot-po-vya-dach, ot-po-vye-dgyech
reservation	**rezerwacja**	re-zer-va-tsya
reserve (to)	**rezerwować** *impf.*, **za-** *pf.* **(rezerwuję, -e)**	re-zer-vo-vach, za-
reserved	**zarezerwowany**	za-re-zer-vo-va-ni
restaurant	**restauracja**	res-taoo-ra-tsya
restaurant car	**wagon restauracyjny**	va-gon res-taoo-ra-tsiy-ni
return (to)	**wracać** *impf.*, **wrócić** *pf.* **(wracam, -a)**	vra-tsach, vroo-cheech
reward	**nagroda**	na-gro-da
ribbon	**wstążka**	fsto^{n}-zhka
rich	**bogaty**	bo-ga-ti
ride	**przejażdżka**	pshe-yazh-dgka
ride (to)	**jeździć, jechać (jeżdżę, jeździ; jadę, jedzie)**	yezh-dgeech, ye-hach

right *not left*	**prawy**	pra-vi
not wrong	**poprawny, słuszny**	po-praw-ni, swoosh-ni
right (to be)	**mieć rację (man . . ., ma . . .)**	myech ra-tsye^{n}
ring	**pierścionek**	pyersh-chyo-nek
ripe	**dojrzały**	doy-zha-wi
rise (to)	**podnosić się** *impf.*, **podnieść się** *pf.* **(podnoszę, podnosi)**	pod-no-sheech she^{n} pod-nyeshch she^{n}
river	**rzeka**	zhe-ka
road	**droga**	dro-ga
road map	**mapa drogowa (samochodowa)**	ma-pa dro-go-va (sa-mo-ho-do-va)
road sign	**znak drogowy**	znak dro-govi
road works	**roboty drogowe**	ro-bo-ti dro-go-ve
rock	**skała**	ska-wa
roller *hair*	**wałek do włosów**	va-wek do vwo-soov
roof	**dach**	dah
room	**pokój**	po-kooy
rope	**lina, sznur**	lee-na, shnoor
rotten	**zgniły**	zgnee-wi
rough	**szorstki**	shor-stkee
round	**okrągły**	o-kro^{n}-gwi
rowing boat	**łodź wiosłowa**	woodg vyo-swo-va
rubber	**guma**	goo-ma
rubbish	**śmieci**	shmye-chee
rucksack	**plecak**	ple-tsak

rude	**nieuprzejmy, niegrzeczny**	nye-oo-pshey-mi, nye-gzhech-ni
ruin	**ruina**	roo-ee-na
rule (to)	**rządzić (rządzę, rządzi)**	zho^{n}-dgeech
run (to)	**biec** *impf.*, **po-** *pf.* **(biegnę, -ie)**	byech, po-

S

sad	**smutny**	smoot-ni
saddle	**siodło/siodełko**	shyo-dwo/shyo-dew-ko
safe	**bezpieczny**	bes-pyech-ni
sail	**żagiel (n)**	zha-gyel
sailing boat	**żaglówka**	zha-gloov-ka
sailor	**marynarz**	ma-ri-nazh
sale *clearance*	**wyprzedaż**	vi-spshe-dazh
for sale	**sprzedaż**	spshe-dazh
salesgirl	**ekspedientka**	eks-ped-yent-ka
salesman	**eskpedient**	eks-ped-yent
salt	**sól**	sool
salt water	**morski**	mor-skee
same	**ten sam, ta sama, to samo**	ten sam, ta sa-ma to sa-mo
sand	**piasek**	pya-sek
sandals	**sandały**	san-da-wi
sanitary towel	**podpaska higieniczna**	pod-pas-ka hee-gye-neech-na

satisfactory	**zadowalający**	za-do-va-la-yo^{n}-tsi
saucer	**spodek**	spo-dek
save (to)	**oszczędzać** *impf.*, **(za)oszczczędzić** *pf.* **(oszczędzam, oszczędza)**	osh-che^{n}-dzach, za-osh-che^{n}-dgeech
rescue	**ratować** *impf.*, **u-** *pf.* **(ratuję, -e)**	ra-to-vach
say (to)	**mówić** *impf.*, **powiedzieć** *pf.* **(mówię, -i)**	moo-veech, po-vye-dgyech
scald (to)	**parzyć** *impf.*, **o-** *pf.* **(parzę-y)**	o-pa-zhich
scarf	**szalik**	sha-leek
scenery	**krajobraz, widok**	kray-o-braz, vee-dok
scent	**zapach**	za-pah
school	**szkoła**	shko-wa
scissors	**nożyczki**	no-zhich-kee
Scotland	**Szkocja**	shkots-ya
Scottish	**szkocki**	shkots-kee
scratch (to)	**drapać** *impf.*, **po-** *pf.* **(drapię, -e)**	dra-pach
screw	**śruba**	shroo-ba
sculpture	**rzeźba**	zhezh-ba
sea	**morze**	mo-zhe
seasickness	**choroba morska**	ho-ro-ba mor-ska
season	**sezon**	se-zon
seat	**miejsce**	myeys-tse

eat belt	**pas bezpieczeństwa**	pas bez-pye-chen-stva
econd	**drugi**	droo-gee
econd class	**druga klasa**	droo-ga kla-sa
ee (to)	**widzieć (widzę, -i)**	vee-dgyech
eem (to)	**wydawać się (wydaję się, -e się)**	vi-da-vach shye^{n}
elf-catering	**żywienie we własnym zakresie**	zhi-vye-nye ve vwas-nim za-kre-shye
elf-contained	**z osobnym wejściem**	zo-sob-nim veysh-chyem
ell (to)	**sprzedawać** *impf.*, **sprzedać** *pf.* **(sprzedaję, -e)**	spshe-da-vach, spshe-dach
end (to)	**posyłać** *impf.*, **posłać** *pf.* **(posyłam, -a)**	po-si-wach, pos-wach
eparate	**oddzielny**	od-dgyel-ni
erious	**poważny**	po-vazh-ni
erve (to)	**obsługiwać** *impf.*, **obsłużyć** *pf.* **(obsługuję, -e)**	ob-swoo-gee-vach ob-swoo-zhich
ervice	**obsługa**	ob-swoo-ga
church	**nabożeństwo**	na-bo-zhen-stvo
everal	**kilka**	keel-ka
ew (to)	**szyć** *impf.*, **u-** *pf.* **(szyję, -e)**	shich, oo-
hade *colour*	**odcień**	od-chen
hade/shadow	**cień**	chen
hallow	**płytki**	pwit-kee

shampoo	**szampon**	sham-pon
shape	**kształt**	kshtawt
share (to)	**dzielić** *impf.*, **po-** *pf.* (**dzielę, -i**)	dgye-leech
sharp	**ostry**	os-tri
shave (to)	**golić (się)** *impf.*, **o- (się)** *pf.* (**golę, -i**)	go-leech, o-
shaving brush	**pędzel do golenia**	pe^n-dzel do go-le-nya
shaving cream	**mydło do golenia**	mi-dwo do go-le-nya
she	**ona**	o-na
sheet	**prześcieradło**	pshesh-chye-rad-wo
shelf	**półka**	poow-ka
shell	**muszla**	moosh-la
shelter	**schronienie, schronisko**	s-hro-nye-nye, s-hro-nees-ko
shine (to)	**świecić,** *impf.*, **za-** *pf.* (**świecę, -i**)	shvye-cheech, za-
shingle	**kamyk**	ka-mik
ship	**statek, okręt**	sta-tek, o-kre^{n}t
shipping line	**linia okrętowa**	lee-nya o-kre^n-to-va
shirt	**koszula**	ko-shoo-la
shock	**szok**	shok
shoe	**but**	boot
shoelace	**sznurowadło**	shnoo-ro-va-dwo
shoe polish	**pasta do butów**	pas-ta do boo-toov
shop	**sklep**	sklep

shopping centre	**centrum handlowe**	tsent-room hand-dlo-ve
shore	**brzeg**	bzheg
short	**krótki**	kroot-kee
shortly	**wkrótce**	fkroot-tse
shorts	**szorty**	shor-ti
shoulder	**ramię**	ra-mye^n
show	**pokaz**	po-kaz
show (to)	**pokazywać** *impf.*, **pokazać** *pf.* **(pokazuję, -e)**	po-ka-zi-vach, po-ka-zach
shower	**prysznic**	prish-neets
shut *closed*	**zamknięte**	zam-knye^n-te
shut (to)	**zamykać** *impf.*, **zamknąć** *pf.* **(zamykam, -a)**	za-mi-kach, zam-kno^{n}ch
side	**strona**	stro-na
sights	**obiekty turystyczne**	o-byek-ti too-ris-tich-ne
sightseeing	**zwiedzanie**	zvye-dza-nye
sign	**znak**	znak
sign (to)	**podpisywać** *impf.*, **podpisać** *pf.* **(podpisuję, -e)**	pod-pee-si-vach, pod-pee-sach
signpost	**drogowskaz**	dro-gov-skaz
silk	**jedwab**	yed-vab
silver	**srebro**	sre-bro
simple	**prosty**	pros-ti
since	**od, odkąd**	od, od-ko^{n}d

sing (to)	śpiewać *impf.*, za- *pf.* (śpiewam, śpiewa)	shpye-vach
single	pojedynczy, jednoosobowy	po-ye-din-chi, yed-no-o-so-bo-vi
single room	pokój jednoosobowy	po-kooy yed-no-o-so-bo-vi
sister	siostra	shyos-tra
sit (to)	siadać *impf.*, usiąść *pf.* (siadam, -a)	shya-dach, oo-shyo^{n}shch
sit down (to)	usiąść *pf.* (siedzę, -i)	oo-shyo^{n}shch
size	rozmiar	roz-myar
skate (to)	jeździć na łyżwach (jeżdżę ..., jeździ)	yezh-dgeech na wizh-vah
ski (to)	jeździć na nartach (jeżdżę, -i)	yezh-dgeech na nar-tah
skid (to)	poślizgnąć się *pf.*	posh-leezg-no^{n}ch shye^{n}
skirt	spódnica	spoo-dnee-tsa
sky	niebo	nye-bo
sleep (to)	spać	spach
sleeper	wagon sypialny	va-gon si-pyal-ni
sleeping bag	śpiwór	shpee-voor
sleeve	rękaw	re^{n}-kav
slice	kawałek	ka-va-wek
slip	halka	hal-ka
slippers	pantofle	pan-tof-le
slowly	powoli	po-vo-li
small	mały	ma-wi
smart	elegancki, szykowny	e-le-gan-tskee, shi-kov-ni

smell	zapach	za-pah
smell (to)	pachnieć *intrans.*, wąchać *trans.* (wącham, -a)	pah-nyech, vo^n-hach
smile (to)	uśmiechać się *impf.*, uśmiechnąć się *pf.* (uśmiecham, -a)	oo-shmye-hach shye^n, oo-shmye-hno^{n}ch she^n
smoke (to)	palić *impf.*, za- *pf.* (palę, -i)	pa-leech, za-
smoking compartment	dla palących	dla pa-lo^n-tsih
(no) smoking	dla niepalących	dla nye-pa-lo^n-tsih
snack	przekąska	pshe-ko^{n}s-ka
snorkel	maska pływacka	mas-ka pwi-vats-ka
snow	śnieg	shnyeg
(it is) snowing	pada śnieg	pa-da shnyeg
so	tak	tak
soap	mydło	mi-dwo
soap powder	proszek do prania	pro-shek do pra-nya
sober	trzeźwy	tzhezh-vi
sock	skarpetka	skar-pet-ka
soft	miękki	mye^{n}k-kee
sold	sprzedany	spshe-da-ni
sold out	wysprzedany	vi-spshe-da-ni
sole *shoe*	podeszwa	po-desh-va
solid	solidny, trwały	so-leed-ni, trva-wi
some	niektóre, trochę	nye-ktoo-re, tro-he^n

somebody	ktoś	ktosh
something	coś	tsosh
sometimes	czasem	cha-sem
somewhere	gdzieś	gdgyesh
son	syn	sin
song	piosenka	pyo-sen-ka
soon	wkrótce	fkroot-tse
sort	gatunek, rodzaj	ga-too-nek, ro-dzay
sound	dźwięk	dgvye^{n}k
sound and light show	widowisko światło i dźwięk	vee-do-vees-ko shvyat-wo ee dgvye^{n}k
sour	kwaśny	kfash-ni
south	południe	po-wood-nye
souvenir	pamiątka	pa-myo^{n}t-ka
space	przestrzeń	pshe-stshen
spanner	klucz do nakrętek	klooch do na-kre^{n}-tek
spare	zapasowy	za-pa-so-vi
speak (to)	mówić (mówię, -i)	moo-veech
speciality	specjalność	spets-yal-noshch
spectacles	okulary	o-koo-la-ri
speed	szybkość	shib-koshch
speed limit	ograniczenie szybkości	o-gra-nee-che-nye shib-kosh-chee
spend (to)	wydawać *impf.*, wydać *pf.* (wydaję, -e)	vi-da-vach vi-dach
spice	przyprawa	pshi-pra-va

spoon	**łyżka**	wizh-ka
sport	**sport**	sport
sprain (to)	**zwichnąć** *pf.*	zveeh-no^{n}ch
spring	**wiosna**	vyos-na
spring *water*	**źródło**	zhrood-wo
square *noun*	**plac**	plats
adj.	**kwadratowy**	kva-dra-to-vi
stable *noun*	**stajnia**	stay-nya
stage	**scena**	stse-na
stain	**plama**	pla-ma
stained	**poplamiony**	po-pla-myo-ni
stairs	**schody**	s-ho-di
tale	**nieświeży**	nye-shvye-zhi
stalls	**parter**	par-ter
stamp	**znaczek**	zna-chek
stand (to)	**stać (stoję, stoi)**	stach
star	**gwiazda**	gvyaz-da
start (to)	**zaczynać** *impf.*, **zacząć** *pf.* **(zaczynam, -a)**	za-chi-nach, za-cho^{n}ch
station	**stacja**	stats-ya
statue	**pomnik**	pom-neek
stay (to)	**zatrzymywać się** *impf.*, **zatrzymać się** *pf.* **(zatrzymuję się, -e)**	za-tshi-mi-vach shye^{n} za-tshi-mach shye^{n}
step	**stopień**	sto-pyen

steward(ess)	**steward(essa)**	**ste-vard, ste-var-des-sa**
stick	**patyk, kij**	**pa-tik, keey**
stiff	**sztywny**	**shtiv-ni**
still *not moving*	**nieruchomy**	**nye-roo-ho-mi**
sting	**użądlić, ukłuć**	**oo-zho^n-dleech, oo-kwooch**
stocking	**pończocha**	**pon-cho-ha**
stolen	**ukradziony**	**oo-kra-dgo-ni**
stool	**taboret**	**ta-bo-ret**
stone	**kamień**	**ka-myen**
stop (to)	**zatrzymywać (się)** ***impf.*****, zatrzymać** ***pf.*** **(zatrzymuję się, -e)**	**za-tshi-mi-vach, za-tshi-mach**
store	**sklep**	**sklep**
straight	**prosty**	**pros-ti**
straight on	**prosto**	**pros-to**
strap	**rzemień, pasek**	**zhe-myen, pa-sek**
stream	**strumień**	**stroo-myen**
street	**ulica**	**oo-lee-tsa**
street map	**plan miasta**	**plan myas-ta**
string	**sznurek**	**shnoo-rek**
strong	**silny**	**sheel-ni**
student	**student**	**stoo-dent**
style	**styl, fason**	**stil, fa-son**
suburb	**przedmieście, peryferie**	**pshed-myesh-chye, pe-ri-fer-ye**
subway	**przejście podziemne**	**pshey-shchye pod-zhyem-ne**

suddenly	**nagle**	nag-le
suede	**zamsz**	zamsh
suit *ladies'*	**kostium**	kos-tyoom
men's	**garnitur**	gar-nee-toor
suitcase	**walizka**	va-leez-ka
summer	**lato**	la-to
sun	**słońce**	swon-tse
sunbathing	**opalanie się**	o-pa-la-nye shye^n
sunburn	**poparzenie słoneczne**	po-pa-zhe-nye swo-nech-ne
sunglasses	**okulary słoneczne**	o-koo-la-ri swo-nech-ne
sunhat	**kapelusz słoneczny**	ka-pe-loosh swo-nech-ni
sunny	**słoneczny**	swo-nech-ni
sunshade	**markiza**	mar-kee-za
suntan cream	**krem do opalania**	krem do o-pa-la-nya
supper	**kolacja**	ko-la-tsya
sure	**pewny**	pev-ni
surfboard	**deska surfingowa**	des-ka ser-feen-go-va
surgery	**pokój przyjęć lekarza**	po-kooy pshi-ye^{n}ch le-ka-zha
surgery hours	**godziny przyjęć (pacjentów)**	go-dgee-ni pshi-ye^{n}ch, (pats-yen-toov)
surprise	**niespodzianka**	nyes-po-dgyan-ka
suspender belt	**podwiązki**	pod-vyo^{n}z-kee
surroundings	**otoczenie**	o-to-che-nye
sweat	**pot**	pot
sweater	**sweter**	sve-ter

sweet	**słodki**	swot-kee
sweets	**słodycze**	swo-di-che
swell (to)	**puchnąć** *impf.*, **s-** *pf.* **(puchnę, -ie)**	pooh-no^{n}ch
swim (to)	**pływać (pływam, -a)**	pwi-vach
swimming pool	**basen pływacki**	ba-sen pwi-vats-kee
swings	**huśtawka**	hoosh-tav-ka
switch *light*	**kontakt**	kon-takt
synagogue	**synagoga**	si-na-go-ga

T

table	**stół**	stoow
tablecloth	**obrus**	o-broos
tablet	**tabletka**	tab-let-ka
tailor	**krawiec**	kra-vyets
take (to)	**brać** *impf.*, **wziąć** *pf.* **(biorę, bierze)**	brach, vzhyo^{n}ch
talk (to)	**mówić, rozmawiać (mówię, -i, rozmawiam, -a)**	moo-veech, roz-ma-vyach
tall	**wysoki**	vi-so-kee
tampon	**tampon**	tam-pon
tank	**zbiornik**	zbyor-neek
tanned	**opalony**	o-pa-lo-ni
tap	**kran**	kran
tapestry	**tkanina**	tka-nee-na

taste	**smak**	smak
taste (to)	**kosztować** *impf.*, **s-** *pf.* **(kosztuję, -e)**	kosh-to-vach
tax	**podatek**	po-da-tek
taxi	**taksówka**	tak-soof-ka
taxi rank	**postój taksówek**	pos-tooy tak-soo-vek
tea	**herbata**	her-ba-ta
teach (to)	**uczyć** *impf.*, **na-** *pf.* **(uczę, -y)**	oo-chich, na-
tear	**rozdarcie**	roz-dar-chye
tear (to)	**drzeć** *impf.*, **po-** *pf.* **(drę, drze)**	dzhech
telegram	**telegram**	te-le-gram
telephone	**telefon**	te-le-fon
telephone (to)	**telefonować** *impf.*, **za-** *pf.* **(telefonuję, -e)**	te-le-fo-no-vach, za-
telephone call	**rozmowa telefoniczna**	roz-mo-va te-le-fo-neech-na
television	**telewizja**	te-le-veez-ya
telex	**telex**	te-leks
tell (to)	**powiedzieć** *pf.*	po-vye-dgyech
temperature	**temperatura**	tem-pe-ra-too-ra
temple	**świątynia**	shvyo^{n}-ti-nya
temporary	**tymczasowy, prowizoryczny**	tim-cha-so-vi, pro-vee-zo-rich-ni
tennis	**tenis**	te-nees
tent	**namiot**	na-myot

tent peg	**kołek namiotowy**	ko-wek na-myo-to-vi
tent pole	**maszt**	masht
terrace	**taras**	ta-ras
than	**niż**	neezh
thank you	**dziękuję**	dgye^{n}-koo-ye^{n}
that	**tamten**	tam-ten
theatre	**teatr**	te-atr
their, theirs	**ich**	eeh
them	**im, ich**	eem, eeh
then	**potem, wtedy**	po-tem, fte-di
there	**tam**	tam
there is	**jest**	yest
there are	**są**	so^{n}
thermometer	**termometr**	ter-mo-metr
these	**te, ci**	te, chee
they	**oni, one**	o-nee, o-ne
thick	**gęsty, gruby**	ge^{n}s-ti, groo-bi
thief	**złodziej**	zwo-dgyey
thin	**cienki, rzadki**	chyen-kee, zhad-kee
thing	**rzecz**	zhech
think (to)	**myśleć (myślę, -i)**	mish-lech
thirsty (to be)	**być spragnionym**	bich sprag-nyo-nim
this	**ten, ta, to**	ten, ta, to
those	**tamci, tamte**	tam-chee, tam-te
though	**chociaż**	ho-chyazh

thread	**nitka**	neet-ka
through	**przez**	pshez
throw (to)	**rzucać** *impf.*, **rzucić** *pf.* **(rzucam, -a)**	zhoo-tsach, zhoo-cheech
thunder	**grzmot**	gzhmot
thunderstorm	**burza**	boo-zha
ticket	**bilet**	bee-let
ticket office	**kasa biletowa**	ka-sa bee-le-to-va
tide	**przypływ**	pshi-pwiv
tie	**krawat**	kra-vat
sport	**remis**	re-mees
tight	**ciasny, szczelny**	chas-ni, shchel-ni
tights	**rajstopy**	ray-sto-pi
time	**czas**	chas
timetable	**rozkład jazdy**	roz-kwad yaz-di
tin	**puszka**	poosh-ka
tin opener	**otwieracz do puszek**	ot-vye-rach do poo-shek
tip	**napiwek**	na-pee-vek
tip (to)	**dać napiwek** *pf.* **(daję ..., -e)**	dach na-pee-vek
tired	**zmęczony**	zme^{n}-cho-ni
to	**do**	do
tobacco	**tytoń**	ti-ton
tobacco pouch	**woreczek na tytoń**	vo-re-chek na ti-ton
together	**razem**	ra-zem

toilet	**toaleta, ubikacja, ustęp, klozet**	to-a-le-ta, oo-bee-ka-tsya, oos-te^{n}p, klo-zet
toilet paper	**papier toaletowy**	pa-pyer to-a-le-to-vi
tomorrow	**jutro**	yoo-tro
tongue	**język**	ye^{n}-zik
too *excessive*	**zbyt**	zbit
also	**rownież**	roov-nyezh
too much/many	**za dużo**	za doo-zho
toothbrush	**szczoteczka do zębów**	shcho-tech-ka do ze^{n}-boov
toothpaste	**pasta do zębów**	pas-ta-do ze^{n}-boov
toothpick	**wykałaczka**	vi-ka-wach-ka
top	**góra, szczyt**	goo-ra, shchit
torch	**latarka elektryczna**	la-tar-ka e-lek-trich-na
torn	**podarty**	po-dar-ti
touch (to)	**dotykać** *impf.*, **dotknąć** *pf.* **(dotykam, -a)**	do-ti-kach, dot-kno^{n}ch
tough	**twardy, wytrzymały**	tvar-di, vi-tchi-ma-wi
tour	**wycieczka**	vi-chyech-ka
tourist	**turysta**	too-ris-ta
tourist office	**biuro turystyczne**	byoo-ro too-ris-tich-ne
towards	**w kierunku**	fkye-roon-ko
towel	**ręcznik**	re^{n}ch-neek
tower	**wieża**	vye-zha
town	**miasto**	myas-to
town hall	**ratusz**	ra-toosh

toy	**zabawka**	**za-bav-ka**
traffic	**ruch uliczny**	**rooh oo-leech-ni**
traffic jam	**korek, zator**	**ko-rek, za-tor**
traffic lights	**światła regulujące ruch uliczny**	**shvyat-wa re-goo-loo-yo^n-tse rooh oo-leech-ni**
trailer	**przyczepa**	**pshi-che-pa**
train	**pociąg**	**po-chyo^{n}g**
tram	**tramwaj**	**tram-vay**
transfer (to)	**przewozić** *impf.*, **przewieźć** *pf.* **(przewożę, przewozi)**	**pshe-vo-zheech pshe-vyezhch**
transit	**tranzyt**	**tran-zit**
translate (to)	**tłumaczyć** *impf.*, **prze-** *pf.* **(tłumaczę, -y)**	**twoo-ma-chich, pshe-**
travel (to)	**podróżować (podróżuję, -e)**	**po-droo-zho-vach**
travel agent	**biuro podróży**	**byoo-ro pod-roo-zhi**
traveller	**podróżny**	**pod-roozh-ni**
travellers' cheques	**czek podróżniczy**	**chek pod-roozh-nee-chi**
treat (to)	**traktować** *impf.*, **po-** *pf.* **(traktuję, -e)**	**trak-to-vach**
treatment	**leczenie**	**le-che-nye**
tree	**drzewo**	**dzhe-vo**
trip	**wycieczka**	**vi-chyech-ka**
trouble	**kłopot**	**kwo-pot**
trousers	**spodnie**	**spod-nye**

true	prawdziwy	praw-dgee-vi
trunk *luggage*	kufer	koo-fer
trunks	spodenki kąpielowe	spo-den-kee ko^{n}-pye-lo-ve
truth	prawda	prav-da
try, try on (to)	próbować, mierzyć *impf.*, s-, z- *pf.* (próbuję, -e mierzę, -y)	proo-bo-vach, mye-zhich
tunnel	tunel	too-nel
turn (to)	skręcać *impf.*, skręcić *pf.* (skręcam, -a)	skre^{n}-tsach, skre^{n}-cheech
turning	zakręt, przecznica	za-kre^{n}t, pshe-chnee-tsa
tweezers	pincetka	peen-tset-ka
twin beds	dwa pojedyncze łóżka	dva po-ye-din-che woozh-ka
twisted	zwichnięty, skręcony	zveeh-nye^{n}-ti, skre^{n}-tso-ni
typewriter	maszyna do pisania	ma-shi-na do pee-sa-nya

U

ugly	brzydki	bzhit-kee
umbrella	parasol	pa-ra-sol
uncle	wujek	voo-yek
uncomfortable	niewygodny	nye-vi-god-ni
unconscious	nieprzytomny	nye-pshi-tom-ni
under	pod	pod
underground	podziemny	pod-zhyem-ni
underneath	pod spodem	pod spo-dem
understand	rozumieć *impf.*, z- *pf.* (rozumiem, -e)	ro-zoo-myech

underwear	**bielizna**	bye-leez-na
university	**uniwersytet**	oo-nee-ver-si-tet
unpack (to)	**rozpakować** *pf.* **(rozpakowuję, -e)**	roz-pa-ko-vach
until	**do** (+*gen.*)	do
unusual	**niezwykły**	nyez-vik-wi
up	**w górę, do góry**	v goo-re^n, do goo-ri
upstairs	**na górze**	na goo-zhe
urgent	**pilny**	peel-ni
us	**nas** (*acc.*), **nam** (*dat.*)	nas, nam
USA	**USA**	oo-ess-a
use (to)	**używać** *impf.*, **użyć** *pf.* **(żywam, -a)**	oo-zhi-vach, oo-zhich
useful	**pożyteczny**	po-zhi-tech-ni
useless	**bezużyteczny**	bez-oo-zhi-tech-ni
usual	**zwykły, normalny**	zvik-wi, nor-mal-ni

V

vacancies	**do wynajęcia**	do vi-na-ye^n-chya
vacant	**wolny, do wynajęcia**	vol-ni, do vi-na-ye^n-chya
valid	**ważny**	vazh-ni
valley	**dolina**	do-lee-na
valuable	**cenny, wartościowy**	tsen-ni, var-tosh-chyo-vi
value	**wartość**	var-toshch
vase	**wazon**	va-zon
vegetables	**jarzyny**	ya-zhi-ni

vegetarian	**jarski**	yar-skee
vein	**żyła**	zhi-wa
velvet	**aksamit**	a-ksa-meet
ventilation	**wentylacja**	ven-ti-la-tsya
very little	**bardzo mało**	bar-dzo ma-wo
very very much	**bardzo**	bar-dzo
vest	**podkoszulek**	pot-ko-shoo-lek
video cassette	**kaseta wideo**	ka-se-ta vee-de-o
video recorder	**magnetowid**	ma-gne-to-veed
view	**widok**	vee-dok
villa	**willa**	veel-la
village	**wieś**	vyesh
vineyard	**winnica**	veen-nee-tsa
violin	**skrzypce**	skship-tse
visa	**wiza**	vee-za
visibility	**widoczność**	vee-doch-noshch
visit	**wizyta**	vee-zi-ta
visit (to)	**odwiedzać *impf.*, odwiedzić *pf.* (odwiedzam, -a)**	od-vye-dzach, od-vye-dgeech
voice	**głos**	gwos
voltage	**napięcie**	na-pye^{n}-chye
voucher	**kupon**	koo-pon
voyage	**podróż**	pod-roozh

W

wait (to)	**czekać** *impf.*, **za-** *pf.* **(czekam, -a)**	che-kach
waiter	**kelner**	kel-ner
waiting room	**poczekalnia**	po-che-kal-nya
waitress	**kelnerka**	kel-ner-ka
wake (to)	**budzić się** *impf.*, **z-** *pf.* **(budzę się, -i)**	boo-dgeech shye^{n}
Wales	**Walia**	val-ya
walk	**spacer**	spa-tser
walk (to)	**spacerować (spaceruję, -e)**	spa-tse-ro-vach
wall	**ściana, mur**	shchya-na, moor
wall plug	**kontakt**	kon-takt
wallet	**portfel**	port-fel
want (to)	**chcieć (chcę, -e)**	hchyech
wardrobe	**szafa**	sha-fa
warm	**ciepły**	chye-pwi
wash (to)	**myć (się)** *impf.*, **u-** *pf.* **(myję -e)**	mich, oo-
washbasin	**umywalka**	oo-mi-val-ka
waste	**odpadki, strata, marnowanie**	od-pad-kee, stra-ta mar-no-va-nye
waste (to)	**marnować** *impf.*, **z-** *pf.* **(marnuję, -e)**	mar-no-vach
watch	**zegarek**	ze-ga-rek
water	**woda**	vo-da

waterfall	**wodospad**	vo-dos-pad
waterproof	**wodoszczelny, nieprzemakalny**	vo-do-shchel-ni, nye-pshe-ma-kal-ni
water skiing	**narty wodne**	nar-ti vod-ne
wave	**fala**	fa-la
way	**droga**	dro-ga
we	**my**	mi
wear (to)	**nosić** *impf.*, **nieść** *pf.* **(noszę, -si)**	no-sheech, nyeshch
weather	**pogoda**	po-go-da
weather forecast	**prognoza pogody**	prog-no-za po-go-di
wedding ring	**obrączka ślubna**	o-bro^{n}ch-ka shloob-na
week	**tydzień**	ti-dgyen
weigh (to)	**ważyć** *impf.*, **z-** *pf.* **(ważę, -y)**	va-zhich
weight	**waga**	va-ga
welcome	**mile widziany**	mee-le vee-dgya-ni
well	**dobrze**	dob-zhe
well (water)	**studnia**	stood-nya
Welsh	**walijski**	va-leey-ski
west	**zachód**	za-hood
wet	**mokry**	mo-kry
what?	**co?**	tso
wheel	**koło**	ko-wo
wheelchair	**wózek inwalidzki**	voo-zek een-va-leedz-kee
when?	**kiedy?**	kye-di

where?	**gdzie?**	gdgye
whether	**czy**	chi
which?	**który** *m*, **która** *f*, **które** *n*?	ktoo-ri, ktoo-ra, ktoo-re
while	**podczas gdy**	pod-chas gdi
who?	**kto?**	kto
whole	**cały**	tsa-wi
whose?	**czyj** *m*, **czyja** *f*, **czyje** *n*?	chiy, chi-ya, chi-ye
why?	**dlaczego?**	dla-che-go
wide	**szeroki**	she-ro-kee
widow	**wdowa**	vdo-va
widower	**wdowiec**	vdo-vyets
wife	**żona**	zho-na
wild	**dziki**	dgee-kee
win (to)	**wygrywać** *impf.*, **wygrać** *pf.* **(wygrywam, -a)**	vi-gri-vach, vi-grach
wind	**wiatr**	vyatr
window	**okno**	ok-no
wine merchant	**winiarnia**	vee-nyar-nya
wing	**skrzydło**	skshid-wo
winter	**zima**	zhee-ma
winter sports	**sporty zimowe**	spor-ti zhee-mo-ve
wire	**drut**	droot
wish (to)	**chcieć (chcę, -e)**	hchyech
with	**z (+*instr.*)**	z
within	**wewnątrz**	vev-no^{n}ch

without	**bez** (+*gen.*)	bez
woman	**kobieta**	ko-bye-ta
wonderful	**cudowny**	tsoo-dov-ni
wood *forest*	**las**	las
timber	**drzewo**	dzhe-vo
wool	**wełna**	vew-na
word	**słowo**	swo-vo
work	**praca**	pra-tsa
work (to)	**pracować (pracuję, -e)**	pra-tso-vach
worry (to)	**martwić się** *impf.*, **z-** *pf.* **(martwię się, martwi się)**	mar-tvich shye^n
worse	**gorszy** *adj.*, **gorzej** *adv.*	gor-shi, go-zhey
worth (to be)	**być wart**	bich vart
wrap (to)	**owijać** *impf.*, **owinąć** *pf.* **(owijam, -a)**	o-vee-yach, o-vee-no^{n}ch
write (to)	**pisać** *impf.*, **na-** *pf.* **(piszę, -e)**	pee-sach
writing paper	**papier listowy**	pa-pyer lees-to-vi
wrong	**zły, nieprawidłowy**	zwi, nye-pra-veed-wo-vi
wrong (to be)	**mylić się** *impf.*, **po-** *pf.* **(mylę się, -i się)**	mi-leech shye^n

X

xerox	**ksero**	kse-ro
X-ray	**prześwietlenie**	pshe-shvye-tle-nye

Y

yacht	**jacht**	yaht
year	**rok**	rok
yes	**tak**	tak
yesterday	**wczoraj**	fcho-ray
yet	**jeszcze**	yesh-che
nevertheless	**a jednak**	a yed-nak
you	**ty**	ti
young	**młody**	mwo-di
your, yours	**twój** *m*, **twoja** *f*, **twoje** *n*	tfooy, tfo-ya, tfo-ye
youth hostel	**schronisko młodzieżowe**	s-hro-nees-ko mwo-dgye-zho-ve

Z

zip	**zamek błyskawiczny**	za-mek bwis-ka-veech-ni
zoo	**zoo**	zo-o

INDEX